SpringerBriefs in Sociology

SpringerBriefs in Sociology are concise summaries of cutting-edge research and practical applications across the field of sociology. These compact monographs are refereed by and under the editorial supervision of scholars in Sociology or cognate fields. Volumes are 50 to 125 pages (approximately 20,000- 70,000 words), with a clear focus. The series covers a range of content from professional to academic such as snapshots of hot and/or emerging topics, in-depth case studies, and timely reports of state-of-the art analytical techniques. The scope of the series spans the entire field of Sociology, with a view to significantly advance research. The character of the series is international and multi-disciplinary and will include research areas such as: health, medical, intervention studies, cross-cultural studies, race/class/gender, children, youth, education, work and organizational issues, relationships, religion, ageing, violence, inequality, critical theory, culture, political sociology, social psychology, and so on. Volumes in the series may analyze past, present and/or future trends, as well as their determinants and consequences. Both solicited and unsolicited manuscripts are considered for publication in this series. SpringerBriefs in Sociology will be of interest to a wide range of individuals, including sociologists, psychologists, economists, philosophers, health researchers, as well as practitioners across the social sciences. Briefs will be published as part of Springer's eBook collection, with millions of users worldwide. In addition, Briefs will be available for individual print and electronic purchase. Briefs are characterized by fast, global electronic dissemination, standard publishing contracts, easy-to-use manuscript preparation and formatting guidelines, and expedited production schedules. We aim for publication 8-12 weeks after acceptance.

Mark Tessler

Social Science Research in the Arab World and Beyond

A Guide for Students, Instructors and Researchers

Mark Tessler
Department of Political Science
University of Michigan
Ann Arbor, MI, USA

This work was supported by Carnegie Corporation of New York

ISSN 2212-6368　　　　　　　ISSN 2212-6376　(electronic)
SpringerBriefs in Sociology
ISBN 978-3-031-13837-9　　　ISBN 978-3-031-13838-6　(eBook)
https://doi.org/10.1007/978-3-031-13838-6

© The Editor(s) (if applicable) and The Author(s) 2023. This book is an open access publication.
Open Access This book is licensed under the terms of the Creative Commons Attribution 4.0 International License (http://creativecommons.org/licenses/by/4.0/), which permits use, sharing, adaptation, distribution and reproduction in any medium or format, as long as you give appropriate credit to the original author(s) and the source, provide a link to the Creative Commons license and indicate if changes were made.
The images or other third party material in this book are included in the book's Creative Commons license, unless indicated otherwise in a credit line to the material. If material is not included in the book's Creative Commons license and your intended use is not permitted by statutory regulation or exceeds the permitted use, you will need to obtain permission directly from the copyright holder.The use of general descriptive names, registered names, trademarks, service marks, etc. in this publication does not imply, even in the absence of a specific statement, that such names are exempt from the relevant protective laws and regulations and therefore free for general use.
The publisher, the authors, and the editors are safe to assume that the advice and information in this book are believed to be true and accurate at the date of publication. Neither the publisher nor the authors or the editors give a warranty, expressed or implied, with respect to the material contained herein or for any errors or omissions that may have been made. The publisher remains neutral with regard to jurisdictional claims in published maps and institutional affiliations.

This Springer imprint is published by the registered company Springer Nature Switzerland AG
The registered company address is: Gewerbestrasse 11, 6330 Cham, Switzerland

(**a**) Arab Barometer Planning Meeting - Amman July 2010;
(**b**) Carnegie Social Science Research Workshop - Kuwait January 2019

To Pat
My Love and Companion in Adventures,
Now as Then

Preface

Why have I written this book?

I have written this slender volume in the hope that students, instructors, and researchers, particularly in the Arab world, will find it useful. Toward this end, an Arabic language translation is being prepared and published by Qatar University Press. With respect to content and the intended audience, the volume is designed for readers who seek a better understanding of disciplinary social science research—what is sometimes described as theory-driven and data-based social research.

The focus of disciplinary social science research is on descriptions and explanations of variance, the latter involving causal inference, and on the discovery of findings and insights that are potentially generalizable. The chapters devote attention to the logic and conceptual foundations of disciplinary political and social science research, as well as to the analysis and presentation of quantitative data, and to a considerable extent, qualitative data as well. The volume does not assume prior knowledge or strong ability in mathematics.

I am only a few short years away from retirement, after more than five decades in academia, and this has led me to reflect on the thematic lines of my professional career that have positioned and motivated me to write this volume. Two interrelated themes stand out, and they are probably two sides of the same coin.

One is the promotion of mutual appreciation and constructive interaction between disciplinary social science and an approach that is usually described, at least in the West, as "area studies." The objective of area studies research is usually thick description, which is the acquisition and informed and critical evaluation of as much relevant factual information as possible about a particular concern that characterizes a particular place and time, a place that may be foreign to the researcher or research team. This will, in most cases, require considerable time in the field, in the place that is the focus of the research, and a knowledge of local cultures and languages.

Area studies research is sometimes disparaged by social scientists in the West and elsewhere. One charge is that it is not scientific and therefore unavoidably subjective. Another is that it is ideographic rather than nomothetic, meaning that it offers information only to those with an interest in the particular place and time on which it focuses and, therefore, little, if anything, to those seeking insights that are generalizable—or at least broadly applicable under conditions that can be specified. I do not find these criticisms entirely persuasive. Most and perhaps all social science research is subjective, with replication being necessary to build confidence that the findings of an investigation are correct, and I see no reason to believe that area studies as an approach to research is incapable of producing insights that may be broadly applicable.

My view is that both disciplinary social science research and area studies research are capable of providing valuable information and insight, and that each, accordingly, deserves respect as a useful approach to the design and conduct of social science research. Moreover, I further contend that there are instances, and undoubtedly many instances, in which elements of both approaches will be needed to answer as fully as possible the questions that motivate a research project. In other words, it is not just that different kinds of research questions require different approaches to social inquiry, so that, as a result, each has a place; it is also that there is not always a single *right* approach to the study of a question or concern that motivates a social science research project. Investigators will often need to draw upon both of these approaches in order to produce the most instructive findings.

The second thematic line of my professional career that leads to the present volume is the promotion of broader familiarity with, and a deeper understanding of, disciplinary social science research in the region that has been the focus of my more scholarly work, among those in this region who may not have had an opportunity to learn about this approach to political and social science inquiry. The region, of course, is the Middle East and North Africa and, secondarily, sub-Saharan Africa.

My activities and efforts in this regard do not reflect a belief that disciplinary social science research is the only legitimate and effective way to investigate social and political phenomena. Nor even do I believe that it is necessarily the most valuable and important of the approaches to research that are available to a social scientist. But I do believe that at least a basic knowledge of this approach belongs in the conceptual and methodological tool kit of a social scientist. What we are calling "disciplinary" social science is widely practiced, and not only by Western scholars. Moreover, there are almost certainly questions to be investigated for which this approach needs to be considered and may, in fact, offer the best fit.

Each of these thematic lines has guided my academic and professional career: Knowledge of disciplinary social science is important, and social scientists who are not familiar with it, who are skilled in other approaches, should learn about it; and disciplinary social science should not disparage area studies research but should rather open itself to the possibility that it may not, by itself, provide all of the conceptual and methodological tools needed to design and carry out a social science research project, especially, but not only, one in a place that is foreign to the investigator.

So what does a career guided in significant measure by these thematic lines look like? To answer this question, let me outline some of the activities and experiences that have brought me to the present, to a point where retirement is visible on the near horizon and I have written a book, almost certainly my last, devoted to an introductory overview of disciplinary social science research. Some readers may find my trajectory of interest, as they seek to understand the perspectives of this author or as they explore their own career paths; others may choose to skip this somewhat self-indulgent description of the experiences that have brought me to this point. I begin with my study and dissertation research in Tunisia, and it is in part for a subset of my readers and in part for myself, I guess, that I go forward from there to review what I have done and where I have been during the last five plus decades.

* * *

My introduction to social science research and the disciplinary social science research paradigm came very quickly when I entered the Ph.D. program in political science at Northwestern University. When I told my undergraduate advisor that I had received a three-year fellowship to study political science and African studies at Northwestern, he congratulated me, but he also asked if I realized that the political science department at Northwestern had a very "behavioral" orientation. At the time, I did not know what this meant; only when I began coursework at Northwestern did I learn that the term "behavioral" referenced what I and others call the disciplinary social science paradigm mentioned above.

With the goal of preparing us to design and carry out original research, my first-year program of study at Northwestern included courses devoted to the logic and method of disciplinary social science research. Attention was devoted to conceptual considerations, as well as research methods and data analysis, the latter including work with qualitative as well as quantitative data. I also took a course on applied social statistics and learned Fortran, a computer programming language. At the time, Northwestern was one of only a handful of political science departments at U.S. universities with a doctoral program that had a behavioral orientation. My training was, therefore, significantly different from that received by many of my political science peers in doctoral programs at other top universities.

At the end of my first year at Northwestern, my graduate advisor presented me with an opportunity to study and do research in Tunisia, and thus began my deep engagement with a particular place and time. There was, first, a year of study at the University of Tunis, in advanced classes in which Tunisian professors taught Tunisian students and for which I received a *Certificat de sociologie islamique et maghrébine*. Although not explicitly identified as such, the area studies paradigm provided the framework and established the goals for this extremely valuable year of study.

I began my dissertation research in Tunisia a year later, having returned to Northwestern for exams during the interim. My year of fieldwork in Tunisia included a public opinion survey conducted in the capital and three small towns in different parts of the country. I conducted most of the interviews myself, and this added to my understanding of Tunisia and its citizens. The research design and methodology of my dissertation were developed within the framework of the disciplinary paradigm. I formulated and gathered data with which to test a series of hypotheses about factors shaping the attitudes of ordinary citizens toward important and much-debated social and political issues. Among these issues were the role that Islam should play in national political affairs and the degree to which the place of women should be equal to that of men in education, work, and other social and political domains.

My study would not have been meaningful had it not also been guided by a strong, or at least relatively strong, knowledge of Tunisia and, in particular, by knowledge about the modernist project of the government at the time, by some understanding of the underlying normative orientations that influenced how Tunisians thought about issues like political religion and women's status, and by an awareness of the diverse and varying views about these and other similar considerations that characterized the Tunisian public. This knowledge and understanding, which owed much to my previous year of study at the University of Tunis, and also to my residence in the university's men's residence hall during this period, constituted the kind of thick description associated with an area studies approach to social inquiry.

Jumping ahead, I was pleased to have succeeded in publishing my dissertation in a coauthored book, *Tradition and Identity in Changing Africa* (Harper and Row 1973). Several of my chapters, and those of my two coauthors, both anthropologists, included thick descriptions of the places in which we conducted our studies, with special attention, of course, to factors pertaining to the topics and issues we were investigating. Other chapters, by contrast, connected our research to the relevant scholarly literature, set forth hypotheses and causal stories that moved our inquiries from description to explanation, and then presented and analyzed our survey data in order to test our propositions and assess the breadth of their applicability.

I was pleased that our book received a number of very positive reviews. One was by Elizabeth Colson, a prominent anthropologist who did not work in North Africa and did not herself do quantitative research. Colson wrote at the time, "This is a ground-breaking exciting book... a fine answer to those who are pessimistic about the chances of anthropology becoming a science with testable propositions related to some general theory." But while Colson recognized and appreciated our focused integration of area studies and disciplinary social science scholarly perspectives, others complained, for example, that we did not present enough descriptive ethnographic information and chose to focus instead on "mere opinions and reported conduct." To this reviewer, our book was a "poorly conceived and premature venture."

These reviews, especially the latter, reflect the opposition at this time of many who studied other countries and world regions to the incorporation of elements of the disciplinary social science paradigm into their studies and research. This opposition has for the most part dissipated and disappeared, at least in the USA and much of Europe, over the last couple of decades. But it was very real at the time, and it may to some extent persist in a number of areas.

Accordingly, and as expected, at least in hindsight, I had difficulty publishing scholarly articles based on my dissertation and subsequent research in North Africa and the Middle East. Journal editors routinely sent my submissions to one reviewer whose own work was in line with the area studies research paradigm and to another whose own work was in line with the disciplinary social science research paradigm. Both reviewers usually recommended against publication, one complaining that there was little to be learned from my theory-driven and data-based study and the other faulting me for an unwelcome excess of detailed, descriptive, and largely unnecessary case-specific information.

I eventually learned how to present my research findings in a way that was acceptable to reviewers with differing perspectives on research design and methodology, and so I eventually amassed a credible record of publication. The tension between the area studies and the disciplinary social science research paradigms nevertheless persisted, at least for a time.

It is at this juncture that I published, in 1999, *Area Studies and Social Science: Strategies for Understanding Middle East Politics* (Indiana University Press). Based on an international conference that I hosted and to which I invited social scientists from the USA and Egypt, the goal of this edited volume, as stated in the introduction, was to offer "a collection of essays and research reports by scholars who are grounded in both area studies and their respective social science disciplines... In most cases, authors either take a self-conscious look at some portion of their past scholarship or present the results of a current research project, making explicit and then evaluating the relationship of this work to both their academic discipline and the field of Middle East studies."

As noted earlier, the tension between practitioners of area studies scholarship and practitioners of disciplinary social science research is much more limited today. Based on the American experience, and certainly the situation elsewhere, although probably not everywhere, it is fair to say that today's doctoral students in comparative politics and those who received their degrees in the last decade or two are grounded both in the disciplinary social science paradigm and in the histories, cultures, and languages of the regions or countries they study. The depth of the skill set and knowledge these individuals possess varies, of course. But the debate is essentially over, or at least coming to an end: Both disciplinary and area studies research have their place and a contribution to make, and the best research in comparative politics will very often require elements of both approaches.

It did take a while to get to this point, and some might argue that my assessment of the present is a bit too optimistic. In any event, the debate did not appear to be over at the time of my conference and the 1999 volume. The situation at the time is described in the following paragraph taken from the book's introduction:

> The area studies controversy, as it is known, has been particularly tense in political science. Thus, in an article entitled "Political Scientists Clash over Value of Area Studies" *The Chronicle of Higher Education* reported the charge that a focus on individual regions leads to work that is mushy. The most important criticism reviewed in the article is the contention that area studies specialists are hostile to social science theory, meaning that they have no interest in either the development or application of insights that transcend particular times and places. [The discussion elsewhere of these charges and counter-charges includes coverage] in *PS: Political Science & Politics*, a quarterly journal of the American Political Science Association. In June 1997, for example, the journal featured a section containing three articles on "Controversies in the Discipline: Area Studies and Comparative Politics." Articles in the prominent scholarly journal *Daedalus* have also explored this issue. They note that while the controversy may be most pronounced in political science, it is by no means limited to that discipline.

Committed to our discipline and also to the regions and countries we study, this is the situation in which I and similarly minded peers found ourselves. It is within this context that we designed and conducted our investigations, sought to publish our findings, and looked for opportunities to reduce the gap between disciplinary and area studies research paradigms. It is precisely with this in mind that *Area Studies and Social Science: Strategies for Understanding Middle East Politics* was conceived and published.

The structure and content of most political science Ph.D. programs in the USA and some other countries is today similar to the training I received at Northwestern University many years ago. Political science doctoral students in comparative politics and many other subfields are grounded, as was I, in the logic and method of disciplinary social science. This sometimes brings a charge that students spend too much time learning advanced research methods and not enough time learning about the places from which their data are drawn. This charge may be warranted in some instances, but students trained in comparative politics at many universities today, and certainly in the strongest doctoral programs, will have spent considerable time in the field and will have invested heavily in learning a new language.

As the discussion heretofore indicates, the pathway from the time of my graduate training and dissertation research to today's understanding that the paradigms of both area studies and disciplinary social science have much to contribute has been complicated and frequently tense. During this decades-long period, I and others worked to advance appreciation of the contributions that can be made by research that draws upon both scholarly paradigms.

In addition, I sought opportunities to introduce the logic and method of the disciplinary paradigm to students, scholars, and others in the Middle East and Africa. Some contributions were made through publications. For example, in 1987, I published *The Evaluation and Application of Survey Research in the Arab World* (Westview Press). I am the lead author on this book, which is based on an international conference that I convened and for which I obtained grant funds from the Ford Foundation and the Rockefeller Foundation.

Other contributions along the way include teaching, lecturing, consulting, and collaborating on research in the Middle East and Africa. This includes:

- Teaching semester-long courses on applied research design and methodology at the national universities in Zaire (now the Democratic Republic of the Congo), Rwanda, and Liberia
- Serving as a principal investigator on contracts to establish polling units at research institutions in the UAE and Qatar
- Organizing and conducting one or more workshops and capacity-building programs in Qatar, the United Arab Emirates, Kuwait, Bahrain, Oman, Jordan, Palestine, Algeria, Morocco, Madagascar, and Senegal
- Lecturing on disciplinary social science research in many of these same countries and in a number of others, the latter including Sudan, Ivory Coast, Niger, and Mauritania
- Bringing several dozen scholars and research practitioners from Arab countries to Ann Arbor, Michigan, for still other instructional and capacity-building programs and
- Collaborating on multi-year research projects with scholars in Tunisia, Algeria, Morocco, Palestine, the UAE, and Qatar

Still another important initiative, one of a different kind, admittedly, is the founding of the Arab Barometer Public Opinion Research Project. The Arab Barometer is a nonpartisan research network that conducts nationally representative and probability-based surveys in Arab countries in order to provide insight into the social, political, and economic attitudes and values of ordinary citizens across the Arab world. Working with Amaney Jamal, a former student and now a professor and dean at Princeton University, and Khalil Shikaki, a prominent Palestinian political scientist who now directs the Ramallah-based Palestinian Center for Policy and Survey Research, I obtained grant funds to complete the first surveys in seven Arab countries from 2006 through 2009. The American Political Science Association named this first wave of Arab Barometer surveys the best new political science dataset of 2010.

Today, at the time of this writing, in mid-2022, the Barometer has carried out 68 original surveys in seven waves, that is to say at two- or three-year intervals, and conducted face-to-face interviews with more than 100,000 ordinary citizens in sixteen Arab countries. Management and much of the hands-on direction of Arab Barometer is today done by Michael Robbins, another of my former students. Michael's dissertation, based on fieldwork in Jordan and Palestine, was named the best dissertation on Religion and Politics in 2012 by the American Political Science Association.

Arab Barometer surveys are designed and then carried out in close collaboration with Arab scholars and Arab country-based research institutions, all of which are identified on the Arab Barometer website. After careful review, cleaning, and correction as needed, the survey data are placed on the Barometer's website and made available to the public for downloading without charge. In 2021, there were almost 300,000 hits on the Barometer's website and about 30,000 downloads of data and reports. Reports based on Arab Barometer surveys today appear in scores, and perhaps hundreds, of scholarly and journalistic publications in the USA, the Middle East, and elsewhere.

The Arab Barometer is somewhat different than the contributions mentioned above. It is not intended to serve primarily researchers in the Middle East and other world regions. Indeed, the principal consumers and users of Arab Barometer survey data are probably in the USA. But I believe the creation and dissemination of this important resource contributes in its own way to bridging the gap that for a long time separated investigators schooled, respectively, in the area studies and disciplinary social science research paradigms.

Since this overview of a portion of my scholarly and professional career is something of an indulgence, permit me to mention one other important contribution, one that is only indirectly related to the matter of research paradigms but has nonetheless played an important role in promoting scholarly interaction between American and North African scholars in social science (and other) disciplines. This is the establishment in 1984, together with I. William Zartman, Georges Sabbagh, and several others, of the American Institute for Maghrib Studies (AIMS). AIMS is a member of the Washington-based and U.S. Department of Education-funded Council of American Overseas Research Centers.

I was the president of AIMS from 1995 through 2004 and served on the Board of Directors for another dozen years. During the years of my presidency, with leadership shared with my vice-president, Donna Lee Bowen, we raised funds from private as well as government sources, added an AIMS center in Algeria to the ones already present in Tunisia and Morocco, and greatly expanded the institute's activities. These included a summer Arabic language course in Morocco; support for research by both American and North African researchers, especially doctoral students; an annual thematic conference, hosted by one of the AIMS in-country centers, at which American and North African scholars presented the results of their research; and establishment of the *Journal of North African Studies*, which was edited at the time by John Entelis and George Joffe and has since grown into a prominent vehicle for the dissemination of research findings by American, Maghribi, and other scholars.

A final activity and contribution to be mentioned, again only indirectly related to the matter of scholarly paradigms but which did also promote interaction, and frequently collaboration, between American social scientists and their peers in the Middle East and North Africa, are the four multi-year university affiliation partnerships I organized and directed. Three were between the University of Wisconsin-Milwaukee, where I began my academic career, and, respectively, Mohammed V University in Rabat, Morocco; the Hebrew University of Jerusalem in Israel; and Najah National University in Nablus in the occupied West Bank. The fourth affiliation was between the University of Michigan and the University of Algiers in Algeria. The first of these affiliations began in 1986 and ran for five years. The last ran for four years and concluded in 2006.

I secured grant funds to support these partnerships, with additional funds provided by some of the participating universities. In each case, with exchanges usually going in both directions, faculty from one university spent time at the other university, often remaining for a full academic year. Visiting faculty sometimes taught courses but sometimes focused only on research or visited to give lectures or meet for purposes of administration.

As stated, there is no reason why others should be interested in this selective and uneven journey down memory lane. But as I reflect on the timetable for my approaching retirement, I have been thinking about these thematic lines of my career, or at least this service dimension of my career. It is with these reflections in mind and the hope of making a meaningful contribution before I depart from academic life that I have prepared the present Arab-focused text on disciplinary social science research.

Ann Arbor, MI   Mark Tessler

Acknowledgments

Preparation of this guide to social science research in the Arab world was made possible by a generous grant from the Carnegie Corporation of New York (CCNY). The ambitious title of the project that was funded is "Understanding Marginalized Communities in the Arab World through Social Science Research: Gaining Insight, Enhancing Capacity, and Building Collaborations to Impact the Region." This is one of several CCNY-funded projects that support social science research in Arab societies. The introductory chapter in this volume provides information about a number of these important and very consequential projects.

The extraordinary encouragement and support of two CCNY program officers, Hillary Weisner and Nehal Amer, are acknowledged with very sincere and special thanks.

Preparation of the guide is not the only activity that the CCNY grant has supported. The project also brought together young Arab scholars and professionals for two years of workshops and a final international conference. Working with these impressive young women and men on the design and conduct of social science research contributed significantly to my thinking about the kind of guide to research that would be helpful to these and other Arab (and non-Arab) social scientists. I very happily acknowledge the indirect but nonetheless significant contribution of the workshop participants.

My partners in administering the CCNY grant are Amaney Jamal of Princeton University and Michael Robbins of the Arab Barometer. Permit me to mention that both of these accomplished scholars received their doctorate degrees in political science at the University of Michigan. Amaney, Michael, and I collaborated closely on the design and conduct of the workshops, and Amaney and Michael deserve much of the credit for the success of the project.

Amaney, Michael, and I were very ably assisted by Abdul-Wahab Kayyali, a young Jordanian scholar and musician. He contributed significantly to both the efficiency and the collegiality of the workshops.

Amaney, Michael, and I manage the Arab Barometer survey project, which is described in the introductory chapter and utilized frequently in subsequent chapters to provide examples and exercises. Together with Khalil Shikaki, a prominent Palestinian political scientist, Amaney and I established the Barometer in 2006, after which it was named the best new dataset by the American Political Science

Association. We currently co-direct the Barometer. Michael leads the Barometer's team and directs operations, including the design as well as the implementation of surveys and associated activities. He deserves much of the credit for moving the Barometer from its modest beginnings to the prominence and visibility it enjoys today.

I also acknowledge with thanks the help of Lana Shehadeh, an Arab-American political scientist who teaches at the Ramallah Campus of the Arab American University in the West Bank. Lana arranged for early drafts of several chapters to be read and reviewed by students in her research methodology class. The volume has benefitted from the observations and suggestions Lana passed along.

Finally, I owe special thanks to those who assisted me in writing this guide. Michael Robbins and Abdul-Wahab Kayyali each wrote one of the four appendices. The other two were written by Rebecca Savelsberg and Irene Morse, advanced doctoral students in the University of Michigan's political science graduate program.

Rebecca and Irene, along with Kallan Larsen, at the time a graduate student in Michigan's survey methodology program, assisted me in almost all phases of the preparation of this guide, from drafting or redrafting paragraphs to editing and proofreading. I worked closely with each of them and I benefitted enormously from their intelligence, knowledge of social science research design and methods, and commitment to the project.

Contents

1 Introduction: Origins, Approach, and an Arab Sensibility 1
   1.1 Origins and Institutional Connections 1
   1.2 The Difficult to Define Middle Ground 5
   1.3 Options and Choices 8
   1.4 The Arab Dimension 11
   1.5 The Chapters 13

2 Univariate Analysis: Variance, Variables, Data, and Measurement .. 19
   2.1 Thinking About Research 19
   2.2 Variance and Variables 20
       2.2.1 The Concept of Variance 20
       2.2.2 Units of Analysis and Variance 22
       2.2.3 Univariate Distributions 25
       2.2.4 Qualitative Research 28
       2.2.5 Descriptive Statistics 31
       2.2.6 Visual Descriptions 34
   2.3 Data Collection and Measurement 37
       2.3.1 Types of Data and Measurement Scales 37
       2.3.2 Data Sources and Data Collection 38
       2.3.3 Conceptual Definitions and Operational Definitions 40
       2.3.4 Measurement Quality 42
       2.3.5 Capturing Variance 47

3 Bivariate Analysis: Associations, Hypotheses, and Causal Stories ... 51
   3.1 Description, Explanation, and Causal Stories 51
   3.2 Hypotheses and Formulating Hypotheses 56
   3.3 Describing and Visually Representing Bivariate Relationships 65
   3.4 Probabilities and Type I and Type II Errors 72
   3.5 Measures of Association and Bivariate Statistical Tests 77

4 Multivariate Analysis: Causation, Control, and Conditionality 87
   4.1 Causal Inference 87
       4.1.1 Covariance and Causation 87
       4.1.2 Temporal Sequence 90
       4.1.3 Multivariate Regression 93

		4.1.4	Control Variables	103
	4.2	Third Variable Possibilities		109
		4.2.1	Other "Third" Variables	109
		4.2.2	Direct and Indirect Relationships	109
		4.2.3	Disaggregation/Conditional Effects	113
		4.2.4	Scope Conditions	119
		4.2.5	Experiments	125

5 Reprise and Conclusion: Overview, Audience, and Uses of the Guide ... 135

Appendices ... 141
- Appendix 1: Fieldwork and Ethics ... 141
  - Pre-Arrival and Preparation ... 141
  - First Steps in the Field ... 142
  - Best Practices of Data Collection and Preservation ... 143
  - Managing Subjectivity and Ensuring the Safety of Collaborators ... 144
  - After the Field ... 145
- Appendix 2: Research Ethics ... 146
  - Informed Consent ... 146
  - Protecting Confidentiality ... 147
  - Trauma and Sensitive Topics ... 148
  - Fieldwork as an Unequal Exchange ... 148
  - Internal Review Boards ... 149
  - Ethics and the Bigger Picture ... 150
- Appendix 3: Survey Research ... 150
  - The Arab Barometer ... 150
  - Sampling Methods ... 150
  - Survey Mode ... 152
  - Survey Questions ... 155
  - Conclusion ... 157
- Appendix 4: Software for Statistics and Data Analysis ... 157
  - Stata ... 158
  - R ... 158
  - SPSS ... 159
  - Excel and Google Sheets ... 159

About the Author

Mark Tessler is Samuel J. Eldersveld Collegiate Professor of Political Science at the University of Michigan. Between 2005 and 2013, he also served as the University's Vice Provost for International Affairs, leading many of the university's global engagement initiatives. He has received the University of Michigan's Distinguished Faculty Achievement Award, which honors senior faculty who have consistently demonstrated outstanding achievements in scholarly research and/or creative endeavors. He has also received the award given by the Department of Political Science in highest recognition of excellence in undergraduate education.

Professor Tessler has studied and/or conducted field research in Tunisia, Israel, Morocco, Egypt, Palestine (West Bank and Gaza), and Qatar. He has also taught at several universities in sub-Saharan Africa. He is co-founder and co-director, with Amaney Jamal, of the Arab Barometer survey project, which, since its establishment in 2006, has carried out 68 large probability-based and nationally representative surveys. There are sixteen Arab countries in which at least one Arab Barometer survey has been conducted. As of spring 2022, slightly more than 100,000 men and women have been interviewed.

Many of Professor Tessler's scholarly publications examine the nature, determinants, and political implications of the attitudes and values, including those pertaining to governance, to women, and to Islam, held by ordinary citizens in the Middle East. Among the fifteen books he has authored, coauthored, or edited are *The Evaluation and Application of Survey Research in the Arab World* (1987); *Area Studies and Social Science: Strategies for Understanding Middle East Politics* (1999); *Public Opinion in the Middle East: Survey Research and the Political Orientations of Ordinary Citizens* (2011); *Islam and Politics in the Middle East: Explaining the Views of Ordinary Citizens* (2015), supported by a Carnegie Scholar award from the Carnegie Corporation of New York; and *Religious Minorities in Non-Secular Middle Eastern and North African States* (2020).

Professor Tessler has directed social research capacity-building and institutional development projects in Algeria, the UAE, and Qatar. He has organized and taught seminars on social science research in Algeria, the UAE, Kuwait, Bahrain, Oman, Qatar, Palestine, and Ann Arbor.

Professor Tessler has also written extensively on the Israeli-Palestinian conflict. His book, *A History of the Israeli-Palestinian Conflict* (2009), has received national honors and awards.

Introduction: Origins, Approach, and an Arab Sensibility

This guide offers readers a concise overview of the elements of social science research, from topic to design to data and analysis. By incorporating examples of research in Arab societies and including exercises using data from the Arab Barometer survey project, the guide situates social scientific concepts and methods in the social and political environment of the Arab world. It will, therefore, be of particular relevance to social scientists who study the Arab region, including, and perhaps especially, Arab scholars who conduct social science research.

The guide does not go into as much depth as do textbooks on the theory and methodology of social science inquiry, but it provides much more information than would an annotated checklist or glossary. Accordingly, with a particular audience and application in mind, the guide seeks to find the middle ground between too much information and not enough information. This introductory chapter discusses the following topics: the origins of this guide and the context in which it has been prepared; what it does and does not cover and the audience for which it is most likely to prove useful; the approach to social science research that has guided decisions about what to cover and what to emphasize; the Arab Barometer, a 16-year old multi-country survey research project with which this guide has a special connection; and a brief summary of the five substantive chapters and the four appendices.

1.1 Origins and Institutional Connections

The idea for this guide to social science research began to take shape when our Arab Barometer team was invited by the Carnegie Corporation of New York, hereafter CCNY, to develop and submit a proposal for the advancement of social science research in the Arab world. In consultation with the very knowledgeable and engaged CCNY program officers, Hillary Weisner and Nehal Amer, a plan was developed to recruit young Arab scholars based at universities or other research institutions and to work with these men and women to develop research and capacity-building opportunities. The proposed project received generous Carnegie

Corporation funding through grants to be administered by the University of Michigan and Princeton University. The project's title reflects both its ambitious goals and the intended beneficiaries: "Understanding Marginalized Communities in the Arab World through Social Science Research: Gaining Insight, Enhancing Capacity, and Building Collaborations to Impact the Region."

The young Arab social scientists participating in the Marginalized Communities project came from Egypt, Iraq, Jordan, Kuwait, Lebanon, Morocco, Palestine, Sudan and Tunisia. These women and men participated in a series of workshops devoted to the theory and method of social science research and to the development by each participant of an original and publishable research project. Examples of the topics on which participants produced publishable, and published, papers are "Quality of Life among Older Syrian Refugees in Jordan: A Quantitative Study," "Perceptions of Sub-Saharan Immigrants about Morocco," and "Are More Educated Women Less at Risk of Experiencing Intimate Partner Violence? Evidence from Tunisia." The preparation of this guide to social science research was also one of the deliverables that the Arab Barometer team happily agreed to provide.

This was by no means the first time that the Carnegie Corporation of New York had supported and helped to initiate projects focused on social science research in the Arab world. On the contrary, for the last two decades, if not more, CCNY has been encouraging and supporting the conduct of social science research both in the Arab world and by scholars from this region. Capacity-building activities have been an important part of many of these projects. An example, beginning in 2013, is the provision of two-year grants to American universities for "mobility fellowships in support of social scientists from the Arab region." Fellowship recipients spent a semester or year at a U.S. research university, where they worked on research projects and collaborated with local faculty members. For example, from fall 2014 to spring 2018, the University of Michigan, one of the participating universities, hosted six Arab social scientists from, respectively, Morocco, Tunisia, Palestine, and Oman. Two were political scientists, and the other four were from the fields, respectively, of sociology, history, women's studies, and development studies.

One of the most important Carnegie-supported projects devoted to building social science research capacity in the Arab world has been developed and led by the American Political Science Association. Designed for Arab doctoral students in Political Science and other social science disciplines and known informally as the APSA-MENA Workshops Program, the project enables teams of Arab and U.S.-based scholars to plan a pair of workshops devoted to research on an issue of both academic and policy significance. Following a call for applications, the team selects about two dozen participants, three or four of whom may be doctoral students at U.S. universities, and then plans the agenda for the workshops.

For example, workshops devoted to research on petroleum rich countries in the Arab world and elsewhere were planned by social scientists from Kuwait, Qatar, and the U.S. in 2017. Workshops were held in Qatar in May and Kuwait in December, and sessions were divided between those devoted to reading and discussing relevant scholarly literature and those devoted the design and development of an original research project by each participant. In 2016, to give another example, a team of

Table 1.1 Seven Waves of Arab Barometer Surveys

Country	Wave 1 2007	Wave 2 2011	Wave 3 2013	Wave 4 2016	Wave 5 2018	Wave 6 2020	Wave 7 2022
Algeria	X	X	X	X	X	X	X
Bahrain	X						
Egypt		X	X	X	X		X
Iraq		X	X		X	X	X
Jordan	X	X	X	X	X	X	X
Kuwait			X		X		X
Lebanon	X	X	X	X	X	X	X
Libya			X		X	X	X
Mauritania							X
Morocco	X		X	X	X	X	X
Palestine	X	X	X	X	X		X
Qatar				X	X		
Saudi Arabia		X					
Sudan		X	X				X
Tunisia		X	X	X	X	X	X
Yemen	X	X	X		X		

social scientists from Egypt and the U.S. organized a pair of workshops devoted to research on associational life and civil society. The workshops were held in Beirut and Cairo.

These few examples, and there are many others, give a sense of the important investment that the Carnegie Corporation has made, and continues to make, in providing opportunities and building capacity to strengthen social science research in the Arab world.

The Arab Barometer has made a different kind of investment in social science research in the Arab world. The Arab Barometer is a nonpartisan research network that conducts public opinion surveys in the Arab region in order to provide insight into the attitudes, values, and concerns of ordinary citizens. Since its establishment in 2006, the Arab Barometer has conducted 68 large, probability-based, and nationally representative surveys organized into seven temporal waves. There are 16 Arab countries in which at least one survey has been conducted; in three of these countries, a survey has been conducted in all seven waves; there are another three in which a survey has been conducted in six of the seven waves; and there are three more in which there has been a survey in five of the seven waves. Table 1.1 shows, as of 2022, where and when Arab Barometer surveys have been carried out. With the exception of Wave VI, when the coronavirus pandemic required phone surveys, all Arab Barometer surveys have been conducted through face-to-face interviews. Slightly more than 100,000 men and women have been interviewed at the time of this writing.

The following topics are generally covered, some in greater depth than others, in Arab Barometer surveys: corruption, economic concerns, extremism, gender issues, governance, international relations, political institutions, religion, social justice, and youth. The Arab Barometer survey instrument is thoroughly evaluated and revised at the start of each new wave of surveys. The topic and format of many questions asked in previous surveys are retained in order to maximize comparability over time. Questions on topics that are no longer relevant are deleted, and new questions on important topics not covered previously are added. In Wave IV, for example, a battery of items designed to measure attitudes toward the Islamic State was added, and in Wave V a battery on sexual harassment and intimate partner violence was added. Beginning in Wave IV, survey experiments were added to the Arab Barometer interview schedule. Finally, when needed, small changes are made in the instrument to be used in specific countries. Questions may be added to assess attitudes toward important local concerns. Questions that are not relevant or too sensitive may be removed.

Arab Barometer surveys are subjected to extensive assessment and quality control procedures, including both before and after a survey has been carried out. The Barometer's multi-country Steering Committee, and representatives of in-country partner institutions in some instances, oversee construction of the interview schedule and selection of the questions to be asked, with the primary version in Arabic and a secondary version in English. Thereafter, interviewer training is carried out in participating countries and, as is standard procedure in serious survey research, the survey instrument is pretested and if necessary refined. Following conduct of the surveys, the data are reviewed and cleaned by members of the Arab Barometer leadership team. Information provided by enumerators about each interview, such as whether or not other persons were present during the interview, is considered to assess the likelihood that distortions were introduced. Reliability and validity are assessed, particularly for questions about topics that might be sensitive, and tests are run to identify any interviews that might have been fabricated by an enumerator. Following this review, undertaken at the completion of each survey, a final dataset is prepared and placed on the Arab Barometer website for examination or downloading by others, and Barometer datasets have in fact been downloaded hundreds of times by individuals in many different countries.

This makes the Arab Barometer the largest repository of reliable and publicly available data on the views of men and women in the Arab world. Although designed primarily for use in scholarly or policy-relevant research, and increasingly for instructional purposes as well, Arab Barometer surveys also perform the very important function of giving voice to the needs, concerns, and aspirations of ordinary citizens in Arab countries.

Arab Barometer data can also be used by interested persons who do not wish to download the wave-specific or country-specific data, possibly because they do not have the necessary software or perhaps have not had sufficient training in the analysis of quantitative social science data. These individuals can make use of the Online Analysis Tool, which is available in both English and Arabic. The tool will show the distribution of responses to any question or questions, separately, if desired, for either all respondents or subsets of respondents with different demographic profiles—showing the response distributions separately for women and men, for example. The online analysis tool will show these distributions for any specified wave or waves and for any specified country or countries. The image below shows the output of the Online Analysis Tool when asked to provide the Tunisian Wave III responses to the question, "How would you evaluate the current economic situation in your country?"

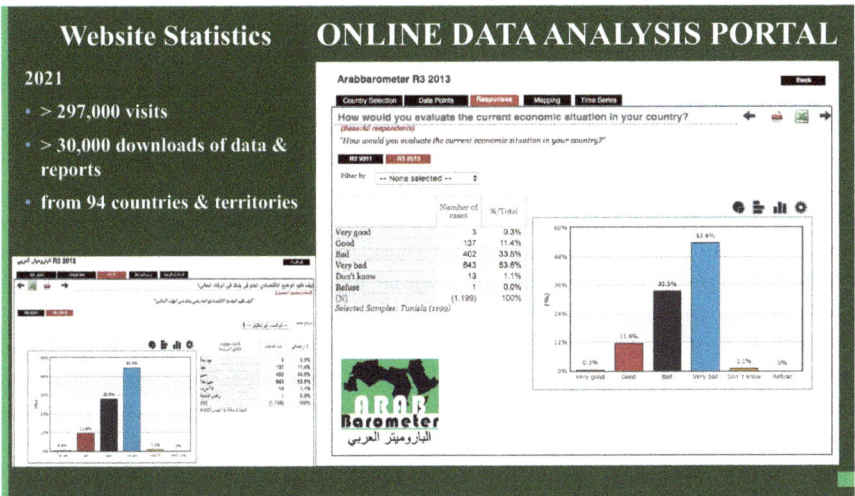

In addition to the data, the survey instrument, and the Online Analysis Tool, the Arab Barometer website contains a great deal of additional information that will be useful to persons interested in the views of Arab publics. Some of the information is technical or methodological. This may not be of general interest, but persons using Arab Barometer data should be familiar with it. The information is also instructive for persons interested in designing new surveys. The Arab Barometer website also contains numerous reports, short articles, and blog posts. Most of these are available in both Arabic and English. They are organized by topic, making them easy to find.

1.2 The Difficult to Define Middle Ground

With support and encouragement from the Carnegie Corporation of New York and with direction and substance provided by the Arab Barometer leadership team, the present guide to the design and implementation of social science research, with particular reference to the Arab world, has been prepared in the hope that it will prove to be a useful supplement to existing textbooks on the theory and methodology of social science inquiry.[1] A direct and substantive discussion of the elements of

---

[1] Among the textbooks that will be very helpful are John Gerring, *Social Science Methodology: A Unified Approach*. Cambridge: Cambridge University Press, 2012; Henry Brady and David Collier,

social science research begins in the next chapter. Before turning to this chapter, however, it will be useful for readers to know something of the assumptions and choices that have shaped the preparation of this guide to social science research in the Arab world and beyond. Accordingly, we turn now to a brief account of some of these assumptions and choices: the question of depth, the question of breadth, and the intended audience.

The Question of Depth This guide to the design and conduct of social science research seeks to situate itself at an appropriate and helpful middle ground between textbooks, on the one hand, for which these chapters are by no means a substitute, and on the other, study guides that are little more than checklists of key concepts and terms or glossaries with two- or three-sentence definitions. Readers should approach this guide to social science research with the sense of a continuum ranging from a detailed and very thorough approach on the one hand to a limited and very introductory approach on the other. The present volume seeks to make its contribution at an intermediate point on this continuum, a point that is distant from each of the two poles.

Specifying the degree of detail that defines this intermediate space is to at least some degree an exercise in decision-making that is unavoidably subjective, and in the end perhaps also arbitrary. There is also a significant degree of subjectivity and attendant variation associated with the concepts, methods and applications about which the guide offers information. The guide does not provide the amount of information about any of these concepts, methods and applications that is comparable to that available in textbooks on social science research, of which there are many. So, it definitely is not a textbook, or even what might be called a textbook light, which would be distinguished primarily by the presence of illustrative examples drawn from social or political research in Arab societies. Even with respect to the subjects discussed in relative detail, it will often be necessary to consult a textbook in order to arrive at a fuller and more complete understanding of the meaning, utility, advantages, disadvantages, and assumptions of a particular concept or method. Turning to a textbook will, of course, be even more necessary for a full understanding of concepts, methods and applications discussed in relatively less detail.

Although turning to a textbook is often necessary for an in-depth understanding of a concept or method, the guide is, nonetheless, much more than a checklist or glossary. It provides a valuable foundation for thinking about tasks and operations, conceptual as well as methodological, that are necessary elements of systematic theory-driven and evidence-based social science research. Further, the guide offers not only an introduction to the elements that must be considered in the design and implementation of social science research, but also provides an understanding of

---

ed., *Rethinking Social Inquiry: Diverse Tools, Shared Standards*. Plymouth, UK: Roman & Littlefield, 2010; and Gary King, Robert Keohane, and Sidney Verba. *Designing Social Inquiry: Scientific Inference in Qualitative Research*. Princeton: Princeton University Press, 1994. For a valuable text on survey research, see Robert Groves, et al., *Survey Methodology*. Hoboken, NJ: John Wiley & Sons, 2009.

how these elements fit together to define the stages and give analytical coherence to a research project.

The Question of Breadth The challenge of finding a helpful and instructive middle ground between a thorough and in-depth account and a largely superficial account of social science research theory and method pertains not only to the amount of detail to be provided when discussing a particular topic or subtopic; it also pertains to the number of topics and subtopics to be discussed. The goal here is to cover enough ground to give a meaningful understanding of the whole as well as the important parts of the research process in social science, and to do so without taking numerous side-trips into the finer points, what some would call the minutia, of the research process. Thus, with respect to scope as well as depth, the guide seeks a kind of equilibrium between too much and too little—and for those familiar with the reference, it seeks an equilibrium that is the "Goldilocks" point.

The Audience This middle ground approach to content helps to define the audience for which the guide will be most useful. It will not provide enough detail for individuals whose professional aspirations give an important place to the design and conduct of social science research. To those with such aspirations who are at an early stage in their professional journey, it offers a well-informed point of departure and a helpful guide for selecting the topics and subtopics to which they should devote more attention. But these individuals will soon enough need to engage with and master details and specificities that are below the depth and beyond the scope of the present text.

For others, those who seek a meaningful understanding of social science research but have no interest or need for the kind of mastery required of professional researchers, the guide provides a clear and coherent overview and synthesis of relevant concepts and procedures. Among those who fit this description, those who are the primary audience for which this guide is intended, might be:

- university students taking an introductory or middle level class on the theory and method of social science research, with the present text assigned along with a textbook on the theory and method of social science research;
- other university students majoring in a social science or a relevant professional school discipline, the latter to include public health, public policy, and education, among others;
- men and women who would be part of a social science research team in which others take the lead and have primary responsibility for analytical and methodological details; and
- those who by interest or profession regularly consume, and perhaps must also utilize in their own work, publications and other papers that report the findings of research projects.

These latter categories suggest that beyond the university setting, which is where most of those for whom this guide is intended are to be found, there are many professions for which an understanding of social science research will be helpful and perhaps even necessary.

There is an additional and very important consideration pertaining to the audience for this guide. Although it will be of value to others, this guide is intended in particular for social scientists who conduct research in the Arab world and, perhaps especially, for social scientists *from* the Arab world. Discussions of concepts, methods, and applications are regularly accompanied by examples from theory-driven and evidence-based social science research in Arab societies on topics of concern to Arab publics. These examples demonstrate the relevance and value of this approach to social science research; they show that the fruits of such research can be meaningful insights and deeper understandings.

Many of the research reports discussed for purposes of illustration have been published in prominent and high impact Western scholarly journals. This demonstrates that insights derived from the study of Arab society are often of value to social scientists and others whose own research does not have an Arab world focus. This shows, in other words, that there should not be, and is not, an epistemological barrier between Arab social science and social science elsewhere. Each draws upon, and contributes to, the framing, findings, and insights of the other. This guide exposes and clarifies the recursive relationship between Arab social science research and social science research more generally.

It remains the case, however, that many of the published research reports presented in this guide to illustrate various concepts, methods, and applications have been authored by Western social scientists. Many of these are based on in-depth fieldwork, frequently involving collaboration with local counterparts. Some of the studies discussed for purposes of illustration are the work of Arab social scientists, but most are not, and this identifies a potentially non-trivial limitation in the degree to which Arab scholars, investigators, and students will find these illustrations to be entirely instructive. The addition of examples based on research projects designed and led by Arab investigators will make this guide more instructive and valuable, and readers are encouraged to seek out and consider such examples. Finding and discussing such examples might be a particularly useful assignment in courses that ask students to read the present volume.

1.3 Options and Choices

In addition to making clear that this guide to the design and conduct of social science research self-consciously situates itself in the middle ground between textbooks, on the one hand, and annotated checklists and glossaries, on the other, the elements of social science research discussed in the chapters to follow also reflect options and choices of a different kind. These choices pertain to the general approach to social science research that is emphasized, to the primacy that is given to particular units and levels of analysis, and to the chosen balance between quantitative research and qualitative research. It will be helpful for readers to be familiar with these options and choices, and with the reasons particular choices have been made, as they turn to the chapters that follow.

Additionally, these are precisely the kind of decisions about approach and emphasis that an investigator must make when selecting and framing a research question, as well as designing a program of research addressed to this question. Important research questions can often be meaningfully studied from a variety of approaches and perspectives, only one of which is the positivist approach discussed below and in the following chapters. Similarly, it is often the case that there is not only one "correct" unit and level of analysis and not only one "correct" decision about whether the investigation should collect and analyze quantitative data or qualitative data or some combination of the two. The nature of the research question and the investigator's own interests and objectives are, of course, paramount, as they should be. Indeed, neophyte researchers are routinely advised to select a topic about which they are passionate. Nevertheless, the concerns discussed here represent common choices that investigators must make, whether or not they are aware of doing so.

The Approach The approach to research discussed in this volume is often described as "positivist." Positivism refers to investigations that rely on empirical evidence, that is to say factual knowledge acquired through direct observation, measurement, or experiments. Positivism does not refer only to factual knowledge that is quantified, or quantifiable, and thus suitable for statistical analysis. It also refers to factual knowledge, that is to say data based on observation, that is qualitative.

The kind of social science research that is the focus of the present guide is also sometimes described by the term "causal inference." The goal in such research is to identify and evaluate cause and effect relationships that help to explain not only *what* the world looks like but also how and *why* it behaves the way it does; the goal, in other words, is to move from description and prediction to explanation. A search for insights and understandings that have explanatory power references first the way that research questions are selected and framed, and only thereafter the kind of data that are sought and the way in which these data are used and analyzed. This usually involves the specification of one or more conceptually-defined causal relationships and the mechanisms that tell how and why the presumed cause impacts the presumed effect. This may be described as a "causal story," and it should be made explicit when formulating research questions that ask about cause and effect.

Also to be noted with respect to causal inference is the importance and meaning of the term "inference." The term references the fact that causation usually cannot be directly observed and must instead be inferred. The analysis is designed to build as strong a case as possible that a relationship presumed to be causal actually is causal, that it does, therefore, have explanatory power. But, with the partial exception of experiments, causation usually cannot be proved, and so it must be inferred and then evaluated in light of the strengths and weaknesses of the case for causation that a researcher is able to build. The evidence with which the case is constructed includes the findings that analysis of the data has produced. It also includes the degree to which the causal story makes sense and is persuasive.

Social science research projects characterized by both positivism and causal inference are also sometimes described as theory-driven and data-based. It is not necessary to be concerned with the differences between these terms. They sometimes overlap in discussions about the approach of a particular research project or set of projects, and the logic of the terms themselves will become more familiar and clear in the chapters ahead. The point to be retained here is that there are various approaches to social science research, all of them valid and frequently used, and that theory-driven evidence-based inquiry is only one among a number of approaches, albeit the one that probably is most widely used today. Other approaches, which are beyond the scope of this volume, include studies that are normative and do not seek empirical grounding; projects that develop innovative methods of observation but seek only thick description and do not lay a foundation for causal inference and explanation; and lines of inquiry that construct formal theoretical models that are developed deductively and are not necessarily evaluated with reference to factual knowledge and empirical evidence.

Units and Levels of Analysis Unit of analysis refers to the entity whose actions or attributes a research project seeks to describe and explain. Level of analysis just describes research about that unit. If investigators are interested in voting behavior, for example, they can interview individuals, men and women, to learn whether they did or did not vote in the last election. The unit of analysis is the individual, the person who either did or did not vote, and a study that interviewed individuals about their voting behavior would be described as an investigation at the individual level of analysis.

The unit and level of analysis may be determined by the questions a research project seeks to answer. Given the topic, there may be only one right and obvious unit and level. But many subjects can be studied at any one of several levels of analysis. Rather than investigate whether, and then why, each member of a population of individuals did or did not vote, researchers may deem it more productive to describe and explain voter turnout across a number of countries. In this case, country is the unit of analysis, and the study itself is being conducted at the country level of analysis. Still other units and levels of analysis may also be relevant for a study of voting, and the researcher will have to decide which one or ones to pursue. Further, the choice will be based not only on the investigator's particular and idiosyncratic interests but also on an understanding of the level at which the phenomenon to be studied actually operates.

The conceptual and methodological considerations discussed in the chapters to follow give examples in which sometimes the individual and sometimes the country is the unit and level of analysis. More frequent, however, are individual-level examples, and the reason for this, in part, is because of the availability and convenience of using Arab Barometer survey data to illustrate important points, Arab Barometer data being based, of course, on interviews with individuals. But the principles and methods, as the chapters will make clear, apply in the same way to different units and levels of analysis. Indeed, Arab Barometer survey data can be aggregated to capture variance in which country is the unit of analysis, thereby laying a foundation for comparison across countries and/or over time.

Quantitative and Qualitative Analysis Much of the discussion and a disproportionate number of examples in the chapters to follow will involve quantitative analysis. This is partly because of the availability and convenience of using Arab Barometer survey data for illustrations and exercises. But this is also, and even more, because data management and analysis methods are not the same for quantitative data and qualitative data, and familiarity with the former is necessary for the investigation of many topics, or at least for the consumption of a significant proportion of the social science research that is being carried out at the present time and made available through publications or other dissemination vehicles.

The present volume's emphasis on quantitative data and analysis is not to imply that working with qualitative data is less valuable. Studies based on qualitative data can also be theory-driven and evidence-based, just as a study based on quantitative data can eschew explanation and limit itself to description. The conceptual and analytical aspects of research that provide a foundation for causal inference, that come into play when moving beyond description and proposing relationships that may have explanatory power, are just as available and relevant in qualitative research as in quantitative research. The important point, then, is that theory-driven and evidence-based research, research seeking to make the case for causal inference, is not confined to investigations that gather and analyze quantitative data. Research that gathers and analyzes qualitative data may also be theory-driven and evidence-based, and a few examples of such studies are presented and discussed in Chap. 2.

1.4 The Arab Dimension

What, if anything, makes the information presented in this guide of special relevance for social scientists who study society and politics in the Arab world? Put differently, and perhaps better, how can this information be introduced and discussed in ways that make it especially relevant for social scientists conducting research in the Arab world, or who are themselves Arab social scientists? And this despite a possible limitation noted earlier: that many of the research projects presented as examples in this guide were carried out in Arab societies by Western investigators.

This is a non-trivial question that requires a meaningful response. At the same time, the elements of theory-driven and evidence-based social science inquiry that are described and discussed in the chapters to follow are not relevant only for certain political environments, be these Arab or Western or other. On the contrary, they are relevant for social science research in general, and hence in many, and potentially almost all, social, political, and economic environments. Accordingly, then, there is not a specifically Arab social science research methodology. Nor is there one specifically for Muslims or the Middle East or, equally important, for the United States or Europe or Africa or other.

Political conditions in some Arab countries may for a time limit the ability to carry out research and apply the elements of this broadly-applicable approach and methodology, and conditions on the ground may make some research designs more useful than others. And of course, a theory-driven and evidence-based investigation may not be the approach best suited to the questions and objectives of a particular research project. But if the political conditions in an Arab country make it difficult or even impossible to implement the research design that best suits the questions being investigated, the barriers to feasibility are not the result of the country's Arab character; they are the result, rather, of the political conditions. Investigators in a non-Arab country characterized by the same political conditions would face the same barriers. Similarly, in the absence of these or other limiting conditions, the opportunities for conducting research would be the same in Arab and non-Arab countries.

It is thus with facts on the ground that an Arab dimension begins to appear. It is in their application that the concepts and methods discussed in this guide take on the flavor of a society. Accordingly, the chapters to follow illustrate many of the concepts and methods they introduce with examples of real-world research projects in the Arab region, projects in which the selection and application of particular conceptual considerations and methodological techniques can easily be seen. It is in this way, here through exposure and explanation and elsewhere through the design and conduct of real and lived research experiences, that a connection is made between the elements of social science research in general and in the abstract and the on-the-ground reality of a society, in this case an Arab society—or Arab societies, actually, since there are large societal, political, and economic differences across the Arab world, and indeed, within Arab countries. Notwithstanding the need for more examples based on research projects designed and carried out by Arab social scientists, the illustrations provided in the chapters that follow demonstrate the applicability to Arab milieu, as to other milieu, of the approach to social science research that is the focus of this guide.

Even here there are limitations in the degree to which this becomes an Arab story. On the one hand, there really is not an "Arab" story. There are very important differences among the societies and political communities to be found in the Arab world, differences possibly large enough to outweigh any commonalities that might exist and to call into question the existence of observations or knowledge to which the differentiating term "Arab" can be legitimately applied. On the other hand, research questions and research findings that are relevant to the Arab world, or to a substantial part of it, do not cease to be interesting or relevant beyond the borders of the region. So, in a certain sense, the search for a uniquely Arab research agenda, let alone an Arab research approach or methodology, is for the most part illusory.

These considerations notwithstanding, genuine and deep familiarity with the elements of social science research is acquired not by reading about them and thinking about them in the abstract, unrelated to their application in an actual research endeavor. On the contrary, it is exactly by their application in real-world research endeavors that this deep familiarity is acquired, and such experience must be sought and obtained by the investigator herself; its provision is beyond the scope of the present guide. But by including examples drawn from actual research in Arab societies, the chapters in this guide encourage readers to put themselves in the place of the investigator. In this way, the elements of social science research are to be considered and understood by readers from the perspective of their application in a real or imagined research project addressed to important on-the-ground concerns in one or more Arab societies.

Thinking about real-world applications will increase the perceived relevance for readers of the concepts and methods being discussed, thus contributing to learning about them and understanding more fully their place in the research process. In addition, however, this will bring an Arab sensibility to their thinking about social science research. As they reflect on the places and issues in the Arab region that are central to the research exemplars described in the text, and as they perhaps also reflect on a project they would themselves design and conduct, their thinking about facts on the ground will strengthen the sense of a connection between the principles of social science research and the Arab arena, or arenas, in which these principles will be applied.

There is one additional way, and an important way, in which this guide seeks to develop and communicate an Arab sensibility. This is by drawing on the Arab Barometer in a number of instances in the chapters that follow. The nature and value of the Arab Barometer survey project were discussed earlier, and the data it provides are an invaluable resource for examining the nature and determinants of the attitudes, values, concerns, and preferences of Arab publics. The chapters that follow build a connection to the Arab world by using Arab Barometer data to illustrate procedures, give examples, and suggest exercises. The latter can easily be done using the Online Analysis Tool on the Arab Barometer website. As readers consider possibilities and make decisions about the countries and time periods from which to take data to complete a suggested exercise, the sense of a connection between the principles of social science research, on the one hand, and the reality of the Arab world, on the other, will again be strengthened. Readers may also imagine their own exercises, looking into the nature and distribution of attitudes toward selected issues or just exploring response distributions without any previously selected research question. Here again, and even more fully, readers will immerse themselves in the world of Arab publics, guided by their own questions but also by the principles of social science research.

1.5 The Chapters

There are five chapters in this guide. They are based on and ordered by the number of variables to be considered. Chapter 2 deals with variables one at a time, and hence is devoted to univariate analysis. Chapter 3 deals with variables two at a time and the possible relationships between two variables. This, of course, is bivariate analysis. Chapter 4 considers the different ways that analyses can be enriched if they involve three or more variables. This can be described as multivariate possibilities.

As discussed briefly below, the three chapters may also be described and named by the principal conceptualizations and methodologies they discuss. Chapter 2 focuses on variance, a concept that is central to theory-driven and evidence-based research. It is, therefore, labelled *Variance, Variables, Data, and Measures*. Chapter 3 builds on the notion of variance and asks either why something varies, on what does it depend, or what difference does it make. The chapter is appropriately named *Associations, Hypotheses, and Causal Stories*. Chapter 4 discusses the many ways that the analysis of data can be enriched and made both more rigorous and more informative by the addition of more variables. This ranges from testing hypotheses and evaluating causal stories with models that include control variables to specifying in conceptual terms the conditions under which confirmed hypotheses do and do not apply. Consistent with these concerns, the chapter is named *Causation, Control, and Conditionality*.

Variance, Variables, Data, and Measures Chapter 2 is devoted to univariate analysis, which is concerned with description. The phenomena in which social science is interested for research purposes differ in either degree or kind, hence the variance. Also essential in this connection is unit of analysis, which is the entity that varies and the level at which that variance occurs. Considering research at the individual level of analysis, for example, meaning that the unit of analysis is the individual, there is an almost infinite number of ways in which an attitude or value, hence a normative orientation, or a pattern of behavior, can vary across a set of individuals. Some think and/or behave in one way, whereas others are different. This applies equally to a set of countries. Some countries are characterized by one set of attributes or have had one kind of experience, whereas other countries are characterized by different sets of attributes or have had different kinds of experiences. And of course, there is a vast array of other units of analysis, including provinces, political parties, charitable organizations, religious movements, and many, many more.

The objective of univariate analysis, as will be discussed in Chap. 2, is description. It is to determine and describe the distribution of ways that units—read individuals, countries, or some other unit—can and do differ with respect to the phenomenon under study, the phenomenon being a variable since it does in fact vary. For example, suppose again that the unit of analysis is the individual, that a researcher is working with a set of 1000 individuals, and that the variable of interest is interpersonal trust, which is the belief that most people are honest and trustworthy. In this case, the objectives of univariate analysis would be to determine, first, the range of ways that interpersonal trust can vary across the available set of individuals, presumably ranging from very high trust to little or no trust; next, to gather data that will permit each of the 1000 individuals to be assigned a value that records his or her particular level of interpersonal trust; and finally, to present a frequency or percentage distribution of the interpersonal trust values. This information can be presented graphically, as well as in tabular form.

This distribution, sometimes described as a mapping of the variance on a variable of interest, or on several variables of interest with each mapped separately, provides descriptive information. The intent of the researcher may be to build on this description and proceed to bivariate or multivariate analysis. Or description alone may be the objective, with the researcher thus using one or several of the standard graphical and/or statistical ways to display and communicate findings about the distribution of interpersonal trust ratings. The discussion in Chap. 2 includes a summary of the most common ways to display and communicate univariate and descriptive findings.

Two other topics covered in the chapter are data collection and measurement. The former includes a discussion of different methods of data collection and the implications this has for the concepts a researcher wants to study. The latter gives particular attention to the measurement of concepts that cannot be directly observed. This includes a discussion of the criteria by which the quality and suitability of a measure can be evaluated: particularly validity (whether the measure does in fact measure the concept it purports to measure) and reliability (whether the measure is replicable, which in social science often means agreement among a number of presumably valid indicators of the concept).

The term "operationalization" refers to the procedures an investigator uses to measure a concept that is abstract and cannot be directly observed. These measurement procedures are often described as an "operational definition" of the concept. Continuing to focus on interpersonal trust, with individual the unit of analysis and data to be collected by a public opinion survey, the investigator would begin by including in the survey instrument a number of questions that appear to be indicators of interpersonal trust. These might be questions that have been shown in previous surveys to be reliable and valid indicators of the concept, or they might be original questions devised by the researcher, or some of both.

Once the investigator's survey has been completed and the data are ready for evaluation and analysis, she can use any one of several standard statistical or other tests to determine whether each question is reliable and valid in her particular study. It is possible that indicators of a concept that are reliable and valid in some settings are not reliable and valid in other settings. Finally, the investigator will use, singly or in combination, those items that her tests have shown to be, or likely to be, reliable and valid. She might also choose to combine these items and construct a scale or index of interpersonal trust, using one of the available scaling techniques. The questions or multi-question scale that the investigator will then use to rate or categorize each individual with respect to interpersonal trust constitute, as stated, an operational definition of the concept.

Associations, Hypotheses, and Causal Stories In theory-driven and evidence-based social science research, the variable or variables that have been the focus of univariate analysis are often the point of departure for bivariate analysis. The goal of bivariate analysis may simply be to describe the way two variables are related to each other. But in the context considered here, and as discussed in Chap. 3, the objective is to move from description to explanation. Toward this end, the researcher asks *why* the variance occurs—in other words, what determines or accounts for the variance, and/or what difference does it make. Prior to data collection and analysis, a researcher should propose one or more answers to these questions, along with the reasoning that makes them persuasive, or at least plausible. Later, once data have been collected and are ready for analysis, the propositions can be evaluated in order to determine their accuracy.

The proposed answers, that is to say the propositions, are most frequently offered in the form of "if...then" statements, or cause and effect statements, which are usually called hypotheses. Simple and straightforward bivariate hypotheses are composed of a dependent variable and an independent variable. The independent variable is the cause, or the "if" in an "if...then" statement, and the dependent variable is the effect, or the "then" in an "if...then" statement; and a proposed hypothesis, meaning an "if...then" statement, will usually specify how as well as whether the independent and the dependent variable are related.

To continue using interpersonal trust for purposes of illustration, the interest of a researcher in this variable may be either as a dependent variable or as an independent variable, or possibly both. Recalling that the unit of analysis is the individual and that interpersonal trust varies among a population or sample of individuals from a very high level to a very low level, a hypothesis that considers interpersonal trust as a dependent variable will specify what other variable or variables have, or tend to have, an impact on it, either raising it or lowering it or changing it in some other way. If one such variable is level of education, for example, and if the hypothesis posits a direct and positive linear relationship, then the hypothesis simply states that an increase in a person's level of education causes, or disproportionately frequently causes, her level of interpersonal trust to go up. In other words, *if* an individual's level of education increases, *then* her level of interpersonal trust will also generally increase. If the hypothesis is confirmed, it may be said that the variable education helps to account for the variance on interpersonal trust.

The researcher may, of course, posit a hypothesis in which interpersonal trust is an independent variable, and so it posits an answer, or partial answer, to a question about the consequences of a change in interpersonal trust. Perhaps support for gender equality is one of the variables affected by interpersonal trust, such that, if the hypothesis again posits a direct and positive linear relationship, then the hypothesis states that an increase in interpersonal trust tends to bring about, or frequently brings about, an increase in support for gender equality, Once again as an "if...then" statement, *if* an individual's level of interpersonal trust increases, *then* her level of support for gender equality will generally increase as well.

A research project often has more than one hypothesis, and the direct and positive linear relationship in these examples is only one possibility among many. Chapter 3 discusses the way that variables and variable relationships are selected—the process of hypothesis formation—and it introduces and illustrates different kinds of bivariate relationships. In addition, Chap. 3 shows how bivariate relationships can be displayed in charts and graphs. It also discusses the use of bivariate statistics to determine whether an observed bivariate relationship differs significantly from the relationship that would be expected if the variables in the relationship were, in fact, unrelated.

Causation, Control, and Conditionality Chapter 4 provides an overview of the reasons and ways that one or more additional variables might be included in the analysis of a hypothesized bivariate causal relationship. One of these involves the inclusion of control variables, variables that are related to both the independent and dependent variables and might lead to an erroneous conclusion about the hypothesis if not held constant by including them in a multivariate analysis. Without appropriate control variables, the analysis might confirm the hypothesized relationship when in fact this conclusion is not justified. The erroneous and unjustified confirmation of a research hypothesis constitutes a false positive. It is called a Type I error. There is also a Type II error, as this suggests. A Type II error refers to a false negative, when a research hypothesis is rejected, or unconfirmed, when this is in fact an erroneous conclusion.

For example, the hypothesis of a positive linear relationship between a person's level of education and her level of interpersonal trust might appear to be confirmed in a bivariate analysis. It might be the case that if the person's education increases, then her level of interpersonal trust does indeed increase as well. But it might be erroneous to attribute causality to this bivariate association since one or more variables related to both the dependent variable and the independent variable, to both education and interpersonal trust, have not been controlled. Salary, or salary level, is such a variable; and to avoid the risk of making a Type I error, it would be necessary to carry out a multivariate analysis in which salary is included in the analysis. If the relationship between education and interpersonal trust remains strong when salary is included as a control variable, the case for inferring causality will be strengthened. If the hypothesized relationship does not remain strong when the control variable is included, it may be concluded that the bivariate relationship is not a causal relationship.

There are many ways in which the inclusion of one or more additional variables can also make it possible to offer a more refined and complex causal story, and/or to make the story more precise by specifying when, that is to say under what conditions, a particular variable does and does not have explanatory power. One of the possibilities discussed in Chap. 4 is the distinction between a direct and an indirect bivariate relationship. The distinction is discussed and explained in a section of the chapter entitled "Third Variable Possibilities," as is the way that data can be analyzed to determine whether the relationship between an independent variable and a dependent variable is direct or indirect. Determining whether a variable relationship is direct or indirect has the potential to significantly enrich the causal story on which a hypothesis is based.

Additional variables may also constitute conditionalities, which specify in terms of concepts when the findings about a relationship do and do not apply. Returning to the hypothesis that education accounts for variance in interpersonal trust, an analysis of the available data may confirm the relationship and justify risking a Type I error. But if the data come from one particular kind of location, say for example, wealthy MENA countries, the researcher and people interested in her findings will probably want to know whether the relationship is also confirmed and has explanatory power in less affluent MENA countries. Attributes that specify when a finding does and does not apply are called scope conditions. Should further study by the researcher or others gather data from less affluent countries and find that an analysis of these data do not confirm the hypothesis, national wealth will have been established as a scope condition; the hypothesis is confirmed and has explanatory power in countries with one level of national wealth but not in countries with a different level of national wealth.

Chapter 4 also discusses conditional relationships within a set of scope conditions. Testing for this sort of possibility involves disaggregation, which refers to testing a hypothesis separately among different subsets of the units about which the researcher has data. If the researcher expects a relationship to be different for men and women, for example, she might do the test for men and women separately. And if it is found that the hypothesis is confirmed for one sex but not the other, sex will have been found to be a conditionality. As noted earlier, this information will enable the researcher to tell a more complex and potentially instructive causal story.

Chapter 4 will very briefly discuss some of the multivariate statistical methods that are used to test hypotheses and increase confidence in a causal story. A detailed account of multivariate statistics is beyond the scope of Chap. 4, however. The chapter will also briefly discuss the use of multivariate analyses for purposes other than testing hypotheses or identifying conditionalities.

Appendices Four appendices follow Chap. 5. One deals with fieldwork and its challenges, including fieldwork in one country or society carried out by a researcher from a different country or society. A second deals with ethical considerations in social science research, including and particularly, international and cross-cultural social science research. A third appendix gives a somewhat fuller description of survey research methodology. Although surveys are only one of the many ways of collecting or generating social science data, the topic is given more attention here due to the connection of this guide to the Arab Barometer survey project. A final appendix very briefly describes the most widely used software packages for the management and analysis of social science data.

Open Access This chapter is licensed under the terms of the Creative Commons Attribution 4.0 International License (http://creativecommons.org/licenses/by/4.0/), which permits use, sharing, adaptation, distribution and reproduction in any medium or format, as long as you give appropriate credit to the original author(s) and the source, provide a link to the Creative Commons license and indicate if changes were made.

The images or other third party material in this chapter are included in the chapter's Creative Commons license, unless indicated otherwise in a credit line to the material. If material is not included in the chapter's Creative Commons license and your intended use is not permitted by statutory regulation or exceeds the permitted use, you will need to obtain permission directly from the copyright holder.

Univariate Analysis: Variance, Variables, Data, and Measurement

2.1 Thinking About Research

Why are some people in the Arab region more likely than others to vote in elections? Why do some countries but not others have higher levels of satisfaction with their healthcare systems? Why is domestic violence more prevalent in some communities than others? What causes some people but not others to become more politically engaged, or less politically engaged, over time? Every day, we come across various phenomena that make us question how, why, and with what implications do they vary across people, countries, communities, and/or time. These phenomena—e.g. voting, satisfaction with health care, domestic violence, and political engagement—are variables, and the variance they express is the foundation and the point of departure for positivist social science research. Accordingly, they are "variables of interest" in research projects that are motivated by this variance and that seek to answer questions of the kind listed above.

Most research projects begin by describing the variance referenced by the variable or variables of interest. This is description, which is the focus of the present chapter. The research project usually then goes on to propose and evaluate hypotheses about factors that account for some of the variance on the variable of interest. This is explanation, which will be the focus of Chaps. 3 and 4.

In many research projects, the concern for explanation, as expressed in hypotheses, offers a causal story about some of the determinants of the variance on the variable of interest. It offers a cause and effect story in which the variable of interest is the effect. Alternatively, the goal of a research project motivated by the variance on the variable of interest may not be why it varies as it does, but rather, what difference does it make. This is also a cause and effect story, but this time the variable of interest is the cause.

For example, if aggregate voter turnout by country is the variable of interest, an investigator might ask and try to answer the question of why citizens of some countries are more likely to vote than are citizens of other countries. One possibility she might consider, offered only as an illustration, is that higher levels of corruption incentivize voting, such that voter turnout will be higher in countries with more corruption. An investigator might also, or instead, be interested in whether voter turnout is itself a determinant of the variance on a particular and presumably important issue. She might advance for testing the proposition that greater voter turnout helps to explain why some countries have more developed and better-quality infrastructure than other countries.

Before an investigator decides on a variable (or variables) of interest and begins a research project, she must consider why the topic is important, and not only to her but also to the broader society and global community. She must also decide on the causal story she will investigate. Will she seek to identify important determinants of the variance on the variable of interest, and then explicate the ways, or mechanisms, by which these determinants exert influences? Or will she choose to consider the variable of interest as a determinant, and then investigate whether, and also how, the variable of interest exerts influence on the variance of other variables?

As stated, the variable of interest has been chosen because the investigator considers it important, and because identifying its relationships with other variables will contribute to a better understanding of political, social, or economic life. The investigator will also want to consider what has been said about the topic in the scholarly literature, and what her investigations have the potential to add to this literature. She will ask whether the topic has for the most part been overlooked, and if not, whether findings from previous research are persuasive or appear to be flawed, or whether there are knowledge gaps that her research can help to fill. By choosing important topics and investigating how and why certain phenomena vary, social science research can make valuable contributions and enrich our knowledge and understanding of societal dynamics.

The variables and variable relationships mentioned above are fictitious, provided only to illustrate that positivist social science research usually begins with the designation of a variable of interest and a description of the way it varies, then proceeds to investigate the nature and direction of its relationships, and very often its causal relationships, with other variables. Of course, designing a research project involves much more than selecting a variable of interest and specifying its relationships to other variables, and this will be the focus of Chaps. 3 and 4. Readers should keep a concern for explanation in mind as they engage with this chapter's emphasis on description.

2.2 Variance and Variables

2.2.1 The Concept of Variance

Once you have decided on a research topic, or while you are deciding whether a particular topic is of interest, the first objective of every researcher should be to understand how a variable varies. Thus, a central preoccupation of this chapter is with the concept of variance, with discovering and then presenting information about the way that the subject or subjects of interest vary. The chapter focuses, therefore, on univariate analysis, that is to say, variables taken one at a time.

The concept of variance is a foundational building block of a positivist approach to social and political inquiry, an approach that refers to investigations that rely on empirical evidence, or factual knowledge, acquired either through direct observation or measurement based on observable indicators. Positivist social science research does not always limit itself to considering variables one at a time, of course. As discussed briefly in the introductory chapter and as a central preoccupation of Chaps. 3 and 4, discerning relationships and patterns of interaction that connect two or more variables is often the objective of inquiry that begins with taking variables one at a time. Often described as theory-driven evidence-based inquiry, positivist social science research that begins with separate descriptions of variance on relevant phenomena, that is to say on the variables of interest to an investigator, frequently does so in order to establish a base for moving from description to explanation, from discerning and describing *how* something varies to shedding light on *why* and/or with what *implications* it varies.

Although discerning and describing variance may not in these instances be the end product of a social scientific investigation, being rather the point of departure for more complex bivariate and multivariate analyses concerned with determinants, causal stories, and conditionalities, it remains important to be familiar with working with variables one at a time. Relevant to this topic are: sources and methods of collecting data on variables of interest; the development of measures that are valid and reliable and capture the variance of interest to an investigator, sometimes requiring the use of indicators to measure abstract concepts that cannot be directly observed; and the use of statistics and graphs to summarize and display variance in order to parsimoniously communicate findings. These are among the topics to which the present chapter devotes attention.

It must also be added that descriptive analysis, that is to say measuring and reporting on the variance associated with particular concepts or variables, need not always be the first stage in an investigation with multivariate objectives. It can be, and often is, an end in and of itself. When the phenomenon being investigated is important, and when the structure and/or extent of its variance are not already known, either in general or in a particular social or political environment, descriptions of variance under these conditions need not be the first step on a multi-step investigatory journey to derive significance but can be, in and of themselves, the end goal of a research project with its own inherent significance.

Finally, while the principle preoccupation of this chapter and the remaining chapters is with what should be done once an investigator has decided on a research question or variables of interest, the first half of this chapter may also be helpful in choosing a research topic. The following sections discuss how to think about and describe variance, not only on the variable(s) of interest but also on other variables that will be included in the research project. Attentiveness to variance, along with the considerations discussed earlier, will help an investigator to think about a research topic and the design of her research project.

2.2.2 Units of Analysis and Variance

Positivist social science research can be conducted with both quantitative and qualitative data and methods, each of which has strengths and limitations. Some topics and questions are best addressed using quantitative data and methods, while others are better suited to qualitative research. Still other researchers utilize both quantitative and qualitative data and methods, often using insights derived from qualitative research to better understand patterns and variable associations that result from the analysis of quantitative data.

This chapter, as well as those that follow, places emphasis on social science research that works with quantitative data. In part, this is because of the volume's connection to the Arab Barometer and the ready availability of the Barometer's seven waves of survey data. Nevertheless, the concept of variance also occupies a foundational position in positivist social science research that works with qualitative data. For this reason, we briefly discuss qualitative research later in the chapter and illustrate its value with several examples.[1] We also discuss what to consider when choosing between different styles of research and types of data.

In this section, we present a few examples from Arab Barometer surveys and other data sources to highlight the importance of describing and understanding the variance of certain phenomena. These examples, which use quantitative data, will also reintroduce the notion of a **unit of analysis**, which is the entity being studied whose status with respect to the variance is being measured. The unit of analysis in studies based on Arab Barometer data is usually, although not always, the individual. These studies investigate how (and very often also why, as discussed in Chaps. 3 and 4) individuals give different responses to the same survey question. An investigator would in effect be asking, what is the range of ways that individuals, that is to say, respondents, answered a question; and how many, or what proportion, of these respondents answered the question in each of the different ways that it could be answered.

Although still somewhat limited in comparison to most other world regions, the number of systematic and high-quality surveys in Arab countries is growing, as is the number of published studies based on these surveys. For example, a study of "Gender Ideals in Turbulent Times," published in *Comparative Sociology* in 2017, used Arab Barometer data to describe the gender-related attitudes of men in Algeria, Egypt, Tunisia, and Yemen. After describing the variance on the attitudes of men in each country, the authors considered the impact of religiosity on this variable of interest and found that the impact of religiosity on attitudes about women varies in instructive ways across the four countries.[2]

---

[1] Readers who wish to further explore the conduct of qualitative data and methods research may find the following source helpful: Gary King, Robert Keohane, and Sidney Verba, *Designing Social Inquiry: Scientific Inference in Qualitative Research* (Princeton University Press, 1994).

[2] Jaime Kucinskas and Tamara van der Does, "Gender Ideals in Turbulent Times: An Examination of Insecurity, Islam, and Muslim Men's Gender Attitudes during the Arab Spring." *Comparative Sociology* 16 (2017): 340–368.

2.2 Variance and Variables

Another example, and one with objectives that clearly involve description, uses data from earlier surveys in Kuwait in 1988, 1994, and 1996 to map continuity and change in Kuwaiti social and political attitudes. Led by a team of Kuwaiti, Egyptian, and American scholars, and published in *International Sociology* in 2007, the study found, among other things, that support for democracy increased over time but attitudes pertaining to the status of women did not change. Consistent with their focus on description, the authors note that their study serves as a "baseline" for later research seeking to take account of differences in Kuwait and other nations.[3]

Country is another commonly used unit of analysis in social science research, including quantitative work. Studies in which country is the unit of analysis might compute a country-level measure by aggregating data on the behavior or attitudes of the individuals who live in that country.[4] For example, respondents in a nationally representative survey of citizens of voting age might be asked if they voted in a given election, and responses might then be aggregated to develop a country-level measure of voter turnout. In comparing countries for descriptive and/or explanatory purposes, the country-level measure might be a single value based on an average, such as the percent who voted. Or it might involve the comparison of response distributions across the countries included in the study.

Measures of both kinds have been used, for example, in the reports of Arab Barometer findings that have been published in *Journal of Democracy* after each wave of surveys. In 2012, for instance, *JoD* published "New Findings on Arabs and Democracy." The article presented and compared findings about attitudes and understandings related to democracy and about Islam's role in political affairs in countries included in the first and second wave of Arab Barometer surveys. It reported, for instance, that the percentage of ordinary citizens agreeing that "it would be better if more religious people held public office" varied from a low of 17.6 percent in Lebanon to a high of 61.0 percent in Palestine in the first wave of surveys, and in the second wave, from a low of 14.3 percent in Lebanon to a high of 61.1 percent in Yemen.[5] Thus, the individual-level data from the Arab Barometer survey was aggregated by country to create statistics at the country-level.

Of course, measuring variance across countries, making country the unit of analysis, in other words, does not involve only the aggregation of individual-level data about the country's citizens. Numerous commonly used country-level measures are produced by important international institutions, such as the United Nations, the World Bank, the Arab League, and many others. The measures themselves are numerous and very diverse, ranging, for example, from Gross Domestic Product to the UN's Human Development Index, which is based on the proportion of school

---

[3] Katherine Meyer, Helen Rizzo, and Yousef Ali, "Changed Political Attitudes in the Middle East: The Case of Kuwait." *International Sociology* 22, 7 (May 2007): 289–324.

[4] Aggregating, here, refers to the construction or calculation of a measure pertaining to a larger unit based on the summing or averaging of smaller units inside the larger unit.

[5] Mark Tessler, Amaney Jamal, and Michael Robbins. "New Findings on Arabs and Democracy." *Journal of Democracy* 23, 4 (October 2012): 89–103.

aged children actually in school, the unemployment rate, and other quality of life indicators.

Without attempting to be comprehensive, and for the broader purpose of insisting on the need to be self-aware and designate the unit of analysis in systematic social science research, it may be useful to present a small number of additional examples. On the one hand, there are quasi-academic institutions that present and regularly update ratings of countries on important concepts and variables. One example among many is Freedom House, which rates countries each year with respect to political rights and civil liberties. It awards 0 to 4 points for each of 10 political rights indicators and 15 civil liberties indicators, giving a total score from 0 to 100. In 2019, it awarded a total of 34 points to Algeria, 37 points to Morocco, and 70 points to Tunisia.

Country-level measures are also produced by individual scholars and scholarly teams for use in data-based research on particular topics or issues. A good example is the scholarly literature on what has been called the "Resource Curse," which considers the proposition that oil and mineral wealth impedes democracy. There are active debates about both theory and method in this field of research, and one result has been the development of country-level measures of key concepts and variables. Among the measures developed by an important early study, for example, is an index of oil-reliance. Scores for the 25 most oil-reliant countries at the time of the study ranged from 47.58 (Brunei) to 3.13 (Columbia). Among Arab countries, Kuwait was judged to be the most oil-reliant and given a score of 46.14. Other Arab countries judged sufficiently oil-reliant to be rated include Bahrain (45.60), Yemen (38.58), Oman (38.43), Saudi Arabia (33.85), Qatar (33.85), Libya (29.74), Iraq (23.48), Algeria (21.44), and Syria (15.00).[6] Although subsequently used in multivariate analysis to test resource curse hypotheses, this country-level index, like numerous others in which country is the unit of analysis, offers valuable descriptive information.

Individual and country are not the only units of analysis, of course. Among the many others are community and group, with numerous possibilities for describing the attributes with respect to which these units vary. Size, location, administrative structure, ethnicity and/or religion, and economic well-being are only a few of the possibilities. Each attribute is a concept and variable with respect to which the units—communities, groups—differ, and descriptions of this variance in the form of univariate distributions can be very useful. An innovative example comes from a study of Lebanese communities that sought to assign to each community a measure pertaining to public goods provision and also to governance structure. In advance of exploring the connection between these two variables, the investigator needed to develop measures of each and present these in univariate descriptions. Interestingly, an attribute related to community governance that turned out to be particularly important was whether the community was dominated by a single faction or whether

---

[6] See Michael Ross, "Does Oil Hinder Democracy." *World Politics* 53 (April 2001): 325–61. Oil reliance is measured by the value of fuel-based exports divided by GDP.

there was competition for community leadership.[7] The cross-community variance associated with this concept—community governance—was mapped in the initial, descriptive portion of the project, which involved univariate analysis and variables being considered one at a time.

2.2.3 Univariate Distributions

Before continuing the discussion of variance, and also taking a brief detour into working with qualitative data, the nature and value of univariate analysis and the presentation of descriptive information can be further illustrated by presenting univariate distributions of answers to four questions asked in Arab Barometer surveys. First, we'll look at responses to two questions about the Islamic State; and second, we'll consider responses to two questions about sexual harassment and domestic violence. These issues are obviously important, and in all four cases, variance in the experience, behavior, and attitudes of ordinary citizens is at best imperfectly known. Accordingly, particularly since samples in Arab Barometer surveys are probability-based and nationally representative, there can be little doubt that univariate distributions of responses given by the individuals interviewed by the Arab Barometer team are valuable and instructive with regard to Arab society at large.

The first example, which was explored in the fourth wave of Arab Barometer surveys, in 2016–2017, concerns Arab attitudes toward the Islamic State. Findings, presented in the top half of Table 2.1, are based on surveys in Jordan, Lebanon, Palestine, Tunisia, Algeria, and Morocco, taken together. The table shows that the overwhelming majority of those interviewed have very negative attitudes toward the Islamic State. At the same time, small minorities agree with the goals of the Islamic State and believe its actions to be compatible with the teachings of Islam.

The second example, which was explored during the fifth and sixth waves of Arab Barometer surveys, in 2018–2019 and 2020–2021, deals with sexual harassment and domestic violence, very important issues about which the variance within and across countries in the Arab world (and elsewhere) is not well-known. Accordingly, once again, discerning and then describing the variance with respect to relevant experiences or behaviors make a very valuable social scientific contribution, and this is quite apart from whatever, if anything, might be learned through bivariate and multivariate analyses in subsequent phases of the research. The lower half of Table 2.1, based on all of the respondents in the 12 countries surveyed in Wave V of the Arab Barometer, shows how people answered questions about unwanted sexual advances and in-household physical abuse. It shows that substantial majorities have not experienced physical sexual harassment and do not reside in a household in which there has been domestic violence.

---

[7] Daniel Corstange, *The Price of a Vote in the Middle East: Clientelism and Communal Politics in Lebanon and Yemen* (Cambridge University Press, 2016).

Table 2.1 Univariate frequency and percentage distributions based on responses to questions about the Islamic State, unwanted sexual advances, and in-household physical abuse

Survey item	To what extent do you agree with the goals of the Islamic State? (Arab Barometer Wave IV)			
Response options	Agree to a large extent	Somewhat agree	Somewhat disagree	Disagree to a large extent
Frequency	45	120	288	5720
Percentage	0.7	1.9	4.7	92.7
Survey item	Some people think that the Islamic State does not represent true Islam while others think that it is truthful to Islam. What do you think? (Arab Barometer Wave IV)			
Response options	Certainly represents true Islam	Represents true Islam	Does not represent true Islam	Certainly does not represent true Islam
Frequency	120	177	336	5470
Percentage	2.0	2.9	5.5	89.6
Survey item	Some people have also experienced unwanted sexual advances, like being touched in public places. How often have you experienced unwanted sexual advances in public in the past 12 months? (Arab Barometer Wave V)			
Response options	Never	Rarely	Sometimes	Often
Frequency	20,460	2929	1003	362
Percentage	82.7	11.8	4.1	1.5
Survey item	People handle disagreements in many different ways. Apart from any punishment that might be used to discipline children when they misbehave, has anyone in your household ever experienced being physically abused by another member of your family? [INTERVIEWER: Reply, if asked, I mean pushed, grabbed, or shoved; having an object thrown at you; or being slapped] (Arab Barometer Wave V)			
Response options	Yes		No	
Frequency	3716		21,162	
Percentage	14.9		85.1	

Respondent answers to survey questions can be and frequently are aggregated by country for research projects in which country is the unit of analysis. Table 2.2 shows the distribution by country of one of the Wave IV questions about the Islamic State and one of the Wave V questions about sexual harassment and domestic violence. The construction of univariate distributions in which country is the unit of analysis is simple and straightforward. In most cases, it involves simply totaling the responses of everyone in the country who was surveyed and then calculating the distribution of percentages. Less straightforward, in some instances, is deciding which unit of analysis is most appropriate for the description (and explanation) of the variance that an investigator seeks to discern.

A third example from Arab Barometer data further illustrates the choice among units of analysis that a researcher may have to make. The variance in this case refers to voting, and specifically to whether or not the respondent voted in the last parliamentary election in her country. Based on responses to the question about voting in Wave V surveys, and again aggregating data from the surveys in Jordan,

2.2 Variance and Variables

Table 2.2 Selected country-level univariate percentage distributions

	To what extent do you agree with the goals of the Islamic State? (%)				Domestic physical abuse (%)				Voted in last election (%)	
	Agree to a large extent	Some-what agree	Some-what disagree	Disagree to a large extent	Never	Rarely	Some-times	Often	Yes	No
Algeria	1.3	3.5	9.2	86.0	73.7	15.9	7.6	2.8	20.8	79.2
Jordan	0.1	0.3	0.5	99.1	94.1	4.2	0.8	0.1	51.5	48.5
Lebanon	0.3	1.1	6.6	92.0	81.5	11.5	4.9	2.1	63.8	36.2
Morocco	0.2	0.5	2.9	96.4	79.0	13.6	5.9	1.5	41.5	54.9
Palestine	1.7	4.7	11.4	82.2	89.2	7.3	2.5	0.9	42.3	57.7
Tunisia	0.5	1.2	0.4	97.9	94.2	4.4	0.4	1.0	48.1	51.9

Lebanon, Palestine, Tunisia, Algeria, and Morocco, 45.5 percent of the individuals interviewed say they voted and 54.5 say they did not. This may be exactly what an investigator wishes to know, and it may be a point of departure for a study that asks about the attributes of individuals who are more likely or less likely to vote.

Alternatively, an investigator may not be very interested in how often individuals vote but rather in the variance in voting across a sample of countries. In this case, the variable of interest to a researcher is voter turnout; and as seen in Table 2.2, turnout ranges across the six countries from a low of 20.8 percent in Algeria to a high of 63.8 in Lebanon. Whether it is individual-level voting or country-level turnout that references the variance of interest to an investigation, and whether, therefore, the relevant unit of analysis is the individual or the country, depends, of course, on the goals of the researcher. Either one may be most relevant, and it is also possible that both will be relevant in some studies.

Readers are encouraged to access the Arab Barometer website, arabbarometer.org, and take a closer look at the data. The website's online analysis tool permits replication of the response distributions shown in Tables 2.1 and 2.2. Additionally, responses to topically associated questions not shown in these tables can also be accessed. In addition, the online analysis tool permits the conduct of simple mapping operations, operations that involve disaggregating the data and examining the variance that characterizes specific subsets of the population, such as women, older individuals, or less religious individuals.

2.2.4 Qualitative Research

While this volume places emphasis on social science research that works with quantitative data, the concepts of variance and unit of analysis also occupy a foundational position in positivist social science research that works with qualitative data. In positivist qualitative social science research, as in quantitative research, the initial objective is to discern the various empirical manifestations of each concept of interest to an investigator, and then to assign each unit on which the investigator has data to one of the empirical manifestations of each concept. The resulting frequency or percentage distributions provide potentially valuable descriptive information, as they do in quantitative research.

As in quantitative research, the objectives of a qualitative study may be descriptive, in which case no more than univariate distributions are needed. Alternatively, again as in quantitative research, these distributions on variables of interest to the investigator may be the beginning stage of research projects that aspire to explanation as well as description, and that, for this reason, anticipate bivariate and/or multivariate analysis. In any of these instances, the point that deserves emphasis is that the notion of variance is central to most positivist inquiry, be it quantitative or qualitative.

A small number of examples involving qualitative research may be mentioned very briefly to illustrate this point. Among these are two studies based on fieldwork in Lebanon, one by Daniel Corstange of Columbia University and one by Melani

2.2 Variance and Variables

Cammett of Harvard University. Both projects included the collection and analysis of qualitative data.

The unit of analysis in the Corstange study is the community, some of which were villages and some of which were neighborhoods in larger agglomerations. The variables with respect to which these communities were classified—hence, the variance that Corstange sought to capture—included the inter-religious confessional composition of the community and whether its leadership structure involved competition or was dominated by one group. These qualitative distinctions with respect to which each community was classified were part of Corstange's larger goal of explaining why some communities fared better than others in obtaining needed public goods, such as electricity and water.[8]

The Cammett study involved the construction of a typology based on two variables taken together. Typologies almost always involve qualitative distinctions, even if one or both of the variables used in their construction are themselves quantitative. Typologies can be particularly useful in conceptualizing and measuring variance that involves more than a single dimension.

In the Cammett study, the unit of analysis was the welfare association, more formally defined as a domestic non-state welfare provider, and each was classified according to the presence or absence of a linkage to a political organization and also to an identity-based community. The concatenation of these two dichotomous distributions yielded four categories, each representing a particular "type" of welfare society based on its political and confessional connections taken together. Cammett's distinctions with respect to type, as is usually the case with typologies, reference qualitative variance. Among the larger goals of the Cammett study, based on the proposition that the motivations of Lebanese welfare societies are not entirely charitable, was to discern whether and how welfare society type was related to the characteristics of those that the association tended to serve and how it made decisions.[9]

The unit of analysis in another study, conducted in Palestine by Wendy Pearlman of Northwestern University, was the Palestinian national movement. The project focused on the movement's resistance to the Zionist project prior to Israeli independence and to Israel's occupation of the West Bank and Gaza following the war of June 1967. The variable of interest to Pearlman was whether resistance activities were essentially non-violent or included significant violence, often directed at Israeli citizens who did not live in the West Bank or Gaza. Pearlman gathered information about resistance activities over time, beginning with the post-World War I period, and then classified each instance of resistance according to whether the national movement used non-violent or violent methods in pursuit of its goals. The larger goal of Pearlman's research project was not only to describe the variance in national

---

[8] Corstange op. cit.
[9] Melani Cammett, *Compassionate Communalism: Welfare and Sectarianism in Lebanon* (Cornell University Press, 2014).

movement resistance activities but also to test hypotheses about determinants of this variance.[10]

A final example is provided by an older but very important study by Tunisian sociologist Elbaki Hermassi. Hermassi's project focuses on Tunisia, Algeria, and Morocco, and country is the unit of analysis. An important qualitative variable in Hermassi's study is the character of the governing regime at independence, 1956 for Tunisia and Morocco and 1962 for Algeria. Tunisia at independence was governed by Western-educated leaders who were supported by a mass-membership political party; in Algeria, the country was led by a military-civilian coalition backed by the military and without a popular grass-roots institutional base; and in Morocco, the king sat at the top of a political system that included a parliament in which the largest party had Islamist origins.[11]

Hermassi uses this country-level variation in political regime to address and answer an important question: Why did the three countries arrive at independence with such differing political systems? After all, each was part of the Arab west and each was colonized by the French. To answer this question, Hermassi takes his readers on a sophisticated and insightful historical journey that can only be hinted at here. He identifies and describes differences among the three countries—making distinctions that are also qualitative—at critical historical periods and junctures. These include differences in pre-colonial society, differences in the character of French colonialism, and differences in the origins and leadership of the nationalist movement and the struggle for independence. The classification of the three countries during each of these time periods is anchored in thick description and extensive historical detail.

These qualitative differences between the three North African countries define a multi-stage temporal sequence through which Hermassi and his readers travel using a method known as process tracing. Country-level qualitative differences during one time period help to explain country-level qualitative differences during the time period that followed, leading in the end to an explanation of the reasons that the countries began their respective political lives at independence with very different governing regimes.

Although brief, and beyond the central, quantitative, focus of this research guide, this overview of qualitative social science research suggests several take-aways, all of which apply to quantitative social science research as well. One is that the concept of variance is no less relevant to qualitative social science investigations than it is to quantitative social science research. A second is that measuring and describing qualitative variance still involves specifying the unit of analysis. A third is that typologies, which make qualitative distinctions among units of analysis, are a useful technique for capturing the variance on concepts defined by more than one attribute

---

[10] Wendy Pearlman, *Violence, Non-Violence, and the Palestinian National Movement* (Cambridge University Press, 2011).

[11] Elbaki Hermassi, *Leadership and National Development in North Africa* (University of California Press, 1979).

or experience. A fourth is that the variance being measured may be among different entities at the same point in time, among the same entity at different points in time, or among different entities at different points in time. And finally, these examples illustrate the importance of fieldwork and deep knowledge of the circumstances of the unit of analysis and variables on which the research project will focus.

2.2.5 Descriptive Statistics

While we often want to know only whether a variable has very much or very little variance across our unit of analysis, it can also be useful to understand how to calculate variance mathematically. In addition, we may also want to describe a variable's distribution of values (numbers) in other ways, such as giving the average value of a variable or identifying the value in a distribution that occurs most frequently (mode). Two ways of describing variance are central tendency and dispersion. There are descriptive statistics for both central tendency and dispersion that can be calculated mathematically.

Measures of **central tendency** are the mean, the median, and the mode. The **mean,** or average, is the sum of all observations for a variable divided by the total number of observations. The **median** is the "middle" value in a variable's distribution of values; it is the value that separates the higher half from the lower half of the values in a distribution. The **mode** is the value in a distribution that appears most often.

It is important to understand that measures of central tendency—the mean, median, and mode—do not tell us how spread out a distribution of values is. The values might be clustered in the middle, spread out evenly, or clustered at the extremes, with each of the distributions having the same mean. Measures of **dispersion** can be calculated to determine the degree to which the values of a variable differ from the mean, or how spread out the distribution is. Two of the most important measures of dispersion are the **variance** and **standard deviation**. The standard deviation, which is the square root of the variance, is one of the most frequently used ways to determine and show the dispersion of a distribution. The **interquartile range** is another measure of dispersion. It shows how spread out the middle 50 percent of the distribution is by subtracting the value of the 25th percentile from the value of the 75th percentile.

Calculating the Variance The variance expresses the degree to which the values in a variable's distribution of values differ from one another. As a descriptive statistic, it is a measure of how much the values differ from the mean. For example, if satisfaction with a country's healthcare system is measured on a scale of 1 to 4, with 4 indicating a high level of satisfaction, and if every individual in a study chooses 4 to express her opinion, there is no variance. The mean will be 4 and none of the ratings given by these individuals differs from the mean. Alternatively, if some participants in the study choose 2, others choose 3, and still others choose 4 to express their opinion, there is variance. We calculate the degree of variance, or dispersion, by squaring the difference between the value and the mean for each participant in the study, then summing the squared deviations for all participants, and then dividing this sum by the number of participants minus 1.[12] These calculations are expressed by the following formula, and its application is shown in an exercise below.

$$s^2 = \Sigma\, (x_i - \bar{x})^2/(n-1)$$

where s^2 is the variance, x_i is the value for each individual, $\bar{x}$ is the mean, and n is the number of individuals.

In the example above, the unit of analysis is the individual. How much variance do you think there is in satisfaction with the healthcare system at the country level in the MENA region? Do you think it is about the same in every country, or do you think it is much higher in some countries and much lower in others? Offer only your "best guess."

You can use the online analysis tool on the Arab Barometer's website, following the steps shown below, to evaluate the accuracy of your best guess.

- Click on the following link: https://www.arabbarometer.org/survey-data/data-analysis-tool/.
- Click "AB Wave V—2018," click "Select all," and click "See results."
- Click "Evaluation of public institutions and political attitudes."
- Click "Satisfaction with the healthcare system in your country."

You can see that there is quite a bit of variance. Which two countries have the most different levels of satisfaction with their healthcare system? Which countries are most similar to each other? Do you have any ideas about why they are similar?
Do you think the variance across the countries would be greater, about the same, or lesser if the cross-country variance was calculated using only male respondents? You can evaluate your answer by adding a filter:

- Click "Add filter"
- Click "Gender"
- Click "Apply"

An example based on the tables below, Tables 2.3 and 2.4, further illustrates computation of the variance. In one case, the unit of analysis is the individual. In the other, country is the unit of analysis. The variable of interest in each case is satisfaction with the country's healthcare system, which is measured on a 1 to 4 scale with 4 being very satisfied and 1 being very dissatisfied.

---

[12] The divisor is n-1 if the analysis is based on data from a sample, or subset, of a larger population. If the analysis is based on data from the entire population, the divisor is n.

2.2 Variance and Variables

Table 2.3 Unit of analysis: individual

Respondent	Satisfaction with healthcare system (1–4 scale)		
	Jordan	Iraq	Tunisia
1	4	3	4
2	4	3	4
3	3	3	3
4	1	4	3
5	2	2	1

Table 2.4 Unit of analysis: country

Country	Average level of public satisfaction with healthcare system (1–4 scale)[a]
Iraq	3.3
Jordan	2.6
Lebanon	3.5
Palestine	2.6

[a]Based on data from Wave V (2018–2019) of the Arab Barometer

First are some questions based on Table 2.3, in which the unit of analysis is the individual. You should be able to answer the questions without doing any major calculations.

- What is the mean of the healthcare system ratings by the individuals in each of the three countries?
- In which of the three countries is the variance of healthcare system ratings by individuals greatest? In which is the variance lowest?

We can now calculate the variance of ratings by the five individuals in Jordan. Thereafter, you may wish to calculate the variance of ratings by the five individuals in Iraq and in Tunisia. This will permit you to check the accuracy of your earlier estimates of rank with respect to magnitude of the variance among distributions for the three countries. To calculate the variance, we take the following steps:

- Calculate the mean: Average satisfaction with the healthcare system in Jordan = sum of individual values/total number of observations = $(4+4+3+1+2)/5 = 2.8$
- Calculate the sum of squared differences between each value and the mean: $((4-2.8)^2 + (4-2.8)^2 + (3-2.8)^2 + (1-2.8)^2 + (2-2.8)^2) = 1.44 + 1.44 + .04 + 3.24 + .64 = 6.8$
- Divide the sum of the differences squared by the number of observations in the data set minus 1: $6.8/4 = 1.7$

We have determined that the individual-level variance in satisfaction in the healthcare system in Jordan at the individual level is 1.7.

We turn now to variance at the *country* level based on Jordan, Iraq, Lebanon, and Palestine, as shown in Table 2.4. This means we are interested in how much the average values of satisfaction with the healthcare system of these countries differ from each other. Before doing any calculations, do you think the variance will be high or low?

The first step in calculating variance at the country level is to calculate the mean of the "satisfaction with the healthcare system" country scores shown in Table 2.4. Thereafter, following the procedures used when individual was the unit of analysis, the sum of the squared difference between the country-specific values and the mean of all countries together, divided by the number of units (countries) minus one gives the variance. These operations are shown below.

- Mean $= (3.3 + 2.6 + 3.5 + 2.6)/4 = 12/4 = 3$
- Variance $=$ *sum of squared differences between each value and the overall mean/ number of observations minus 1* $= ((3.3-3)^2 + (2.6-3)^2 + (3.5-3)^2 + (2.6-3)^2)/3 = .66/3 = 0.22$

In this example, we see that there is variance in healthcare system satisfaction at the individual level and at the country level. However, variance at the individual level is much higher. Another way to think about this is to say that satisfaction with the healthcare system is more similar across countries than it is across individuals. What in your opinion is the significance of this unit of analysis difference in degree of variance? If you wanted to study healthcare satisfaction in the MENA region, how might this difference in degree of variance influence your research design?

Now, think about your own country or a country in the MENA region that you know well. What do you think is the average level of satisfaction with the healthcare system in this country? How much individual-level variance in healthcare system satisfaction do you think there is? What do you think causes, and thus helps to explain, this individual level variance?

2.2.6 Visual Descriptions

Investigators and analysts will often wish to see and show more about the distribution of a variable than is expressed by univariate measures of dispersion such as the variance or standard deviation, or more about a distribution than is expressed by a measure of dispersion and a measure of central tendency taken together. They may also wish to see and show exactly *how* the variance is distributed. Are the values on a variable clustered at the high and low extremes? Are they spread out evenly across the range of possible values? For these reasons, an analyst will often prepare a frequency distribution to show the variance.

Frequency distributions are a common way of looking at variance. A **frequency distribution** is a univariate table that shows the number of times each distinct value of a variable occurs. As shown for Jordan in Table 2.3, for example, the value "2" appears once and the value "4" appears two times. A percentage distribution shows the percentage of times a value appears in the data—the value "2" is 20 percent of all observations and the value "4" is 40 percent of all observations, Table 2.5.

Table 2.5 Example of a frequency and percentage distribution: satisfaction with the healthcare system in the MENA Region (Arab Barometer Wave V, 2018–2019)

Category	%/Total	Frequency
1 Completely satisfied	5.8%	1545
2 Satisfied	32.3%	8637
3 Dissatisfied	34.2%	9161
4 Completely dissatisfied	27.2%	7289
98 Don't know	0.5%	127
99 Refused to answer	0.1%	22
(N)	(100%)	(26,781)

There are many other ways to visualize the data on a variable. A **bar chart** is a visualization of a frequency distribution, where the bars represent distinct (categorical) responses and the length or height of the bars represents the frequency of each. A **histogram** is similar to a bar chart, but it is used to display groupings of a variable's values. A **pie chart** is similar, but the numerical values of a variable are represented by different "slices," with each representing its proportion of the whole.

You will see examples of all of these visual descriptions in the exercise below. In the Arab Barometer's online analysis tool, frequency distributions are on the left side of the page and charts and graphs are on the right side of the page. Above the charts and graphs on the right side of the page is a legend that permits selecting the particular type of chart or graph that is desired.

> **Exercise 2.1. Units of Analysis, Variance, and Descriptive Charts**
> 1. Go to the data analysis tool on the Arab Barometer website using the following link: https://www.arabbarometer.org/survey-data/data-analysis-tool/
> 2. Choose a wave of the Arab Barometer. For this exercise, let's click "AB Wave V—2018-2019." Select the country or countries you want to examine. For this exercise, click "Select all." Next, click on "See results." This will bring you to a page that says "Select a Survey Topic." Select "General topics."
> 3. Let's begin with looking at a variable at the individual-level of analysis: interpersonal trust. Respondents can choose among the following options: "Most people can be trusted," "I must be very careful in dealing with people," or "Don't Know."
> 4. Click on "Interpersonal Trust." You should now see a table showing the frequency and percentage of responses. On the right side, you should also see a bar chart with the percentage of each response. Congratulations, you have just made two types of frequency distributions! We can see that there is variance in interpersonal trust in the MENA region: 15.7 percent of the individuals surveyed trust most people, while 83.1 percent do not trust others very much. What questions could we ask based on the fact that there is variance in interpersonal trust in the MENA region? We could
>
> (continued)

Exercise 2.1 (continued)

consider other individual-level factors, such as "Does someone's age affect how much they trust other people?" Or country-level factors, such as "Does the amount of corruption in the country in which people live affect how much they trust other people?"

5. We might also be interested in how interpersonal trust varies over time. To see this, click "Time series." How does interpersonal trust vary between 2007 and 2019? Why do you think people started trusting others less after 2013?
6. Suppose you are considering doing research on the question: Does gender affect interpersonal trust in the MENA region? Click "Cross by" and select "Gender." Describe the variance in how much men and how much women in the MENA region trust others.
7. Now, suppose you are interested in how much gender affects interpersonal trust in a certain country, in a certain age group, or in some other category. Click "Select countries," then "Deselect all," and then select Morocco. Describe the variance in interpersonal trust based on gender in Morocco.
8. What are the advantages or disadvantages of studying how gender affects interpersonal trust in the MENA region vs. in Morocco? Which study do you think would be more interesting, or more instructive? We see that the distributions for men and for women in the MENA region look almost identical: 15.6 percent of men trust most people, and 15.8 percent of women trust most people. On the other hand, in Morocco, 19 percent of men and 26 percent of women trust most people. You might conclude from this that you want to pursue this research question in Morocco, and not in the entire MENA region.
9. You may also be interested in how interpersonal trust varies at the country-level. To see this, click "Select countries," "Select all," and "Apply." You should now see the average, or mean, of respondents who selected each response category in each country. There is quite a lot of variance in interpersonal trust at the country-level! Describe the distribution you observe. Are there clusters of countries with similar degrees of interpersonal trust? What might be the reasons these countries have similar degrees of interpersonal trust?
10. Repeat the steps above for two other variables: one that you would like to explore at the individual-level—either in the entire MENA region or in one or more specific countries in which you are particularly interested; and one that you are interested in exploring at the country-level. Describe the variance you observe in each case. Are there individual-level factors that you think might help to explain the variance you observe? Are there country-level factors that you think might help to explain the variance you see?

Arab Barometer data have been used to illustrate the points this chapter makes about variance, variables, univariate analysis, and unit of analysis. This has been done, in part, for convenience, but also because Arab Barometer data are readily available, which offers readers an opportunity to replicate, deepen, or expand on the examples used above. The points being illustrated with Arab Barometer data are, of course, of general significance. Different kinds of examples will be offered in the second half of this chapter.

2.3 Data Collection and Measurement

Remaining to be discussed are two essential and interrelated topics that must be addressed in the design of a research project and then implemented before any analysis can be undertaken. One of these involves data collection, which obviously must precede both the calculation of descriptive statistics and the preparation of graphs and charts. Since most of our examples use Arab Barometer data, our discussion will give special attention to the collection and use of survey data. A fuller overview of survey research is presented in Appendix 3. We will also, however, discuss other sources and methods of data collection and data generation. Even researchers who work with data that have already been collected and cleaned should have an understanding of the sources and processes associated with data collection.

The second essential topic concerns measurement, which merits special attention when the concepts and variables of interest to a researcher are to some degree abstract and cannot be directly observed. In this case, measurement involves the selection and use of **indicators**, phenomena that can be observed and will permit inferences about the more abstract concepts. In survey research, and equally in many other modes of data collection, the concepts and variables to be measured and the indicators to be used must be identified before data collection can begin.

2.3.1 Types of Data and Measurement Scales

Data can be categorized as **categorical or numerical**, and many research projects utilize both types of data. Categorical data is often the main type of data used in qualitative research, although numerical data may also be used.

Categorical data are data that are divided into groups based on certain characteristics, such as gender, nationality, or level of education. Categorical data can either be *nominal* or *ordinal*. Nominal data don't have a logical order to the categories. There is no set order to male or female, for example. Ordinal data do have a logical order. There is an order to primary school education, secondary school education, and university degree, for example. Sometimes categorical data are represented with numbers in datasets to facilitate statistical analyses, such as assigning "female" the number 1, and "male" the number 2. When a researcher does this, they will generally provide a codebook to assist others in understanding what the numbers mean.

Numerical data are data that can be measured with numbers. Numerical data can either be *discrete* or *continuous*. Discrete data can only take on certain values, such as the number of protests that take place in a month—you can't have 3.1 or 3.5 protests. Continuous data are data that can take any value within a certain range, such as the GDP of a country. It could be $20.05 billion USD, $40.26 billion USD, or any other number larger than zero.

2.3.2 Data Sources and Data Collection

There are many different types of data sources, and each of them is useful in different contexts. We will not discuss all of them in detail in this guide, but it may be useful to get an idea of some of the major sources of data.

Existing datasets can be extremely useful for a researcher. Many existing datasets are free and accessible online to everyone. The Arab Barometer, and other similar surveys, such as the Afrobarometer, the World Values Survey, and the European Social Survey, measure diverse attitudes, beliefs, and behaviors in various regions of the world. International organizations, such as the UN and the World Bank, publish data on socioeconomic indicators and other topics on their websites. Most of the datasets are aggregated at the country level, but some data come from surveys or administrative systems and are at the individual or sub-national level. Many countries or administrative units also publish datasets, such as crime statistics.

Many researchers also make the data that they collect available online without charge, such as through Harvard Dataverse or personal or university websites. For example, a recently published dataset accessible through Harvard Dataverse is the Global Parties Survey, which compares the values, issue positions, and rhetoric of over 1000 political parties. Researchers make datasets available not only to make future research easier, but also to increase the transparency and replicability of their own research. This is important, as transparency and replication increase our confidence in researchers' findings and can make their propositions easier to test in other settings.

Archival research involves using documents, images, correspondence, reports, audio or audiovisual recordings, or other objects that already exist. Archival research is commonly used to answer historical research questions. Additional types of records one might access when conducting archival research include medical records, government papers, news articles, personal collections, or even tweets. Archival materials are generally accessed at museums, government offices or, of course, archives. In some cases, a researcher may need to get special permission or training before being allowed to access archival materials. What documents are used depends on the research question. Researchers sometimes use content analysis to categorize or quantify archival documents.

Content analysis is a related research technique that can generate both quantitative and qualitative data. The goal of content analysis is to characterize textual or audio data, such as news articles, speeches of officials, or even a set of tweets. Content analysis can generate quantitative data by counting the frequency, space, or time devoted to certain words, ideas, or themes in the documents being analyzed. Content analysis can generate qualitative data, and sometimes also quantitative data, through directed coding, such as, for example, categorizing certain speeches as either in favor or not in favor of a certain policy. Direct coding is usually done by multiple coders who are instructed to employ a set of coding guidelines, and confidence in the data produced usually requires agreement among the decisions and assignments of the different coders. Sentiment analysis is a type of directed coding in which texts are classified as containing certain emotions, such as positive, negative, sad, angry, happy. Content analysis is most useful when there is a large amount of scattered text from which it is difficult to draw conclusions without analyzing it systematically. More recently, advances in the fields of computational linguistics and natural language processing have allowed researchers to conduct content analysis on much larger amounts of data and have reduced the need for human coders.

Observational research is exactly what it sounds like—observing behavior. Sometimes observational research occurs in a laboratory setting, where aspects of the environment are controlled to test how participants react, but often observational research occurs in public. A researcher might be interested in the gender dynamics of a protest, for example. The researcher might attend the protest and take notes or record who stands where in a crowd, what kinds of things women and their signs say versus what kinds of things men and their signs say. This is a very flexible method of data collection, but it can be difficult to draw conclusions with so many uncontrollable factors.

A *focus group* is a group discussion of a specific topic led by a moderator or interviewer. You have probably heard of focus groups in the context of consumer research. Focus groups are a good way to learn and understand what a target audience thinks about a specific topic. They are sometimes used in the early stages of survey research, before actually conducting the survey. In this connection, focus groups are used to gain ideas and insights that help in developing the survey instrument or in evaluating the clarity and efficacy of a survey instrument that an investigator is planning to use.

Interviews are a way of collecting information by talking with other people. They can be structured, unstructured, or semi-structured. You might conduct interviews of protesters as though you were having a conversation to get a sense of their motivations. This unstructured format might make the respondents feel more at ease and then disclose valuable information you would never have thought to ask. On the other hand, you might also conduct interviews in a structured way, by asking the protesters a predetermined set of questions. This allows you to more easily compare responses between respondents.

Survey research is another way to collect data by asking people questions. The answers people give are the data. You might conduct a survey through face-to-face interviews, as the Arab Barometer does. This means administering a questionnaire face-to-face, with the interviewer asking the questions and recording the responses. You might also conduct a survey using phone calls, text messages, or online messaging. Another method of conducting surveys is having people complete questionnaires in person, online, or through mail. In this case, the surveys are called self-administered rather than interview-administered. We have included more information about survey research in the Appendix of this research guide.

Sampling refers to the fact that it is usually impossible for a researcher to collect all of the data that are relevant for her research project. Sampling is very often a concern in survey research, but it may also be a concern when other data collection procedures are employed. There are some projects for which this is not the case, but these are the exceptions in social science research. In survey research, for example, an investigator may be interested in the political attitudes of all of the adult citizens of her country, but it is very unlikely, virtually impossible, actually, that she or her research team can survey all of these men and women. Or, a researcher may be interested in the gender-related behavior of students in college social science classes, but again, it is virtually impossible for the researcher and her team to observe all of the social science classes in all of the colleges in her country, let alone in other countries.

A *sample* refers to the units about whom or which the researcher will actually collect data, and these are the data she will analyze and with which she will carry out her investigation. *Population* refers to the units in which the researcher is interested, those about whom or which her study seeks to provide information. In the first example above, the population is all of the adult citizens of the researcher's country; and in the second, it is college social science classes in general, meaning virtually all such classes.

The distinction between population and sample raises two important questions that are discussed elsewhere in this guide.

- The first question asks which are the units about whom or which the investigator will collect information. In other words, it asks which members of the population will be included in the sample, and how will those in the sample be selected. The answers lie in the design and construction of the investigator's sample, a topic that is discussed in the appendix on survey research with examples from the Arab Barometer.
- The second question concerns the relationship between the population and the sample. It asks whether, and if so, when, how, and with what degree of confidence, can findings based on analyses of the data in the sample provide information and insight that apply to the population. This important question is taken up in the next chapter.

2.3.3 Conceptual Definitions and Operational Definitions

The indicators and type of data that are best suited for measuring a certain concept depend on how the concept is defined. A **conceptual definition** should specify how we are thinking about variance related to the concept: what is the unit of analysis and what is the variance we want to capture? Take, for example, the concept of quality of healthcare services. If country is the unit of analysis, do we want to capture the amount of healthcare services that the government provides? If so, we might consider measuring the concept by using the percent of the national budget devoted to health and healthcare, or the number of physicians per 100,000 citizens. On the other hand, we may be interested in citizens' perceptions of healthcare service provision. In this case, we may want to measure perceived quality of healthcare services by asking questions, most probably in a survey, such as "Do you find doctors helpful when you are sick?" or "When you have been sick, were you able to obtain the healthcare services you needed?" We will want to conceptualize "quality of healthcare services" differently depending on our research question, and then, accordingly, collect or use data at the appropriate level of analysis.

Once an investigator has formulated and determined her conceptual definitions, she is ready to think about and specify her **operational definitions**. An operational definition describes the data, indicators, and methods of analysis she will use to rate, classify or assign values to the entities in which she is interested. An operational definition, in other words, describes the procedures an investigator will use to measure each of the abstract concepts and variables in her study, concepts and variables that cannot be directly observed.

In formulating an operational definition, an investigator must decide what data and indicators best fit the variance specified in the conceptual definition of each concept and variable in her study that cannot be directly observed or directly measured. She asks, therefore, what data can be obtained or collected, do these data contain the indicators she needs, and of course, what will be the quality of the data.

Returning to the previous illustration, suppose you have decided to measure the satisfaction of individuals with the provision of healthcare services. You need to decide what type of data to use, and in this case, it makes sense to use public opinion data. Perhaps, however, survey data on this topic do not exist, or the survey data that do exist do not ask questions that you would consider good indicators of the concept you want to measure. You might consider administering your own survey, but if this is not feasible, you can consider other types of data and data collection and build your own new dataset, informed and guided by the conceptual definition you are seeking to operationalize. For example, you might collect tweets related to healthcare and use content analysis by coders to rate each tweet on a spectrum ranging from very negative to very positive.

Think of another concept in which you are interested and then ask yourself the following questions. Are you interested in variance at the individual level, country level, or a different level and unit of analysis? What is a conceptual definition that makes clear and gives meaning to the variance of the concept that you seek to measure? What type of data would best measure your variable? What elements that might be good indicators of the variable you seek to measure—questions in a survey, for example—should the dataset contain? How feasible do you think it is to obtain data that will contain these elements?

Researchers cannot always use the data and method of measuring their concepts and variables that are best suited to operationalizing their conceptual definitions.

Collecting data takes time, resources, and certain skill sets. Also significant, certain types of data collection may pose risks to the researcher or the research subjects, and for this reason they must be avoided due to ethical concerns. For example, in some countries it can be dangerous to interview people about their participation in opposition political parties or movements. It is important to consider the trade-offs in using different types of data and, in some cases, different indicators. Which type of data collection is most feasible? What are good indicators of the variance you want to capture? We discuss these questions in the following section.

2.3.4 Measurement Quality

How do we decide whether a certain kind of data or particular survey questions are good indicators of the concept we seek to measure? We want data to be *reliable* and *valid*, which are the criteria by which the quality of a measure may be evaluated. We also want measures that capture all of the variance associated with the concepts and variables to be used in analyses. Attention to these criteria is particularly important if the concept to be measured is abstract and not directly observable. In this case, we will probably be measuring indicators of the concept, rather than the concept itself.

Reliability Reliability refers to the absence of error variance, which means that the observed variance is based solely on the measure, as intended, and not on extraneous factors as well. In survey research, for example, a question will be a reliable measure if the response is based solely on the content of that question and not also on factors such as ambiguous wording, the appearance or behavior of the interviewer, comments by other persons who were present when the interview was conducted, or even the time of day of the interview.

Attention to reliability is no less important in other forms of research. For example, when coding events data from newspapers in order to classify countries or other units of analysis with respect to newsworthy events such as protests, instances of violence, violations of human rights, labor strikes, elections and electoral outcomes, or other attributes, error variance may result from unclear coding instructions, inconsistent newspaper selections, or changing standards about what constitutes an instance of violence or a violation of human rights.

Consistency over multiple trials offers evidence of reliability. In survey research, once again, this means that a question would be answered in the same way—perhaps a response of "somewhat satisfied" to a question about satisfaction with the country's healthcare system—regardless of who was the interviewer or the time of day at which the interview was conducted. In natural science, especially laboratory science, this means that the result of a measuring operation is reproducible.

In social science, evidence of reliability is often provided by consistency among multiple indicators that purport to measure the same concept or variable. This applies not only to questions asked in a survey, but also to data collected or generated in other ways as well. A measure based on multiple indicators that agree with one another can also be described as a unidimensional measure, and unidimensionality across multiple indicators demonstrates that a measure is reliable. For this reason, researchers often seek to use multiple indicators to measure the same concept in order to increase the robustness of their results.

Note also that the values or ratings produced by different indicators need not be absolutely identical. To be consistent with one another, they need only to be strongly correlated. A number of statistical tests are available for determining the degree of inter-indicator agreement, or consistency. Cronbach's alpha is probably the test most frequently used for this purpose. Factor analysis is also frequently used. We discuss some of these statistical techniques in Chaps. 3 and 4.

Table 2.6, which presents hypothetical data on indicators purporting to measure a country's level of development, provides a simplified illustration of three patterns of agreement among multiple indicators. Although the data are fictitious, the indicators might be thought of as Gross Domestic Product, Per Capita National Income, Percentage of the Population below the Poverty Line, the Level of Unemployment, or other potentially reliable indicators of national development. The table illustrates the following three patterns.

- Pattern A indicates strong inter-indicator agreement and hence a high degree of reliability. Even though the ratings are not completely identical, the correlations among them are very strong. Each of the indicators can be used with confidence that it is a reliable measure. Its reliability has been demonstrated by its agreement with other indicators. The items can also be combined to form a scale or index, which, again, can be used with confidence that it is a reliable measure.
- Pattern B indicates the absence of inter-indicator agreement and hence a low level of reliability. It is possible that one of the indicators is a reliable measure of national development, but there is no basis for determining which item is the reliable measure. It is also possible that all are reliable measures but of different dimensions of national development, meaning that the concept and the measure are not unidimensional and, hence, Pattern B does not provide evidence that any indicator or combination of indicators constitutes a reliable measure for the specific concept of concern.
- Pattern C indicates strong inter-indicator agreement among three of the indicators (I-1, I-2, and I-4), and these three, but not the fourth (I-3), may be considered reliable measures and used in the ways described for Pattern A. In the absence of evidence that it is reliable, I-3 should not be used to measure the same concept, national development, that the other three indicators measure.

Validity Validity asks whether, or to what degree, a measure actually measures what it purports to measure. A concern for validity is important whenever the concept or variable to be measured cannot be directly observed, and so the investigator in this case must use an indicator, rather than the concept or variable itself, to capture the relevant variance.

It is useful to think of validity as expressing the congruence between the conceptual definition and the operational definition of a concept or variable. A conceptual definition makes explicit what an investigator understands the concept to mean, and it is important that she provide a conceptual definition when the concept cannot be directly observed, is abstract, and might also be multi-dimensional. By contrast, if

Table 2.6 Patterns of agreement among hypothetical indicators of National Development and Reliability Implications

	Pattern A					Pattern B					Pattern C				
	Indicators					Indicators					Indicators				
	I-1	I-2	I-3	I-4	Mean	I-1	I-2	I-3	I-4	Mean	I-1	I-2	I-3	I-4	Mean
Country 1	4	3	4	4	3.75	1	2	3	4	2.5	4	3	1	4	3.0
Country 2	3	3	3	4	3.25	2	1	4	3	2.5	3	4	2	3	3.0
Country 3	3	4	4	3	3.50	3	4	1	2	2.5	2	2	4	2	2.5
Country 4	2	1	1	2	1.50	4	2	3	1	2.5	2	1	3	2	2.0
Country 5	1	2	1	1	1.25	2	3	1	4	2.5	1	2	4	1	2.0

Level of Development: 4 = Very High, 3 = Somewhat High, 2 = Somewhat Low, 1 = Very Low the concept or variable is familiar and there is a widely shared understanding of what it means, the investigator may make this the basis of her conceptual definition.

The operational definition makes explicit the way that the concept or variable will be measured. What indicator or indicators should an investigator use, and how exactly should she use them? Suppose, for example, that an investigator is designing a study in which country is the unit of analysis and the goal is to measure the degree to which each country is democratic. Her operational definition will spell out how she will capture the cross-country variance in degree of democracy. If you, Dear Reader, were the investigator, what would be your operational definition? What indicator or indicators would you use, and how would you use them?

A concern for validity often emerges when using Arab Barometer survey data. Suppose you wanted to rate or classify individuals with respect to tolerance and interpersonal trust. After offering conceptual definitions of tolerance and interpersonal trust, what would be your operational definitions? What item or items would you feel comfortable treating as indicators of each concept and would you, therefore, include in your questionnaire or survey instrument?

It is important to make clear that validity is not about how well the variance is captured by an operational definition. That is an important concern and one by which the quality of a measure is judged, as discussed in the next section. But validity does not ask how much of the variance is captured but, rather, does the variance that is captured, however complete or incomplete that may be, actually pertain to the concept specified in your conceptual definition.

The standardized tests used to evaluate and classify students are often mentioned to illustrate this point. Do intelligence tests really measure intelligence, or do they rather measure something else—perhaps being the oldest child, perhaps income, perhaps something else? Do university entrance exams, the *tawjihi*, for example, really measure what they purport to measure: the likelihood of success at university? Or do they again measure something else—perhaps growing up in a middle class household? You might find it useful to construct your own operational definition of the concept "likelihood of success at university." What indicators would you use, and how would you use them to construct a measure that would give a rating or score to each student?

An exercise with Arab Barometer survey data provides another illustration, and one in which the importance of the conceptual definition is also demonstrated. Suppose that the variable to be measured is satisfaction with the government, and the goal is to rate each respondent on a five-point scale ranging from $1 =$ no satisfaction at all to $5 =$ very high satisfaction. Do you think, for example, that a question about government corruption is a valid indicator—an indicator of the concept as it is defined in your conceptual definition? What about a question that asks, "Do you think government officials care more about being re-elected than solving important problems for the country's citizens?" What question would you write to attempt to measure the concept of government satisfaction?

Once you have specified your measurement strategy, or operational definition, it may be necessary, or at least very advisable, to offer evidence that your measure is valid—that you can use it to measure a concept with confidence and that it does actually measure that concept. Unlike reliability, which can be demonstrated, validity must be inferred. An investigator will state why it is very likely that the measure does indeed measure the concept it purports to measure, and when appropriate, she will offer evidence or reasoning in support of this assertion.

Face Validity Sometimes, asserting "face validity" is sufficient to establish validity and to persuade consumers of the findings produced by a research project that an operational definition does indeed measure what it purports to measure. This may be the case if there is an apparently very good fit between the conceptual definition and the operational definition of a particular concept or variable. In many cases, however, face validity may not be evident and the assertion of face validity by an investigator is unlikely to be persuasive. Below are brief descriptions of the ways an investigator can support her assertion that a measure is valid. Although different, each involves some sort of comparison.

Construct Validity The measure may be considered valid if it is related to the same phenomena, and in the same way, that the concept being measured is known to be related to the measure. For example, if an investigator conducting a survey seeks to measure interpersonal trust, and if it is known that interpersonal trust is related to personal efficacy, construct validity can be demonstrated by a significant correlation between the investigator's measure of interpersonal trust and a measure of personal efficacy.

Criterion Validity Also sometimes known as *Predictive Validity*. The measure may be considered valid if there is a significant correlation between the results of an investigator's operational definition and a distinct, established, and commonly used measure of the concept or variable the investigator seeks to measure. For example, an investigator using aggregated survey data to classify countries with respect to democracy might assess validity by comparing her country ratings with those provided by Freedom House.

Known Groups The measure may be considered valid if it correctly differentiates between groups that are known to differ with respect to the concept or variable being measured. For example, evidence that the *tawjihi* examination is a valid measure of likelihood of success at university would be provided if university students currently doing well at university have higher exam scores than university students currently doing less well at university.

Inter-Indicator Agreement Inter-indicator agreement builds on the discussion of reliability, particularly on the significance of unidimensionality and the patterns of inter-indicator agreement shown in Table 2.6. If each indicator in a battery of indicators has face validity, and if each one agrees with each of the others, it is very unlikely that they measure something other than the concept or variable they purport to measure.

As noted in the discussion of reliability, various statistical procedures, including Crombach's alpha and factor analysis, can be used to assess the degree to which indicators are inter-correlated and, therefore, taken together, constitute a

2.3 Data Collection and Measurement

unidimensional and reliable measure. And if different indicators possessing face validity all reliably measure the *same* concept or variable, it is reasonable to infer that this concept or variable is indeed the one the investigator seeks to measure and is, therefore, valid as well as reliable.

Content Validity Content validity refers to whether, or to what degree, an operational definition captures a fuller range of the concept's meaning and variance. As discussed in the next section, using multiple indicators increases the likelihood that a measure will possess content validity.

Exercise 2.2. Inter-Indicator Agreement and Reliability and Validity

Which of the following items from Arab Barometer surveys do you think would be most likely to be reliable and valid indicators of support for gender equality? Briefly state the reasons you have selected these particular items, or all of the items, if that is what you chose. Then, referring to the patterns of inter-indicator agreement shown in Table 2.6, describe the pattern that you think the items you have selected would resemble. Finally, describe and explain the implications for reliability and validity of the pattern of inter-indicator agreement that you think the items you have selected would resemble.

1. Do you think it is important for girls to go to high school?
2. A married woman can work outside the home, if she wishes
3. It is acceptable for a woman to be a member of parliament
4. A university education is more important for a boy than a girl
5. Men and women should have equal job opportunities and wages
6. Women have the right to get divorced upon their request
7. A woman can be president or prime minister of a Muslim country
8. A woman should cease to work outside the home after marriage in order to devote full time to home and family
9. A woman can travel abroad by herself, if she wishes
10. On the whole, men make better political leaders than women

---

2.3.5 Capturing Variance

Although reliability and validity are recognized and widely-used criteria for assessing the quality of a measure in social science (and other) research, there is an additional criterion that is important as well. This is the degree to which a measure captures all, as opposed to only some, of the variance associated with the concept that an investigator seeks to measure. This can be described as the completeness of a measure.

If the variance of the concept to be measured is continuous, ranging from low to high or weak to strong, for example, a measure will be flawed if it does not capture the whole of the continuum, or at least the whole of that part of the continuum in which the investigator is interested. Such a measure may be reliable and valid, and in this sense of very good quality. But its utility may still be limited, or it may at least be less than maximally useful, if it captures only some of the variance.

A simplified and hypothetical example of a survey about religious involvement illustrates this point. If an investigator wishes to know how often a respondent attended Friday prayers at the mosque during the past year, her survey instrument should not ask a question like the following: "Over the last year, on average, did you pray at the mosque on Friday at least once a month?" A response of "No" will lump together respondents who never pray at the mosque on Friday and those who do so in two months out of three. A response of "Yes" will lump together those who attend Friday prayers once a month and those who do so every week.

In constructing the survey instrument, the investigator may have had good reason to ask a Yes-No question and make "once a month" the cutting point. But such a cutting point can be implemented during the data analysis phase, if needed, rather than asking the initial survey question in a manner that reduces much of the variance that characterizes the population being surveyed.

A more realistic example, perhaps, would be survey questions that ask about age or income. Ideally, the investigator should ask respondents for their exact age and their exact monthly or annual income. Sometimes this is difficult or impossible, however, in the latter case, perhaps, because the matter is considered sensitive. If this is the case, the investigator may decide to use age and income categories, such as 18–25 years of age and 500–1000 dinars per month. Again, while the data obtained may be reliable and valid and also useful, not all of the variance that characterizes the population has been captured: individuals 19 years of age and individuals 24 years of age are treated as if they have the same age, the variance in their actual ages, therefore, not being captured. Even more variance would remain uncaptured by wider categories or categories with no lower or upper limit, such as 55 years of age or older and, say, 5000 or more dinars a month.

The same concern arises when the data are categorical rather than continuous. Variance in this case refers to a range of types or kinds or categories. As is standard with categorizations, categories should be comprehensive and mutually exclusive, meaning that every member of a population can be assigned to one but only one category.

The challenge here is for the investigator to be knowledgeable about the array of one-and-only-one categories into which she wishes to sort the entities whose attributes she seeks to measure. And in principle, this means she must be knowledgeable about the actual, real-world variance, as well as about the categories relevant for her particular study. With respect to religious affiliation, for example, asking people in Lebanon whether they are Muslim or Christian would leave a great deal of variance uncaptured since there are important subdivisions within each category. Asking only about Muslims and Christians would therefore be appropriate only if the researcher is aware of the subdivisions within each category and has explicitly determined that her project does not require attention to these subdivisions.

There are numerous examples that involve a unit of analysis other than the individual. Consider, for example, a study in several Arab countries in which non-governmental organization, NGO, is the unit of analysis, and the variable of interest is NGO type. The investigator seeks, in other words, to prepare a distribution of NGO types, perhaps to see if the distribution differs from country to country. In this case, the investigator must decide on the categories of NGO type that she will use, and these categories, taken together, must be such that each NGO can be assigned to one and only one category.

To make it easier to assign each NGO to a category of NGO type, the investigator might be inclined to define NGO type very broadly, such as economic, sociocultural, and political NGOs. But this will, again, leave much of the variance uncaptured. Assigning NGOs to the "sociocultural" NGO type category, for example, will group together NGOs that may actually differ from one another with respect to objectives and strategies and perhaps in other ways as well. The investigator must be aware of these within-NGO type differences and make an informed decision about their relevance for her study.

Finally, there is an additional and somewhat different way in which an investigator needs to think about the variance that will and will not be captured, and this concerns the dimensional structure of the concept to be measured. For example, the United Nations has developed an index of human development and it annually gives each of the world's countries a numerical HDI score. Investigators can use the index provided by the UN if it measures a concept that is relevant for their studies. But the HDI is based on a formula that combines a country's situation with respect to health, education, and income, and countries with an identical HDI score are not necessarily the same with respect to the three elements. One country's HDI may be driven up by the excellent quality of its educational system, whereas it might be the excellent quality of its health care system that is driving up the HDI score of another country.

Does this mean that the investigator should abandon the HDI and instead include separate measures of education, income, and health in their analyses? Of course, it depends on the goals of the study. But investigators seeking to measure concepts with multiple dimensions or multiple elements must be aware of these differences and then, in light of the goals of each specific research project, make informed decisions about whether the variance these differences represent does or does not need to be captured.

Other examples, ones in which the individual is the unit of analysis, remind us that attitudes and behavior may also have multiple dimensions or components, and that a researcher must again decide, therefore, whether her investigation will be best served by considering the dimensions separately or by constructing an index that combines them.

Attitudes about immigration, for example, probably have an economic, a cultural, and perhaps a political dimension. Similarly, the important concept of trust has multiple components, including general interpersonal trust, trust in important political institutions, trust in people who belong to a different religion, etc. In cases such as these, the researcher will likely want to ask about each of these dimensions or components. The use of multiple questions will enable the researcher to capture more of the variance associated with attitudes toward immigration or the concept of trust. It will remain, however, for the investigator to decide whether to consider the various elements separately or construct an index that considers them in combination with one another.

* * *

The concepts and procedures discussed in this chapter focus on description, on taking variables one at a time. But while the objectives of a positivist social science research project might be descriptive, and this might well produce valuable information and insight, familiarity with the topics discussed in the present chapter is necessary not only, or even primarily, for investigators with descriptive objectives. An understanding of many of these topics is essential for investigators who seek to explain as well as describe variance. This is not the case for every topic considered. Descriptive statistics and visual descriptions are, as their name indicates, for descriptions, for variables taken one at a time. But most of the other concepts and procedures are building blocks, or points of departure, for research endeavors that seek to explain and, toward this end, carry out bivariate and multivariate analyses. Accordingly, readers of Chaps. 3 and 4 will want to keep in mind, and may occasionally find it helpful to refer back to, the material covered in the present chapter.

Open Access This chapter is licensed under the terms of the Creative Commons Attribution 4.0 International License (http://creativecommons.org/licenses/by/4.0/), which permits use, sharing, adaptation, distribution and reproduction in any medium or format, as long as you give appropriate credit to the original author(s) and the source, provide a link to the Creative Commons license and indicate if changes were made.

The images or other third party material in this chapter are included in the chapter's Creative Commons license, unless indicated otherwise in a credit line to the material. If material is not included in the chapter's Creative Commons license and your intended use is not permitted by statutory regulation or exceeds the permitted use, you will need to obtain permission directly from the copyright holder.

Bivariate Analysis: Associations, Hypotheses, and Causal Stories

3.1 Description, Explanation, and Causal Stories

Every day, we encounter various phenomena that make us question how, why, and with what implications they vary. In responding to these questions, we often begin by considering bivariate relationships, meaning the way that two variables relate to one another. Such relationships are the focus of this chapter.

There are many reasons why we might be interested in the relationship between two variables. Suppose we observe that some of the respondents interviewed in Arab Barometer surveys and other surveys report that they have thought about emigrating, and we are interested in this variable. We may want to know how individuals' consideration of emigration varies in relation to certain attributes or attitudes. In this case, our goal would be *descriptive*, sometimes described as the mapping of variance. Our goal may also or instead be *explanation*, such as when we want to know why individuals have thought about emigrating.

Description Description means that we seek to increase our knowledge and refine our understanding of a single variable by looking at whether and how it varies in relation to one or more other variables. Descriptive information makes a valuable contribution when the structure and variance of an important phenomenon are not well known, or not well known in relation to other important variables.

Returning to the example about emigration, suppose you notice that among Jordanians interviewed in 2018, 39.5 percent of the 2400 men and women interviewed reported that they have considered the possibility of emigrating.

Our objective may be to discover what these might-be migrants look like and what they are thinking. We do this by mapping the variance of emigration across attributes and orientations that provide some of this descriptive information, with the descriptions themselves each expressed as bivariate relationships. These relationships are also sometimes labeled "associations" or "correlations" since they are not considered causal relationships and are not concerned with explanation.

Of the 39.5 percent of Jordanians who told interviewers that they have considered emigrating, 57.3 percent are men and 42.7 percent are women. With respect to age, 34 percent are age 29 or younger and 19.2 percent are age 50 or older. It might have been expected that a higher percentage of respondents age 29 or younger would have considered emigrating. In fact, however, 56 percent of the 575 men and women in this age category have considered emigrating. And with respect to destination, the Arab country most frequently mentioned by those who have considered emigration is the UAE, named by 17 percent, followed by Qatar at 10 percent and Saudi Arabia at 9.8 percent. Non-Arab destinations were mentioned more frequently, with Turkey named by 18.1 percent, Canada by 21.1 percent, and the U.S. by 24.2 percent.

With the variables sex, age, and prospective destination added to the original variable, which is consideration of emigration, there are clearly more than two variables under consideration. But the variables are described two at a time and so each relationship is bivariate.

These bivariate relationships, between having considered emigration on the one hand and sex, age, and prospective destination on the other, provide descriptive information that is likely to be useful to analysts, policymakers, and others concerned with emigration. They tell, or begin to tell, as noted above, what might-be migrants look like and what they are thinking. Still additional insight may be gained by adding descriptive bivariate relationships for Jordanians interviewed in a different year to those interviewed in 2018. In addition, of course, still more information and possibly a more refined understanding, may be gained by examining the attributes and orientations of prospective emigrants who are citizens of other Arab (and perhaps also non-Arab) countries.

With a focus on description, these bivariate relationships are not constructed to shed light on explanation, that is to contribute to causal stories that seek to account for variance and tell *why* some individuals but not others have considered the possibility of emigrating. In fact, however, as useful as bivariate relationships that provide descriptive information may be, researchers usually are interested as much if not more in bivariate relationships that express causal stories and purport to provide explanations.

Explanation and Causal Stories There is a difference in the origins of bivariate relationships that seek to provide descriptive information and those that seek to provide explanatory information. The former can be thought to be responding to *what* questions: What characterizes potential emigrants? What do they look like? What are their thoughts about this or that subject? If the objective is description, a researcher collects and uses her data to investigate the relationship between two variables without a specific and firm prediction about the relationship between them. Rather, she simply wonders about the "what" questions listed above and believes that finding out the answers will be instructive. In this case, therefore, she selects the bivariate relationships to be considered based on what she thinks it will be useful to know, and not based on assessing the accuracy of a previously articulated causal story that specifies the strength and structure of the effect that one variable has on the other.

3.1 Description, Explanation, and Causal Stories

A researcher is often interested in causal stories and explanation, however, and this does usually begin with thinking about the relationship between two variables, one of which is the presumed cause and the other the presumed effect. The presumed cause is the **independent variable,** and the presumed effect is the **dependent variable**. Offering evidence that there is a strong relationship between two variables is not sufficient to demonstrate that the variables are likely to be causally related, but it is a necessary first step. In this respect it is a point of departure for the fuller, probably multivariate analysis, required to persuasively argue that a relationship is likely to be causal. In addition, as discussed in Chap. 4, multivariate analysis often not only strengthens the case for inferring that a relationship is causal, but also provides a more elaborate and more instructive causal story. The foundation, however, on which a multivariate analysis aimed at causal inference is built, is a bivariate relationship composed of a presumed independent variable and a presumed dependent variable.

A hypothesis that posits a causal relationship between two variables is not the same as a causal story, although the two are of course closely connected. The former specifies a presumed cause, a presumed determinant of variance on the dependent variable. It probably also specifies the structure of the relationship, such as linear as opposed to non-linear, or positive (also called direct) as opposed to negative (also called inverse).

On the other hand, a causal story describes in more detail what the researcher believes is actually taking place in the relationship between the variables in her hypothesis; and accordingly, why she thinks this involves causality. A causal story provides a fuller account of operative processes, processes that the hypothesis references but does not spell out. These processes may, for example, involve a pathway or a mechanism that tells how it is that the independent variable causes and thus accounts for some of the variance on the dependent variable. Expressed yet another way, the causal story describes the researcher's understandings, or best guesses, about the real world, understandings that have led her to believe, and then propose for testing, that there is a causal connection between her variables that deserves investigation. The hypothesis itself does not tell this story; it is rather a short formulation that references and calls attention to the existence, or hypothesized existence, of a causal story. Research reports present the causal story as well as the hypothesis, as the hypothesis is often of limited interpretability without the causal story.

A causal story is necessary for causal inference. It enables the researcher to formulate propositions that purport to explain rather than merely describe or predict. There may be a strong relationship between two variables, and if this is the case, it will be possible to predict with relative accuracy the value, or score, of one variable from knowledge of the value, or score, of the other variable. Prediction is not explanation, however. To explain, or attribute causality, there must be a causal story to which a hypothesized causal relationship is calling attention.

An instructive illustration is provided by a recent study of Palestinian participation in protest activities that express opposition to Israeli occupation.[1] There is plenty of variance on the dependent variable: There are many young Palestinians who take part in these activities, and there are many others who do not take part. Education is one of the independent variables that the researcher thought would be an important determinant of participation, and so she hypothesized that individuals with more education would be more likely to participate in protest activities than individuals with less education.

But why would the researcher think this? The answer is provided by the causal story. To the extent that this as yet untested story is plausible, or preferably, persuasive, at least in the eyes of the investigator, it gives the researcher a reason to believe that education is indeed a determinant of participation in protest activities in Palestine. By spelling out in some detail how and why the hypothesized independent variable, education in this case, very likely impacts a person's decision about whether or not to protest, the causal story provides a rationale for the researcher's hypothesis.

In the case of Palestinian participation in protest activities, another investigator offered an insightful causal story about the ways that education pushes toward greater participation, with emphasis on its role in communication and coordination.[2] Schooling, as the researcher theorizes and subsequently tests, integrates young Palestinians into a broader institutional environment that facilitates mass mobilizations and lowers informational and organizational barriers to collective action. More specifically, she proposes that those individuals who have had at least a middle school education, compared to those who have not finished middle school, have access to better and more reliable sources of information, which, among other things, enables would-be protesters to assess risks. More schooling also makes would-be protesters better able to forge inter-personal relationships and establish networks that share information about needs, opportunities, and risks, and that in this way facilitate engaging in protest activities in groups, rather than on an individual basis. This study offers some additional insights to be discussed later.

The variance motivating the investigation of a causal story may be thought of as the "variable of interest," and it may be either an independent variable or a dependent variable. It is a variable of interest because the way that it varies poses a question, or puzzle, that a researcher seeks to investigate. It is the dependent variable in a bivariate relationship if the researcher seeks to know *why* this variable behaves, or varies, as it does, and in pursuit of this objective, she will seek to identify the determinants and drivers that account for this variance. The variable of interest is an independent variable in a particular research project if the researcher seeks to know

---

[1] Dana El Kurd. 2019. "Who Protests in Palestine? Mobilization Across Class Under the Palestinian Authority." In Alaa Tartir and Timothy Seidel, eds. *Palestine and Rule of Power: Local Dissent vs. International Governance*. New York: Palgrave Macmillan.
[2] Yael Zeira. 2019. *The Revolution Within: State Institutions and Unarmed Resistance in Palestine*. New York: Cambridge University Press.

3.1 Description, Explanation, and Causal Stories

Table 3.1 Percentage considering emigration

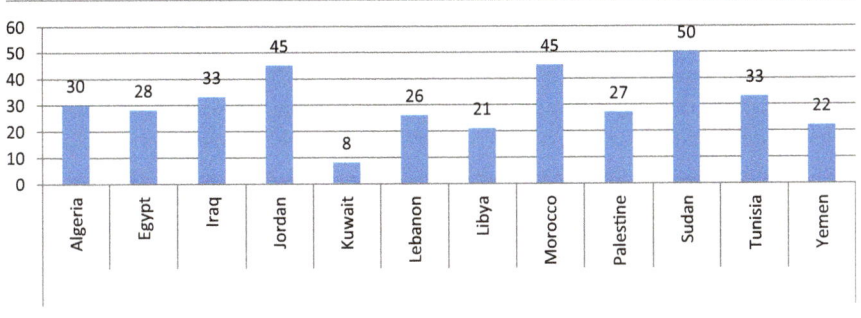

what difference it makes—on what does its variance have an impact, of what other variable or variables is it a driver or determinant.

The variable in which a researcher is initially interested, that is to say the variable of interest, can also be both a dependent variable and an independent variable. Returning to the variable pertaining to consideration of emigration, but this time with country as the unit of analysis, the variance depicted in Table 3.1 provides an instructive example. The data are based on Arab Barometer surveys conducted in 2018–2019, and the table shows that there is substantial variation across twelve countries. Taking the countries together, the mean percentage of citizens that have thought about relocating to another country is 30.25 percent. But in fact, there is very substantial variation around this mean. Kuwait is an outlier, with only 8 percent having considered emigration. There are also countries in which only 21 percent or 22 percent of the adult population have thought about this, figures that may be high in absolute terms but are low relative to other Arab countries. At the other end of the spectrum are countries in which 45 percent or even 50 percent of the citizens report having considered leaving their country and relocating elsewhere.

The very substantial variance shown in Table 3.1 invites reflection on both the causes and the consequences of this country-level variable, aggregate thinking about emigration. As a dependent variable, the cross-country variance brings the question of why the proportion of citizens that have thought about emigrating is higher in some countries than in others; and the search for an answer begins with the specification of one or more bivariate relationships, each of which links this dependent variable to a possible cause or determinant. As an independent variable, the cross-country variance brings the question of what difference does it make—of what is it a determinant or driver and what are the consequences for a country if more of its citizens, rather than fewer, have thought about moving to another country.

3.2 Hypotheses and Formulating Hypotheses

Hypotheses emerge from the research questions to which a study is devoted. Accordingly, a researcher interested in explanation will have something specific in mind when she decides to hypothesize and then evaluate a bivariate relationship in order to determine whether, and if so how, her variable of interest is related to another variable. For example, if the researcher's variable of interest is attitude toward gender equality and one of her research questions asks why some people support gender equality and others do not, she might formulate the hypothesis below to see if education provides part of the answer.

Hypothesis 1. Individuals who are better educated are more likely to support gender equality than are individuals who are less well-educated.

The usual case, and the preferred case, is for an investigator to be specific about the research questions she seeks to answer, and then to formulate hypotheses that propose for testing part of the answer to one or more of these questions. Sometimes, however, a researcher will proceed without formulating specific hypotheses based on her research questions. Sometimes she will simply look at whatever relationships between her variable of interest and a second variable her data permit her to identify and examine, and she will then follow up and incorporate into her study any findings that turn out to be significant and potentially instructive. This is sometimes described as allowing the data to "speak." When this hit or miss strategy of trial and error is used in bivariate and multivariate analysis, findings that are significant and potentially instructive are sometimes described as "grounded theory." Some researchers also describe the latter process as "inductive" and the former as "deductive."

Although the inductive, atheoretical approach to data analysis might yield some worthwhile findings that would otherwise have been missed, it can sometimes prove misleading, as you may discover relationships between variables that happened by pure chance and are not instructive about the variable of interest or research question. Data analysis in research aimed at explanation should be, in most cases, preceded by the formulation of one or more hypotheses. In this context, when the focus is on bivariate relationships and the objective is explanation rather than description, each hypothesis will include a dependent variable and an independent variable and make explicit the way the researcher thinks the two are, or probably are, related. As discussed, the dependent variable is the presumed effect; its variance is what a hypothesis seeks to explain. The independent variable is the presumed cause; its impact on the variance of another variable is what the hypothesis seeks to determine.

Hypotheses are usually in the form of if-then, or cause-and-effect, propositions. They posit that *if* there is variance on the independent variable, the presumed cause, there will *then* be variance on the dependent variable, the presumed effect. This is because the former impacts the latter and causes it to vary.

An illustration of formulating hypotheses is provided by a study of voting behavior in seven Arab countries: Algeria, Bahrain, Jordan, Lebanon, Morocco,

Palestine, and Yemen.[3] The variable of interest in this individual-level study is electoral turnout, and prominent among the research questions is why some citizens vote and others do not. The dependent variable in the hypotheses proposed in response to this question is whether a person did or did not vote in the country's most recent parliamentary election. The study initially proposed a number of hypotheses, which include the two listed here and which would later be tested with data from Arab Barometer surveys in the seven countries in 2006–2007. We will return to this illustration later in this chapter.

Hypothesis 1: Individuals who have used clientelist networks in the past are more likely to turn out to vote than are individuals who have not used clientelist networks in the past.
Hypothesis 2: Individuals with a positive evaluation of the economy are more likely to vote than are individuals with a negative evaluation of the economy.

Another example pertaining to voting, which this time is hypothetical but might be instructively tested with Arab Barometer data, considers the relationship between perceived corruption and turning out to vote at the individual level of analysis.

The normal expectation in this case would be that perceptions of corruption influence the likelihood of voting. Even here, however, competing causal relationships are plausible. More perceived corruption might increase the likelihood of voting, presumably to register discontent with those in power. But greater perceived corruption might also actually reduce the likelihood of voting, presumably in this case because the would-be voter sees no chance that her vote will make a difference. But in this hypothetical case, even the direction of the causal connection might be ambiguous. If voting is complicated, cumbersome, and overly bureaucratic, it might be that the experience of voting plays a role in shaping perceptions of corruption. In cases like this, certain variables might be both independent and dependent variables, with causal influence pushing in both directions (often called "endogeneity"), and the researcher will need to carefully think through and be particularly clear about the causal story to which her hypothesis is designed to call attention.

The need to assess the accuracy of these hypotheses, or any others proposed to account for variance on a dependent variable, will guide and shape the researcher's subsequent decisions about data collection and data analysis. Moreover, in most cases, the finding produced by data analysis is not a statement that the hypothesis is true or that the hypothesis is false. It is rather a statement that the hypothesis is *probably* true or it is *probably* false. And more specifically still, when testing a hypothesis with quantitative data, it is often a statement about the odds, or probability, that the researcher will be wrong if she concludes that the hypothesis is correct—if she concludes that the independent variable in the hypothesis is indeed a

---

[3]Carolina de Miguel, Amaney A. Jamal, and Mark Tessler. 2015. "Elections in the Arab World: Why do citizens turn out?" *Comparative Political Studies* 48, (11): 1355–1388.

significant determinant of the variance on the dependent variable. The lower the probability of being wrong, of course, the more confident a researcher can be in concluding, and reporting, that her data and analysis confirm her hypothesis.

> **Exercise 3.1**
>
> Hypotheses emerge from the research questions to which a study is devoted. Thinking about one or more countries with which you are familiar: (a) Identify the independent and dependent variables in each of the example research questions below. (b) Formulate at least one hypothesis for each question. Make sure to include your expectations about the directionality of the relationship between the two variables; is it positive/direct or negative/inverse? (c) In two or three sentences, describe a plausible causal story to which each of your hypotheses might call attention.
>
> 1. *Does religiosity affect people's preference for democracy?*
> 2. *Does preference for democracy affect the likelihood that a person will vote?*[4]

> **Exercise 3.2**
>
> Since its establishment in 2006, the Arab Barometer has, as of spring 2022, conducted 68 social and political attitude surveys in the Middle East and North Africa. It has conducted one or more surveys in 16 different Arab countries, and it has recorded the attitudes, values, and preferences of more than 100,000 ordinary citizens.
>
> The Arab Barometer website (arabbarometer.org) provides detailed information about the Barometer itself and about the scope, methodology, and conduct of its surveys. Data from the Barometer's surveys can be downloaded in either SPSS, Stata, or csv format. The website also contains numerous reports, articles, and summaries of findings.
>
> In addition, the Arab Barometer website contains an Online Data Analysis Tool that makes it possible, without downloading any data, to find the
>
> (continued)

---

[4] Question 1: Independent variable is religiosity; dependent variable is preference for democracy. Example of hypothesis for Question 1: H1. More religious individuals are more likely than less religious individuals to prefer democracy to other political systems. Question 2: Independent variable is preference for democracy; dependent variable is turning out to vote. Example of hypothesis for Question 2: H2. Individuals who prefer democracy to other political systems are more likely than individuals who do not prefer democracy to other political systems to turn out to vote.

Exercise 3.2 (continued)

distribution of responses to any question asked in any country in any wave. The tool is found in the "Survey Data" menu. After selecting the country and wave of interest, click the "See Results" tab to select the question(s) for which you want to see the response distributions. Click the "Cross by" tab to see the distributions of respondents who differ on one of the available demographic attributes.

The charts below present, in percentages, the response distributions of Jordanians interviewed in 2018 to two questions about gender equality. Below the charts are questions that you are asked to answer. These questions pertain to formulating hypotheses and to the relationship between hypotheses and causal stories.

Jordan in 2018: University Education for Males is More Important than University Education for Females

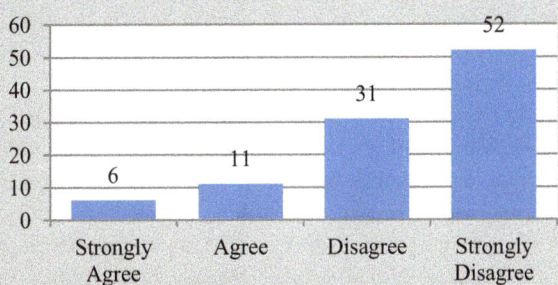

Jordan in 2018: In General, Men are Better at Political Leadership than Women

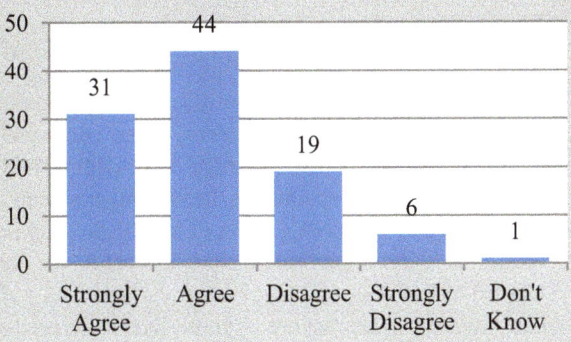

(continued)

Exercise 3.2 (continued)
1. For each of the two distributions, do you think (hypothesize) that the attitudes of Jordanian women are:
   (a) About the same as those of Jordanian men
   (b) More favorable toward gender equality than those of Jordanian men
   (c) Less favorable toward gender equality than those of Jordanian men
2. For each of the two distributions, do you think (hypothesize) that the attitudes of younger Jordanians are:
   (a) About the same as those of older Jordanians
   (b) More favorable toward gender equality than those of older Jordanians
   (c) Less favorable toward gender equality than those of older Jordanians
3. Restate your answers to Questions 1 and 2 as hypotheses.
4. Give the reasons for your answers to Questions 1 and 2. In two or three sentences, make explicit the presumed causal story on which your hypotheses are based.
5. Using the Arab Barometer's Online Analysis Tool, check to see whether your answers to Questions 1 and 2 are correct. For those instances in which an answer is incorrect, suggest in a sentence or two a causal story on which the *correct* relationship might be based.
6. In which other country surveyed by the Arab Barometer in 2018 do you think the distributions of responses to the questions about gender equality are very similar to the distributions in Jordan? What attributes of Jordan and the other country informed your selection of the other country?
7. In which other country surveyed by the Arab Barometer in 2018 do you think the distributions of responses to the questions about gender equality are very different from the distributions in Jordan? What attributes of Jordan and the other country informed your selection of the other country?
8. Using the Arab Barometer's Online Analysis Tool, check to see whether your answers to Questions 6 and 7 are correct. For those instances in which an answer is incorrect, suggest in a sentence or two a causal story on which the *correct* relationship might be based.

We will shortly return to and expand the discussion of probabilities and of hypothesis testing more generally. First, however, some additional discussion of hypothesis *formulation* is in order. Three important topics will be briefly considered. The first concerns the origins of hypotheses; the second concerns the criteria by which the value of a particular hypothesis or set of hypotheses should be evaluated; and the third, requiring a bit more discussion, concerns the structure of the hypothesized relationship between an independent variable and a dependent variable, or between any two variables that are hypothesized to be related.

Origins of Hypotheses Where do hypotheses come from? How should an investigator identify independent variables that may account for much, or at least some, of the variance on a dependent variable that she has observed and in which she is interested? Or, how should an investigator identify dependent variables whose variance has been determined, presumably only in part, by an independent variable whose impact she deems it important to assess.

Previous research is one place the investigator may look for ideas that will shape her hypotheses and the associated causal stories. This may include previous hypothesis-testing research, and this can be particularly instructive, but it may also include less systematic and structured observations, reports, and testimonies. The point, very simply, is that the investigator almost certainly is not the first person to think about, and offer information and insight about, the topic and questions in which the researcher herself is interested. Accordingly, attention to what is already known will very likely give the researcher some guidance and ideas as she strives for originality and significance in delineating the relationship between the variables in which she is interested.

Consulting previous research will also enable the researcher to determine what her study will add to what is already known—what it will contribute to the collective and cumulative work of researchers and others who seek to reduce uncertainty about a topic in which they share an interest. Perhaps the researcher's study will fill an important gap in the scientific literature. Perhaps it will challenge and refine, or perhaps even place in doubt, distributions and explanations of variance that have thus far been accepted. Or perhaps her study will produce findings that shed light on the generalizability or scope conditions of previously accepted variable relationships. It need not do any of these things, but that will be for the researcher to decide, and her decision will be informed by knowledge of what is already known and reflection on whether and in what ways her study should seek to add to that body of knowledge.

Personal experience will also inform the researcher's search for meaningful and informative hypotheses. It is almost certainly the case that a researcher's interest in a topic in general, and in questions pertaining to this topic in particular, have been shaped by her own experience. The experience itself may involve many different kinds of connections or interactions, some more professional and work-related and some flowing simply and perhaps unintentionally from lived experience. The hypotheses about voting mentioned earlier, for example, might be informed by elections the researcher has witnessed and/or discussions with friends and colleagues about elections, their turnout, and their fairness. Or perhaps the researcher's experience in her home country has planted questions about the generalizability of what she has witnessed at home.

All of this is to some extent obvious. But the take-away is that an investigator should not endeavor to set aside what she has learned about a topic in the name of objectivity, but rather, she should embrace whatever personal experience has taught her as she selects and refines the puzzles and propositions she will investigate. Should it happen that her experience leads her to incorrect or perhaps distorted understandings, this will be brought to light when her hypotheses are tested. It is in the testing that objectivity is paramount. In hypothesis formation, by contrast, subjectivity is permissible, and, in fact, it may often be unavoidable.

A final arena in which an investigator may look for ideas that will shape her hypotheses overlaps with personal experience and is also to some extent obvious. This is referenced by terms like creativity and originality and is perhaps best captured by the term "sociological imagination." The take-away here is that hypotheses that deserve attention and, if confirmed, will provide important insights, may not all be somewhere out in the environment waiting to be found, either in the relevant scholarly literature or in recollections about relevant personal experience. They can and sometimes will be the product of imagination and wondering, of discernments that a researcher may come upon during moments of reflection and deliberation.

As in the case of personal experience, the point to be retained is that hypothesis formation may not only be a process of discovery, of finding the previous research that contains the right information. Hypothesis formation may also be a creative process, a process whereby new insights and proposed original understandings are the product of an investigator's intellect and sociological imagination.

Crafting Valuable Hypotheses What are the criteria by which the value of a hypothesis or set of hypotheses should be evaluated? What elements define a good hypothesis? Some of the answers to these questions that come immediately to mind pertain to hypothesis testing rather than hypothesis formation. A good hypothesis, it might be argued, is one that is subsequently confirmed. But whether or not a confirmed hypothesis makes a positive contribution depends on the nature of the hypothesis and goals of the research. It is possible that a researcher will learn as much, and possibly even more, from findings that lead to rejection of a hypothesis. In any event, findings, whatever they may be, are valuable only to the extent that the hypothesis being tested is itself worthy of study.

Two important considerations, albeit somewhat obvious ones, are that a hypothesis should be non-trivial and non-obvious. If a proposition is trivial, suggesting a variable relationship with little or no significance, discovering whether and how the variables it brings together are related will not make a meaningful contribution to knowledge about the determinants and/or impact of the variance at the heart of the researcher's concern. Few will be interested in findings, however rigorously derived, about a trivial proposition. The same is true of an obvious hypothesis, obvious being an attribute that makes a proposition trivial. As stated, these considerations are themselves somewhat obvious, barely deserving mention. Nevertheless, an investigator should self-consciously reflect on these criteria when formulating hypotheses. She should be sure that she is proposing variable relationships that are neither trivial nor obvious.

A third criterion, also somewhat obvious but nonetheless essential, has to do with the significance and salience of the variables being considered. Will findings from research about these variables be important and valuable, and perhaps also useful? If the primary variable of interest is a dependent variable, meaning that the primary goal of the research is to account for variance, then the significance and salience of the dependent variable will determine the value of the research. Similarly, if the primary variable of interest is an independent variable, meaning that the primary goal of the research is to determine and assess impact, then the significance and salience of the independent variable will determine the value of the research.

These three criteria—non-trivial, non-obvious, and variable importance and salience—are not very different from one another. They collectively mean that the researcher must be able to specify why and how the testing of her hypothesis, or hypotheses, will make a contribution of value. Perhaps her propositions are original or innovative; perhaps knowing whether they are true or false makes a difference or will be of practical benefit; perhaps her findings add something specific and identifiable to the body of existing scholarly literature on the subject. While calling attention to these three connected and overlapping criteria might seem unnecessary since they are indeed somewhat obvious, it remains the case that the value of a hypothesis, regardless of whether or not it is eventually confirmed, is itself important to consider, and an investigator should, therefore, know and be able to articulate the reasons and ways that consideration of her hypothesis, or hypotheses, will indeed be of value.

Hypothesizing the Structure of a Relationship Relevant in the process of hypothesis formation are, as discussed, questions about the origins of hypotheses and the criteria by which the value of any particular hypothesis or set of hypotheses will be evaluated. Relevant, too, is consideration of the structure of a hypothesized variable relationship and the causal story to which that relationship is believed to call attention.

The point of departure in considering the structure of a hypothesized variable relationship is an understanding that such a relationship may or may not be linear. In a direct, or positive, linear relationship, each increase in the independent variable brings a constant increase in the dependent variable. In an inverse, or negative, linear relationship, each increase in the independent variable brings a constant decrease in the dependent variable. But these are only two of the many ways that an independent variable and a dependent variable may be related, or hypothesized to be related. This is easily illustrated by hypotheses in which level of education or age is the independent variable, and this is relevant in hypothesis formation because the investigator must be alert to and consider the possibility that the variables in which she is interested are in fact related in a non-linear way.

Consider, for example, the relationship between age and support for gender equality, the latter measured by an index based on several questions about the rights and behavior of women that are asked in Arab Barometer surveys. A researcher might expect, and might therefore want to hypothesize, that an increase in age brings increased support for, or alternatively increased opposition to, gender equality. But these are not the only possibilities. Likely, perhaps, is the possibility of a curvilinear relationship, in which case increases in age bring increases in support for gender equality until a person reaches a certain age, maybe 40, 45, or 50, after which additional increases in age bring decreases in support for gender equality. Or the researcher might hypothesize that the curve is in the opposite direction, that support for gender equality initially decreases as a function of age until a particular age is reached, after which additional increases in age bring an increase in support.

Of course, there are also other possibilities. In the case of education and gender equality, for example, increased education may initially have no impact on attitudes toward gender equality. Individuals who have not finished primary school, those who have finished primary school, and those who have gone somewhat beyond primary school and completed a middle school program may all have roughly the same attitudes toward gender equality. Thus, increases in education, within a certain range of educational levels, are not expected to bring an increase or a decrease in support for gender equality. But the level of support for gender equality among high school graduates may be higher and among university graduates may be higher still. Accordingly, in this hypothetical illustration, an increase in education does bring increased support for gender equality but only beginning after middle school.

A middle school level of education is a "floor" in this example. Education does not begin to make a difference until this floor is reached, and thereafter it does make a difference, with increases in education beyond middle school bringing increases in support for gender equality. Another possibility might be for middle school to be a "ceiling." This would mean that increases in education through middle school would bring increases in support for gender equality, but the trend would not continue beyond middle school. In other words, level of education makes a difference and appears to have explanatory power only until, and so not after, this ceiling is reached. This latter pattern was found in the study of education and Palestinian protest activity discussed earlier. Increases in education through middle school brought increases in the likelihood that an individual would participate in demonstrations and protests of Israeli occupation. However, additional education beyond middle school was not associated with greater likelihood of taking part in protest activities.

This discussion of variation in the structure of a hypothesized relationship between two variables is certainly not exhaustive, and the examples themselves are straightforward and not very complicated. The purpose of the discussion is, therefore, to emphasize that an investigator must be open to and think through the possibility and plausibility of different kinds of relationships between her two variables, that is to say, relationships with different structures. Bivariate relationships with several different kinds of structures are depicted visually by the scatter plots in Fig. 3.4.

These possibilities with respect to structure do not determine the value of a proposed hypothesis. As discussed earlier, the value of a proposed relationship depends first and foremost on the importance and salience of the variable of interest. Accordingly, a researcher should not assume that the value of a hypothesis varies as a function of the degree to which it posits a complicated variable relationship. More complicated hypotheses are not necessarily better or more correct. But while she should not strive for or give preference to variable relationships that are more complicated simply because they are more complicated, she should, again, be alert to the possibility that a more complicated pattern does a better job of describing the causal connection between the two variables in the place and time in which she is interested.

This brings the discussion of formulating hypotheses back to our earlier account of causal stories. In research concerned with explanation and causality, a hypothesis for the most part is a simplified stand-in for a causal story. It represents the causal story, as it were. Expressing this differently, the hypothesis states the causal story's "bottom line;" it posits that the independent variable is a determinant of variance on the dependent variable, and it identifies the structure of the presumed relationship between the independent variable and the dependent variable. But it does not describe the interaction between the two variables in a way that tells consumers of the study why the researcher believes that the relationship involves causality rather than an association with no causal implications. This is left to the causal story, which will offer a fuller account of the way the presumed cause impacts the presumed effect.

3.3 Describing and Visually Representing Bivariate Relationships

Once a researcher has collected or otherwise obtained data on the variables in a bivariate relationship she wishes to examine, her first step will be to describe the variance on each of the variables using the univariate statistics described in Chap. 2. She will need to understand the distribution on each variable before she can understand how these variables vary in relation to one another. This is important whether she is interested in description or wishes to explore a bivariate causal story.

Once she has described each one of the variables, she can turn to the relationship between them. She can prepare and present a visual representation of this relationship, which is the subject of the present section. She can also use bivariate statistical tests to assess the strength and significance of the relationship, which is the subject of the next section of this chapter.

Contingency Tables Contingency tables are used to display the relationship between two categorical variables. They are similar to the univariate frequency distributions described in Chap. 2, the difference being that they juxtapose the two univariate distributions and display the interaction between them. Also called crosstabulation tables, the cells of the table may present frequencies, row percentages, column percentages, and/or total percentages. Total frequencies and/or percentages are displayed in a total row and a total column, each one of which is the same as the univariate distribution of one of the variables taken alone.

Table 3.2, based on Palestinian data from Wave V of the Arab Barometer, crosses gender and the average number of hours watching television each day. Frequencies are presented in the cells of the table. In the cell showing the number of Palestinian men who do not watch television at all, row percentage, column percentage, and total percentage are also presented. Note that total percentage is based on the 10 cells showing the two variables taken together, which are summed in the lower right-hand cell. Thus, total percent for this cell is $342/2488 = 13.7$. Only frequencies are given in the other cells of the table; but in a full table, these four figures – frequency, row percent, column percent and total percent – would be given in every cell.

Table 3.2 Hours watching television by gender (Palestine, Wave V)

Hours watching television		Gender		Total
		Men	Women	
None	Frequency	342	317	659
	Row percent	52%		
	Column percent	28%		
	Total percent	14%		
Up to 2 h		707	652	1359
Up to 5 h		151	260	411
Up to 10 h		11	27	38
10 h or more		5	10	15
Total		1216	1266	2482

> **Exercise 3.3**
> Compute the row percentage, the column percentage, and the total percentage in the cell showing the number of Palestinian women who do not watch television at all.
>
> Describe the relationship between gender and watching television among Palestinians that is shown in the table. Do the television watching habits of Palestinian men and women appear to be generally similar or fairly different? You might find it helpful to convert the frequencies in other cells to row or column percentages.

Stacked Column Charts and Grouped Bar Charts Stacked column charts and grouped bar charts are used to visually describe how two categorical variables, or one categorical and one continuous variable, relate to one another. Much like contingency tables, they show the percentage or count of each category of one variable within each category of the second variable. This information is presented in columns stacked on each other or next to each other. The charts below show the number of male Palestinians and the number of female Palestinians who watch television for a given number of hours each day. Each chart presents the same information as the other chart and as the contingency table shown above (Fig. 3.1).

Box Plots and Box and Whisker Plots Box plots, box and whisker plots, and other types of plots can also be used to show the relationship between one categorical variable and one continuous variable. They are particularly useful for showing how spread out the data are. Box plots show five important numbers in a variable's distribution: the minimum value; the median; the maximum value; and the first and third quartiles (Q1 and Q2), which represent, respectively, the number below which are 25 percent of the distribution's values and the number below which are 75 percent of the distribution's values. The minimum value is sometimes called the lower extreme, the lower bound, or the lower hinge. The maximum value is sometimes

3.3 Describing and Visually Representing Bivariate Relationships   67

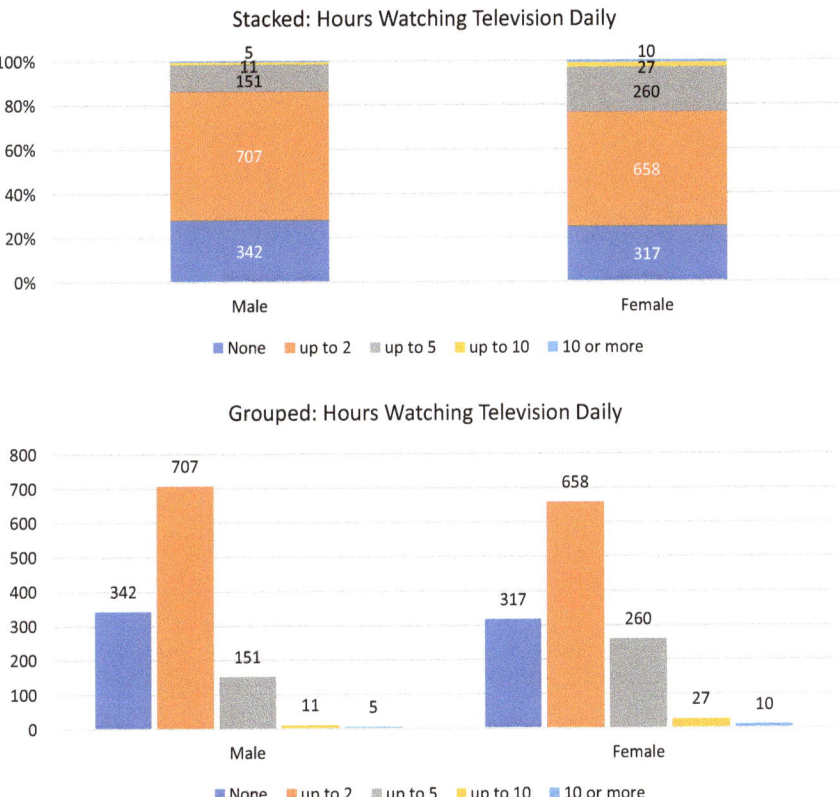

Fig. 3.1 Stacked column charts and grouped bar charts comparing Palestinian men and Palestinian women on hours watching television

called the upper extreme, the upper bound, or the upper hinge. The middle 50 percent of the distribution, the range between Q1 and Q3 that represents the "box," constitutes the interquartile range (IQR). In box and whisker plots, the "whiskers" are the short perpendicular lines extending outside the upper and lower quartiles. They are included to indicate variability below Q1 and above Q3. Values are usually categorized as outliers if they are less than $Q1 - IQR*1.5$ or greater than $Q3 + IQR*1.5$. A visual explanation of a box and whisker plot is shown in Fig. 3.2a and an example of a box plot that uses actual data is shown in Fig. 3.2b.

The box plot in Fig. 3.2b uses Wave V Arab Barometer data from Tunisia and shows the relationship between age, a continuous variable, and interpersonal trust, a dichotomous categorical variable. The line representing the median value is shown in bold. Interpersonal trust, sometimes known as generalized trust, is an important personal value. Previous research has shown that social harmony and prospects for democracy are greater in societies in which most citizens believe that their fellow citizens for the most part are trustworthy. Although the interpersonal trust variable is dichotomous in Fig. 3.2b, the variance in interpersonal trust can also be measured by

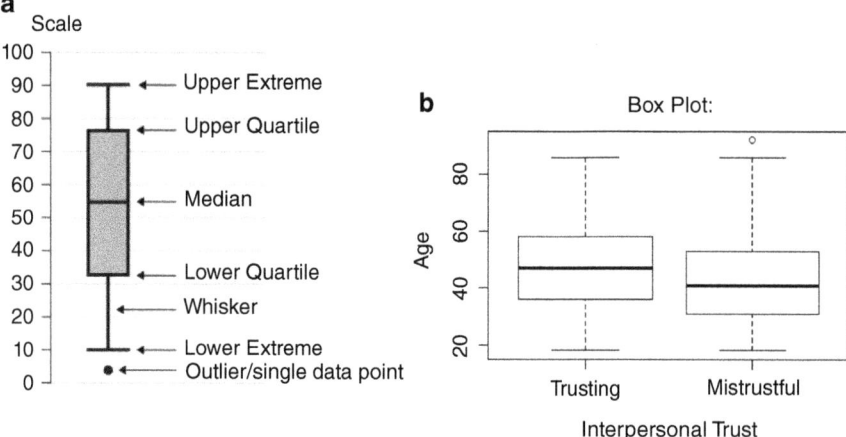

Fig. 3.2 (**a**) A box and whisker plot. (**b**) Box plot comparing the ages of trusting and mistrustful Tunisians in 2018

a set of ordered categories or a scale that yields a continuous measure, the latter not being suitable for presentation by a box plot. Figure 3.2b shows that the median age of Tunisians who are trusting is slightly higher than the median age of Tunisians who are mistrustful of other people. Notice also that the box plot for the mistrustful group has an outlier.

Line Plots Line plots may be used to visualize the relationship between two continuous variables or a continuous variable and a categorical variable. They are often used when time, or a variable related to time, is one of the two variables. If a researcher wants to show whether and how a variable changes over time for more than one subgroup of the units about which she has data (looking at men and women separately, for example), she can include multiple lines on the same plot, with each line showing the pattern over time for a different subgroup. These lines will generally be distinguished from each other by color or pattern, with a legend provided for readers.

Line plots are a particularly good way to visualize a relationship if an investigator thinks that important events over time may have had a significant impact. The line plot in Fig. 3.3 shows the average support for gender equality among men and among women in Tunisia from 2013 to 2018. Support for gender equality is a scale based on four questions related to gender equality in the three waves of the Arab Barometer. An answer supportive of gender equality on a question adds +.5 to the scale and an answer unfavorable to gender equality adds −.5 to the scale. Accordingly, a scale score of 2 indicates maximum support for gender equality and a scale score of −2 indicates maximum opposition to gender equality.

Fig. 3.3 Line plot showing level of support for gender equality among Tunisian women and men in 2013, 2016, and 2018

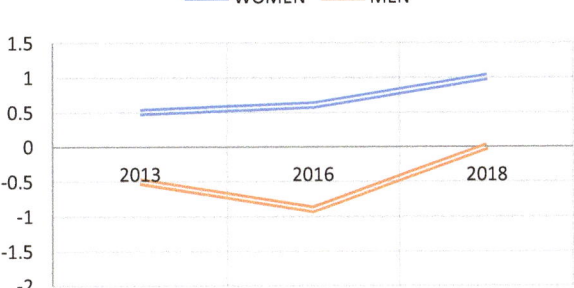

Scatter Plots Scatter plots are used to visualize a bivariate relationship when both variables are numerical. The independent variable is put on the x-axis, the horizontal axis, and the dependent variable is put on the y-axis, the vertical axis. Each data point becomes a dot in the scatter plot's two-dimensional field, with its precise location being the point at which its value on the x-axis intersects with its value on the y-axis. The scatter plot shows how the variables are related to one another, including with respect to linearity, direction, and other aspects of structure. The scatter plots in Fig. 3.4 illustrate a strong positive linear relationship, a moderately strong negative linear relationship, a strong non-linear relationship, and a pattern showing no relationship.[5] If the scatter plot displays no visible and clear pattern, as in the lower left hand plot shown in Fig. 3.4, the scatter plot would indicate that the independent variable, by itself, has no meaningful impact on the dependent variable.

Scatter plots are also a good way to identify outliers—data points that do not follow a pattern that characterizes most of the data. These are also called non-scalar types. Figure 3.5 shows a scatter plot with outliers.

Outliers can be informative, making it possible, for example, to identify the attributes of cases for which the measures of one or both variables are unreliable and/or invalid. Nevertheless, the inclusion of outliers may not only distort the assessment of measures, raising unwarranted doubts about measures that are actually reliable and valid for the vast majority of cases, they may also bias bivariate statistics and make relationships seem weaker than they really are for most cases. For this reason, researchers sometimes remove outliers prior to testing a hypothesis. If one does this, it is important to have a clear definition of what is an outlier and to justify the removal of the outlier, both using the definition and perhaps through substantive analysis. There are several mathematical formulas for identifying outliers, and researchers should be aware of these formulas and their pros and cons if they plan to remove outliers.

---

[5] Mike Yi. "A complete Guide to Scatter Plots," posted October 16, 2019 and seen at https://chartio.com/learn/charts/what-is-a-scatter-plot/

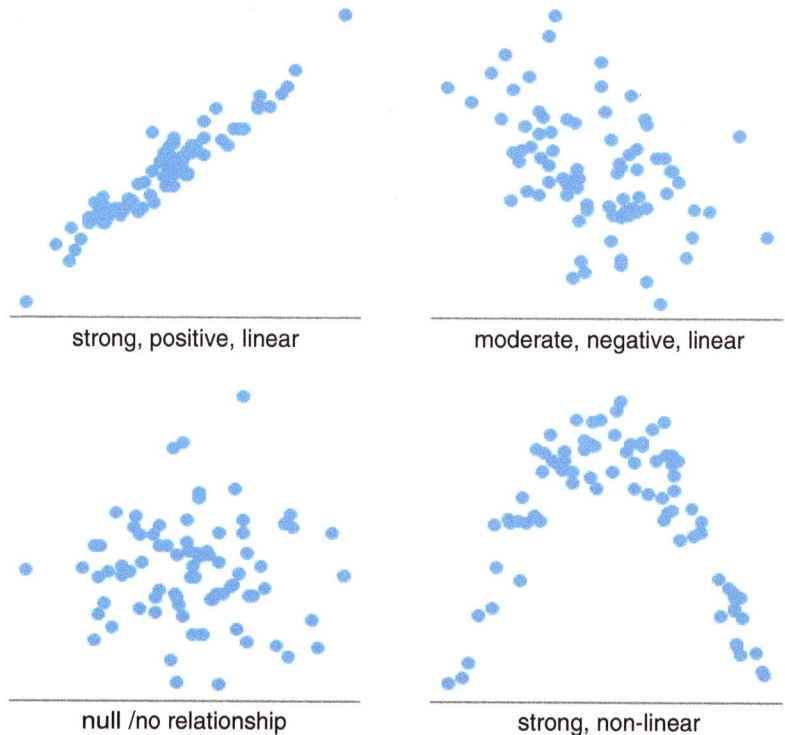

Fig. 3.4 Scatter plots showing bivariate relationships with different structures

Fig. 3.5 A scatter plot with outliers marked in red

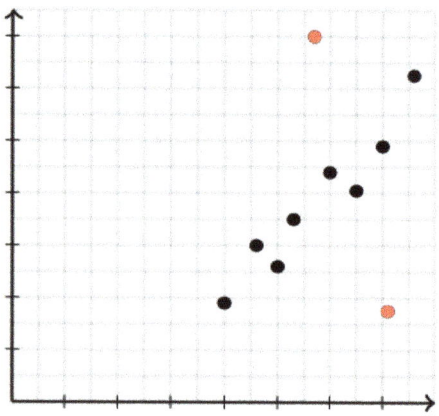

If there are relatively few outliers, perhaps no more than 5–10 percent of the cases, it may be justifiable to remove them in order to better discern the relationship between the independent variable and the dependent variable. If outliers are much

more numerous, however, it is probably because there is not a significant relationship between the two variables being considered. The researcher might in this case find it instructive to introduce a third variable and disaggregate the data. Disaggregation will be discussed in Chap. 4.

> **Exercise 3.4 Exploring Hypotheses through Visualizing Data: Exercise with the Arab Barometer Online Analysis Tool**
> 1. Go to the Arab Barometer Online Analysis Tool (https://www.arabbarometer.org/survey-data/data-analysis-tool/)
>   (a) Select Wave V and a country that interests you
>   (b) Select "See Results"
>   (c) Select "Social, Cultural and Religious topics"
>   (d) Select "Religion: frequency: pray"
>   (e) Questions: What does the distribution of this variable look like? How would you describe the variance?
> 2. Click on "Cross by," then
>   (a) Select "Show all variables"
>   (b) Select "Kind of government preferable" and click
>   (c) Select "Options," then "Show % over Row total," then "Apply"
>   (d) Questions: Does there seem to be a relationship between religiosity and preference for democracy? If so, what might explain the relationship you observe—what is a plausible causal story? Is it consistent with the hypothesis you wrote for Exercise 3.1?
> 3. Questions:
>   (a) What other variables could be used to measure religiosity and preference for democracy? Explore your hypothesis using different items from the list of Arab Barometer variables
>   (b) Do these distributions support the previous results you found? Do you learn anything additional about the relationship between religiosity and preference for democracy?
> 4. Now it is your turn to explore variables and variable relationships that interest you!
>   (a) Pick two variables that interest you from the list of Arab Barometer variables. Are they continuous or categorical? Ordinal or nominal? (Hint: Most Arab Barometer variables are categorical, even if you might be tempted to think of them as continuous. For example, age is divided into the ordinal categories 18–29, 30–49, and 50 and more.)
>   (b) Do you expect there to be a relationship between the two variables? If so, what do you think will be the structure of that relationship, and why?
> 5. Go to the Arab Barometer Online Analysis Tool (https://www.arabbarometer.org/survey-data/data-analysis-tool/)
>
> (continued)

Exercise 3.4 (continued)
(a) Select the wave (year) and the country that interest you
(b) Select one of your two variables of interest
(c) Click on "Cross by," and then select your second variable of interest.
(d) On the left side of the page, you'll see a contingency table. On the right side at the top, you'll see several options to graphically display the relationship between your two variables. Which type of graph best represents the relationship between your two variables of interest?
(e) Do the two variables seem to be independent of each other, or do you think there might be a relationship between them? Is the relationship you see similar to what you had expected

3.4 Probabilities and Type I and Type II Errors

As in visual presentations of bivariate relationships, selecting the appropriate measure of association or bivariate statistical test depends on the types of the two variables. The data on both variables may be categorical; the data on both may be continuous; or the data may be categorical on one variable and continuous on the other variable. These characteristics of the data will guide the way in which our presentation of these measures and tests is organized. Before briefly describing some specific measures of association and bivariate statistical tests, however, it is necessary to lay a foundation by introducing a number of terms and concepts. Relevant here are the distinction between population and sample and the notions of the null hypothesis, of Type I and Type II errors, and of probabilities and confidence intervals. As concepts, or abstractions, these notions may influence the way a researcher thinks about drawing conclusions about a hypothesis from qualitative data, as was discussed in Chap. 2. In their precise meaning and application, however, these terms and concepts come into play when hypothesis testing involves the statistical analysis of quantitative data.

To begin, it is important to distinguish between, on the one hand, the population of units—individuals, countries, ethnic groups, political movements, or any other unit of analysis—in which the researcher is interested and about which she aspires to advance conclusions and, on the other hand, the units on which she has actually acquired the data to be analyzed. The latter, the units on which she actually has data, is her sample. In cases where the researcher has collected or obtained data on all of the units in which she is interested, there is no difference between the sample and the population, and drawing conclusions about the population based on the sample is straightforward. Most often, however, a researcher does not possess data on all of the units that make up the population in which she is interested, and so the possibility of error when making inferences about the population based on the analysis of data in the sample requires careful and deliberate consideration.

This concern for error is present regardless of the size of the sample and the way it was constructed. The likelihood of error declines as the size of the sample increases and thus comes closer to representing the full population. It also declines if the sample was constructed in accordance with random or other sampling procedures designed to maximize representation. It is useful to keep these criteria in mind when looking at, and perhaps downloading and using, Arab Barometer data. The Barometer's website gives information about the construction of each sample. But while it is possible to reduce the likelihood of error when characterizing the population from findings based on the sample, it is not possible to eliminate entirely the possibility of erroneous inference. Accordingly, a researcher must endeavor to make the likelihood of this kind of error as small as possible and then decide if it is small enough to advance conclusions that apply to the population as well as the sample.

The null hypothesis, frequently designated as H0, is a statement to the effect that there is no meaningful and significant relationship between the independent variable and the dependent variable in a hypothesis, or indeed between two variables even if the relationship between them has not been formally specified in a hypothesis and does not purport to be causal or explanatory. The null hypothesis may or may not be stated explicitly by an investigator, but it is nonetheless present in her thinking; it stands in opposition to the hypothesized variable relationship. In a point and counterpoint fashion, the hypothesis, H1, posits that the variables *are* significantly related, and the null hypothesis, H0, replies and says no, they are *not* significantly related. It further says that they are not related in any meaningful way, neither in the way proposed in H1 nor in any other way that could be proposed.

Based on her analysis, the researcher needs to determine whether her findings permit rejecting the null hypothesis and concluding that there is indeed a significant relationship between the variables in her hypothesis, concluding in effect that the research hypothesis, H1, has been confirmed. This is most relevant and important when the investigator is basing her analysis on some but not all of the units to which her hypothesis purports to apply—when she is analyzing the data in her sample but seeks to advance conclusions that apply to the population in which she is interested. The logic here is that the findings produced by an analysis of some of the data, the data she actually possesses, may be different than the findings her analysis would hypothetically produce were she able to use data from very many more, or ideally even all, of the units that make up her population of interest.

This means, of course, that there will be uncertainty as the researcher adjudicates between H0 and H1 on the basis of her data. An analysis of these data may suggest that there is a strong and significant relationship between the variables in H1. And the stronger the relationship, the more unlikely it is that the researcher's sample is a subset of a population characterized by H0 and that, therefore, the researcher may consider H1 to have been confirmed. Yet, it remains at least possible that the researcher's sample, although it provides strong support for H1, is actually a subset of a population characterized by the null hypothesis. This may be unlikely, but it is not impossible, and so, therefore, to consider H1 to have been confirmed is to run the risk, at least a small risk, of what is known as a Type I error. A Type I error is made when a researcher accepts a research hypothesis that is actually false, when she judges to be true a hypothesis that does not characterize the population of which her sample is a subset. Because of the possibility of a Type I error, even if quite unlikely, researchers will often write something like "We can reject the null hypothesis," rather than "We can confirm our hypothesis."

Another analysis related to voter turnout provides a ready illustration. In the Arab Barometer Wave V surveys in 12 Arab countries,[6] 13,899 respondents answered a question about voting in the most recent parliamentary election. Of these, 46.6 percent said they had voted, and the remainder, 53.4 percent, said they had not voted in the last parliamentary election.[7] Seeking to identify some of the determinants of voting—the attitudes and experiences of an individual that increase the likelihood that she will vote, the researcher might hypothesize that a judgment that the country is going in the right direction will push toward voting. More formally:

H1. An individual who believes that her country is going in the right direction is more likely to vote in a national election than is an individual who believes her country is going in the wrong direction.

Arab Barometer surveys provide data with which to test this proposition, and in fact there is a difference associated with views about the direction in which the country is going. Among those who judged that their country is going in the right direction, 52.4 percent voted in the last parliamentary election. By contrast, among those who judged that their country is going in the wrong direction, only 43.8 percent voted in the last parliamentary election.

This illustrates the choice a researcher faces when deciding what to conclude from a study. Does the analysis of her data from a subset of her population of interest confirm or not confirm her hypothesis? In this example, based on Arab Barometer data, the findings are in the direction of her hypothesis, and differences in voting associated with views about the direction the country is going do not appear to be trivial. But are these differences big enough to justify the conclusion that judgements about the country's path going forward are a determinant of voting, one among others of course, in the population from which her sample was drawn? In other words, although this relationship clearly characterizes the sample, it is unclear whether it characterizes the researcher's population of interest, the population from which the sample was drawn.

---

[6] The countries are Algeria, Egypt, Iraq, Jordan, Kuwait, Lebanon, Libya, Morocco, Palestine, Sudan, Tunisia, and Yemen. The Wave V surveys were conducted in 2018–2019.

[7] Not considered in this illustration are the substantial cross-country differences in voter turnout. For example, 63.6 of the Lebanese respondents reported voting, whereas in Algeria the proportion who reported voting was only 20.3 percent. In addition to testing hypotheses about voting in which the individual is the unit of analysis, country could also be the unit of analysis, and hypotheses seeking to account for country-level variance in voting could be formulated and tested.

3.4 Probabilities and Type I and Type II Errors

Unless the researcher can gather data on the entire population of eligible voters, or at least almost all of this population, it is not possible to entirely eliminate uncertainty when the researcher makes inferences about the population of voters based on findings from the subset, or sample, of voters on which she has data. She can either conclude that her findings are sufficiently strong and clear to propose that the pattern she has observed characterizes the population as well, and that H1 is therefore confirmed; or she can conclude that her findings are not strong enough to make such an inference about the population, and that H1, therefore, is not confirmed. Either conclusion could be wrong, and so there is a chance of error no matter which conclusion the researcher advances.

The terms Type I error and Type II error are often used to designate the possible error associated with each of these inferences about the population based on the sample. Type I error refers to the rejection of a true null hypothesis. This means, in other words, that the investigator could be wrong if she concludes that her finding of a strong, or at least fairly strong, relationship between her variables characterizes Arab voters in the 12 countries in general, and if she thus judges H1 to have been confirmed when the population from which her sample was drawn is in fact characterized by H0. Type II error refers to acceptance of a false null hypothesis. This means, in other words, that the investigator could be wrong if she concludes that her finding of a somewhat weak relationship, or no relationship at all, between her variables characterizes Arab voters in the 12 countries in general, and that she thus judges H0 to be true when the population from which her sample was drawn is in fact characterized by H1.

In statistical analyses of quantitative data, decisions about whether to risk a Type I error or a Type II error are usually based on probabilities. More specifically, they are based on the probability of a researcher being wrong if she concludes that the variable relationship—or hypothesis in most cases—that characterizes her data, meaning her sample, also characterizes the population on which the researcher hopes her sample and data will shed light. To say this in yet another way, she computes the odds that her sample does *not* represent the population of which it is a subset; or more specifically still, she computes the odds that from a population that *is* characterized by the null hypothesis she could have obtained, by chance alone, a subset of the population, her sample, that is *not* characterized by the null hypothesis. The lower the odds, or probability, the more willing the researcher will be to risk a Type I error.

There are numerous statistical tests that are used to compute such probabilities. The nature of the data and the goals of the analysis will determine the specific test to be used in a particular situation. Most of these tests, frequently called tests of significance or tests of statistical significance, provide output in the form of probabilities, which always range from 0 to 1. The lower the value, meaning the closer to 0, the less likely it is that a researcher has collected and is working with data that produce findings that differ from what she would find were she to somehow have data on the entire population. Another way to think about this is the following:

- If the researcher provisionally assumes that the population is characterized by the null hypothesis with respect to the variable relationship under study, what is the probability of obtaining from that population, by chance alone, a subset or sample that is not characterized by the null hypothesis but instead shows a strong relationship between the two variables;
- The lower the probability value, meaning the closer to 0, the less likely it is that the researcher's data, which support H1, have come from a population that is characterized by H0;
- The lower the probability that her sample could have come from a population characterized by H0, the lower the possibility that the researcher will be wrong, that she will make a Type I error, if she rejects the null hypothesis and accepts that the population, as well as her sample, is characterized by H1;
- When the probability value is low, the chance of actually making a Type I error is small. But while small, the possibility of an error cannot be entirely eliminated.

If it helps you to think about probability and Type I and Type II error, imagine that you will be flipping a coin 100 times and your goal is to determine whether the coin is unbiased, H0, or biased in favor of either heads or tails, H1. How many times more than 50 would heads have to come up before you would be comfortable concluding that the coin is in fact biased in favor of heads? Would 60 be enough? What about 65? To begin to answer these questions, you would want to know the odds of getting 60 or 65 heads from a coin that is actually unbiased, a coin that would come up heads and come up tails roughly the same number of times if it were flipped many more than 100 times, maybe 1000 times, maybe 10,000. With this many flips, would the ratio of heads to tails even out. The lower the odds, the less likely it is that the coin is unbiased. In this analogy, you can think of the mathematical calculations about an unbiased coin's odds of getting heads as the population, and your actual flips of the coin as the sample.

But exactly how low does the probability of a Type I error have to be for a researcher to run the risk of rejecting H0 and accepting that her variables are indeed related? This depends, of course, on the implications of being wrong. If there are serious and harmful consequences of being wrong, of accepting a research hypothesis that is actually false, the researcher will reject H0 and accept H1 only if the odds of being wrong, of making a Type I error, are very low.

There are some widely used probability values, which define what are known as "confidence intervals," that help researchers and those who read their reports to think about the likelihood that a Type I error is being made. In the social sciences, rejecting H0 and running the risk of a Type I error is usually thought to require a probability value of less than .05, written as $p < .05$. The less stringent value of $p < .10$ is sometimes accepted as sufficient for rejecting H0, although such a conclusion would be advanced with caution and when the consequences of a Type I error are not very harmful. Frequently considered safer, meaning that the likelihood of accepting a false hypothesis is lower, are $p < .01$ and $p < .001$. The next section introduces and briefly describes some of the bivariate statistics that may be used to calculate these probabilities.

Table 3.3 Computing Degrees of Freedom for a Contingency Table

Computing Degrees of Freedom		a			b		
		Variable 2			Variable 2		
		Type a	Type b	Row total	Type a	Type b	Row total
Variable 1	Category a			75			60
	Category b			75			40
	Category c						50
	Column total	100	50	150	75	75	150

3.5 Measures of Association and Bivariate Statistical Tests

The following section introduces some of the bivariate statistical tests that can be used to compute probabilities and test hypotheses. The accounts are not very detailed. They will provide only a general overview and refresher for readers who are already fairly familiar with bivariate statistics. Readers without this familiarity are encouraged to consult a statistics textbook, for which the accounts presented here will provide a useful guide. While the account below will emphasize calculating these test statistics by hand, it is also important to remember that they can be calculated with the assistance of statistical software as well. A discussion of statistical software is available in Appendix 4.

Parametric and Nonparametric Statistics Parametric and nonparametric are two broad classifications of statistical procedures. A parameter in statistics refers to an attribute of a population. For example, the mean of a population is a parameter. Parametric statistical tests make certain assumptions about the shape of the distribution of values in a population from which a sample is drawn, generally that it is normally distributed, and about its parameters, that is to say the means and standard deviations of the assumed distributions. Nonparametric statistical procedures rely on no or very few assumptions about the shape or parameters of the distribution of the population from which the sample was drawn. Chi-squared is the only nonparametric statistical test among the tests described below.

Degrees of Freedom Degrees of freedom (df) is the number of values in the calculation of a statistic that are free to vary. Statistical software programs usually give degrees of freedom in the output, so it is generally unnecessary to know the number of the degrees of freedom in advance. It is nonetheless useful to understand what degrees of freedom represent. Consistent with the definition above, it is the number of values that are not predetermined, and thus are free to vary, within the variables used in a statistical test.

This is illustrated by the contingency tables below, which are constructed to examine the relationship between two categorical variables. The marginal row and column totals are known since these are just the univariate distributions of each variable. $df = 1$ for Table 3.3a, which is a 4-cell table. You can enter any one value in any one cell, but thereafter the values of all the other three cells are determined. Only one number is not free to vary and thus not predetermined. df = 2 for Table 3.3b, which is a 6-cell table. You can enter any two values in any two cells, but thereafter the values of all the other cells are determined. Only two numbers are free to vary and thus not predetermined. For contingency tables, the formula for calculating df is:

Number of columns – 1 (minus 1)* Number of rows – 1 (minus 1)

Chi-Squared Chi-squared, frequently written X^2, is a statistical test used to determine whether two categorical variables are significantly related. As noted, it is a nonparametric test. The most common version of the chi-squared test is the Pearson chi-squared test, which gives a value for the chi-squared statistic and permits determining as well a probability value, or p-value. The magnitude of the statistic and of the probability value are inversely correlated; the higher the value of the chi-squared statistic, the lower the probability value, and thus the lower the risk of making a Type I error—of rejecting a true null hypothesis—when asserting that the two variables are strongly and significantly related.

The simplicity of the chi-squared statistic permits giving a little more detail in order to illustrate several points that apply to bivariate statistical tests in general. The formula for computing chi-squared is given below, with O being the observed (actual) frequency in each cell of a contingency table for two categorical variables and E being the frequency that would be expected in each cell if the two variables are not related. Put differently, the distribution of E values across the cells of the two-variable table constitutes the null hypothesis, and chi-squared provides a number that expresses the magnitude of the difference between an investigator's actual observed values and the values of E.

$$X^2 = \sum \frac{(O - E)^2}{E}$$

X^2 = the test statistic $\sum$ = the sum of

O = Observed frequencies   E = Expected frequencies

The computation of chi-squared involves the following procedures, which are illustrated using the data in Table 3.4.

- The values of O in the cells of the table are based on the data collected by the investigator. For example, Table 3.4 shows that of the 200 women on whom she collected information, 85 are majoring in social science.

3.5 Measures of Association and Bivariate Statistical Tests

Table 3.4 Fields of study of 400 hypothetical male and female university students: testing the hypothesis that female university students are less likely to major in math and natural science than male university students

	Female students	Male students	Column totals (column totals give the univariate distribution for the variable university major)
Social Science	O = 85 E = (200 * 150)/400 = 75 $X^2 = 1.33$	O = 65 E = 75 $X^2 = ?$	O = 150
Math and Natural Science	O = 45 E = (200 * 100)/400 = 50 $X^2 = .33$	O = 55 E = 50 $X^2 = ?$	O = 100
Philosophy and Humanities	O = 50 E = ? $X^2 = ?$	O = 50 E = ? $X^2 = ?$	O = 100
Law, Medicine and Professions	O = 20 E = ? $X^2 = ?$	O = 30 E = ? $X^2 = ?$	O = 50
Row totals (row totals give the univariate distribution for the variable gender)	O = 200	O = 200	N = 400

- The value of E for each cell is computed by multiplying the marginal total of the column in which the cell is located by the marginal total of the row in which the cell is located divided by N, N being the total number of cases. For the female students majoring in social science in Table 3.4, this is: 200 * 150/400 = 30,000/400 = 75. For the female students majoring in math and natural science in Table 3.4, this is: 200 * 100/400 = 20,000/400 = 50.
- The difference between the value of O and the value of E is computed for each cell using the formula for chi-squared. For the female students majoring in social science in Table 3.4, this is: $(85-75)^2/75 = 10^2/75 = 100/75 = 1.33$. For the female students majoring in math and natural science, the value resulting from the application of the chi-squared is: $(45-50)^2/50 = 5^2/75 = 25/75 = .33$.
- The values in each cell of the table resulting from the application of the chi-squared formula are summed (Σ). This chi-squared value expresses the magnitude of the difference between a distribution of values indicative of the null hypothesis and what the investigator actually found about the relationship between gender and field of study. In Table 3.4, the cell for female students majoring in social science adds 1.33 to the sum of the values in the eight cells, the cell for female students majoring in math and natural science adds .33 to the sum, and so forth for the remaining six cells.

A final point to be noted, which applies to many other statistical tests as well, is that the application of chi-squared and other bivariate (and multivariate) statistical tests yields a value with which can be computed the probability that an observed pattern does not differ from the null hypothesis and that a Type I error will be made if the null hypothesis is rejected and the research hypothesis is judged to be true. The lower the probability, of course, the lower the likelihood of an error if the null hypothesis is rejected.

Prior to the advent of computer assisted statistical analysis, the value of the statistic and the number of degrees of freedom were used to find the probability value in a table of probability values in an appendix in most statistics books. At present, however, the probability value, or p-value, and also the degrees of freedom, are routinely given as part of the output when analysis is done by one of the available statistical software packages.

Table 3.5 shows the relationship between economic circumstance and trust in the government among 400 ordinary citizens in a hypothetical country. The observed data were collected to test the hypothesis that greater wealth pushes people toward greater trust and less wealth pushes people toward lesser trust. In the case of all three patterns, the probability that the null hypothesis is true is very low. All three patterns have the same high chi-squared value and low probability value. Thus, the chi-squared and p-values show only that the patterns all differ significantly from what would be expected were the null hypothesis true. They do not show whether the data support the hypothesized variable relationship or any other particular relationship.

As the three patterns in Table 3.5 show, variable relationships with very different structures can yield similar or even identical statistical test and probability values, and thus these tests provide only some of the information a researcher needs to draw conclusions about her hypothesis. To draw the right conclusion, it may also be necessary for the investigator to "look at" her data. For example, as Table 3.5 suggests, looking at a tabular or visual presentation of the data may also be needed to draw the proper conclusion about how two variables are related.

How would you describe the three patterns shown in the table, each of which differs significantly from the null hypothesis? Which pattern is consistent with the research hypothesis? How would you describe the other two patterns? Try to visualize a plot of each pattern.

Pearson Correlation Coefficient The Pearson correlation coefficient, more formally known as the Pearson product-moment correlation, is a parametric measure of linear association. It gives a numerical representation of the strength and direction of the relationship between two continuous numerical variables. The coefficient, which is commonly represented as r, will have a value between -1 and 1. A value of 1 means that there is a perfect positive, or direct, linear relationship between the two variables; as one variable increases, the other variable consistently increases by some amount. A value of -1 means that there is a perfect negative, or inverse, linear relationship; as one variable increases, the other variable consistently decreases by some amount. A value of 0 means that there is no linear relationship; as one variable

3.5 Measures of Association and Bivariate Statistical Tests

Table 3.5 The relationship between economic circumstance and trust in government: testing the hypothesis that greater wealth pushes toward greater trust

	Pattern A. Distribution of observed frequencies				Pattern B. Distribution of observed frequencies				Pattern C. Distribution of observed frequencies			
	No trust	Little trust	Some trust	High trust	No trust	Little trust	Some trust	high trust	No trust	Little trust	Some trust	High trust
Wealthy	30	50	50	30	50	20	0	0	0	0	30	50
Middle class	40	50	50	40	40	50	20	10	10	30	50	40
Working class	20	0	0	20	10	30	50	40	40	50	20	10
Poor	10	0	0	10	0	0	30	50	50	20	0	0
	100	100	100	100	100	100	100	100	100	100	100	100

increases, the other variable neither consistently increases nor consistently decreases.

It is easy to think of relationships that might be assessed by a Pearson correlation coefficient. Consider, for example, the relationship between age and income and the proposition that as age increases, income consistently increases or consistently decreases as well. The closer a coefficient is to 1 or −1, the greater the likelihood that the data on which it is based are *not* the subset of a population in which age and income are unrelated, meaning that the population of interest is not characterized by the null hypothesis. Coefficients very close to 1 or −1 are rare; although it depends on the number of units on which the researcher has data and also on the nature of the variables. Coefficients higher than .3 or lower than −.03 are frequently high enough, in absolute terms, to yield a low probability value and justify rejecting the null hypothesis. The relationship in this case would be described as "statistically significant."

> **Exercise 3.5**
> Estimating Correlation Coefficients from scatter plots
>
> 1. Look at the scatter plots in Fig. 3.4 and estimate the correlation coefficient that the bivariate relationship shown in each scatter plot would yield.
> 2. Explain the basis for each of your estimates of the correlation coefficient.

Spearman's Rank-Order Correlation Coefficient The Spearman's rank-order correlation coefficient is a nonparametric version of the Pearson product-moment correlation. Spearman's correlation coefficient, (ρ, also signified by r_s) measures the strength and direction of the association between two ranked variables.

Bivariate Regression Bivariate regression is a parametric measure of association that, like correlation analysis, assesses the strength and direction of the relationship between two variables. Also, like correlation analysis, regression assumes linearity. It may give misleading results if used with variable relationships that are not linear.

Regression is a powerful statistic that is widely used in multivariate analyses. This includes ordinary least squares (OLS) regression, which requires that the dependent variable be continuous and assumes linearity; binary logistic regression, which may be used when the dependent variable is dichotomous; and ordinal logistic regression, which is used with ordinal dependent variables. The use of regression in multivariate analysis will be discussed in the next chapter. In bivariate analysis, regression analysis yields coefficients that indicate the strength and direction of the relationship between two variables. Researchers may opt to "standardize" these coefficients. Standardized coefficients from a bivariate regression are the same as the coefficients produced by Pearson product-moment correlation analysis.

T-Test The t-test, also sometimes called a "difference of means" test, is a parametric statistical test that compares the means of two variables and determines whether they are different enough from each other to reject the null hypothesis and risk a Type I error. The dependent variable in a t-test must be continuous or ordinal—otherwise the investigator cannot calculate a mean. The independent variable must be categorical since t-tests are used to compare two groups.

An example, drawing again on Arab Barometer data, tests the relationship between voting and support for democracy. The hypothesis might be that men and women who voted in the last parliamentary election are more likely than men and women who did not vote to believe that democracy is suitable for their country. Whether a person did or did not vote would be the categorical independent variable, and the dependent variable would be the response to a question like, "To what extent do you think democracy is suitable for your country?" The question about democracy asked respondents to situate their views on a 11-point scale, with 0 indicating completely unsuitable and 10 indicating completely suitable.

Focusing on Tunisia in 2018, Arab Barometer Wave V data show that the mean response on the 11-point suitability question is 5.11 for those who voted and 4.77 for those who did not vote. Is this difference of .34 large enough to be statistically significant? A t-test will determine the probability of getting a difference of this magnitude from a population of interest, most likely all Tunisians of voting age, in which there is no difference between voters and non-voters in views about the suitability of democracy for Tunisia. In this example, the t-test showed $p < .086$. With this p-value, which is higher than the generally accepted standard of .05, a researcher cannot with confidence reject the null hypotheses, and she is unable, therefore, to assert that the proposed relationship has been confirmed.

This question can also be explored at the country level of analysis with, for example, regime type as the independent variable. In this illustration, the hypothesis is that citizens of monarchies are more likely than citizens of republics to believe that democracy is suitable for their country. Of course, a researcher proposing this hypothesis would also advance an associated causal story that provides the rationale for the hypothesis and specifies what is really being tested. To test this proposition, an investigator might merge data from surveys in, say, three monarchies, perhaps Morocco, Jordan, and Kuwait, and then also merge data from surveys in three republics, perhaps Algeria, Egypt, and Iraq. A t-test would then be used to compare the means of people in republics and people in monarchies and give the p-value.

A similar test, the Wilcoxon-Mann-Whitney test, is a nonparametric test that does not require that the dependent variable be normally distributed.

ANOVA Analysis of variance, or ANOVA, is closely related to the t-test. It may be used when the dependent variable is continuous and the independent variable is categorical. A one-way ANOVA compares the mean and variance values of a continuous dependent variable in two or more categories of a categorical independent variable in order to determine if the latter affects the former.

ANOVA calculates the F-ratio based on the variance between the groups and the variance within each group. The F-ratio can then be used to calculate a p-value.

Table 3.6 Bivariate visual representations and bivariate statistical tests for pairs of variables possessing particular characteristics

Types of variables	Visual representation	Measures of association and statistical tests
Numerical (both)	Scatter plot Line plot	Pearson correlation coefficient, Spearman's rank-order correlation coefficient Linear regression
Categorical (both)	Contingency table Bar chart Stacked column chart	Chi-squared test T-test and Wilcoxon-Mann-Whitney test (when the dependent variable is ordinal) Logistic regression
One numerical, one categorical	Bar chart Line plot Box plot	T-test Wilcoxon-Mann-Whitney test (when the dependent variable is ordinal) Linear and Logistic regression One-way ANOVA

However, if there are more than two categories of the independent variable, the ANOVA test will not indicate which pairs of categories differ enough to be statistically significant, making it necessary, again, to look at the data in order to draw correct conclusions about the structure of the bivariate relationships. Two-way ANOVA is used when an investigator has more than two variables.

Table 3.6 presents a summary list of the visual representations and bivariate statistical tests that have been discussed. It reminds readers of the procedures that can be used when both variables are categorical, when both variables are numerical/continuous, and when one variable is categorical and one variable is numerical/continuous.

Bivariate Statistics and Causal Inference It is important to remember that bivariate statistical tests only assess the association or correlation between two variables. The tests described above can help a researcher estimate how much confidence her hypothesis deserves and, more specifically, the probability that any significant variable relationships she has found characterize the larger population from which her data were drawn and about which she seeks to offer information and insight.

The finding that two variables in a hypothesized relationship are related to a statistically significant degree is not evidence that the relationship is causal, only that the independent variable is related to the dependent variable. The finding is consistent with the causal story that the hypothesis represents, and to that extent, it offers support for this story. Nevertheless, there are many reasons why an observed statistically significant relationship might be spurious. The correlation might, for example, reflect the influence of one or more other and uncontrolled variables. This will be discussed more fully in the next chapter. The point here is simply that bivariate statistics do not, by themselves, address the question of whether a statistically significant relationship between two variables is or is not a causal relationship.

3.5 Measures of Association and Bivariate Statistical Tests

Only an Introductory Overview As has been emphasized throughout, this chapter seeks only to offer an introductory overview of the bivariate statistical tests that may be employed when an investigator seeks to assess the relationship between two variables. Additional information will be presented in Chap. 4. The focus in Chap. 4 will be on multivariate analysis, on analyses involving three or more variables. In this case again, however, the chapter will provide only an introductory overview. The overviews in the present chapter and the next provide a foundation for understanding social statistics, for understanding what statistical analyses involve and what they seek to accomplish. This is important and valuable in and of itself. Nevertheless, researchers and would-be researchers who intend to incorporate statistical analyses into their investigations, perhaps to test hypotheses and decide whether to risk a Type I error or a Type II error, will need to build on this foundation and become familiar with the contents of texts on social statistics. If this guide offers a bird's eye view, researchers who implement these techniques will also need to expose themselves to the view of the worm at least once.

* * *

Chapter 2 makes clear that the concept of variance is central and foundational for much and probably most data-based and quantitative social science research. Bivariate relationships, which are the focus of the present chapter, are building blocks that rest on this foundation. The goal of this kind of research is very often the discovery of causal relationships, relationships that explain rather than merely describe or predict. Such relationships are also frequently described as accounting for variance. This is the focus of Chap. 4, and it means that there will be, first, a dependent variable, a variable that expresses and captures the variance to be explained, and then, second, an independent variable, and possibly more than one independent variable, that impacts the dependent variable and causes it to vary.

Bivariate relationships are at the center of this enterprise, establishing the empirical pathway leading from the variance discussed in Chap. 2 to the causality discussed in Chap. 4. Finding that there is a significant relationship between two variables, a statistically significant relationship, is not sufficient to establish causality, to conclude with confidence that one of the variables impacts the other and causes it to vary. But such a finding is necessary.

The goal of social science inquiry that investigates the relationship between two variables is not always explanation. It might be simply to describe and map the way two variables interact with one another. And there is no reason to question the value of such research. But the goal of data-based social science research is very often explanation; and while the inter-relationships between more than two variables will almost always be needed to establish that a relationship is very likely to be causal, these inter-relationships can only be examined by empirics that begin with consideration of a bivariate relationship, a relationship with one variable that is a presumed cause and one variable that is a presumed effect.

Against this background, with the importance of two-variable relationships in mind, the present chapter offers a comprehensive overview of bivariate relationships, including but not only those that are hypothesized to be causally related. The chapter considers the origin and nature of hypotheses that posit a particular relationship between two variables, a causal relationship if the larger goal of the research is explanation and the delineation of a causal story to which the hypothesis calls attention. This chapter then considers how a bivariate relationship might be described and visually represented, and thereafter it discusses how to think about and determine whether the two variables actually are related.

Presenting tables and graphs to show how two variables are related and using bivariate statistics to assess the likelihood that an observed relationship differs significantly from the null hypothesis, the hypothesis of no relationship, will be sufficient if the goal of the research is to learn as much as possible about whether and how two variables are related. And there is plenty of excellent research that has this kind of description as its primary objective, that makes use for purposes of description of the concepts and procedures introduced in this chapter. But there is also plenty of research that seeks to explain, to account for variance, and for this research, use of these concepts and procedures is necessary but not sufficient. For this research, consideration of a two-variable relationship, the focus of the present chapter, is a necessary intermediate step on a pathway that leads from the observation of variance to explaining how and why that variance looks and behaves as it does.

Open Access This chapter is licensed under the terms of the Creative Commons Attribution 4.0 International License (http://creativecommons.org/licenses/by/4.0/), which permits use, sharing, adaptation, distribution and reproduction in any medium or format, as long as you give appropriate credit to the original author(s) and the source, provide a link to the Creative Commons license and indicate if changes were made.

The images or other third party material in this chapter are included in the chapter's Creative Commons license, unless indicated otherwise in a credit line to the material. If material is not included in the chapter's Creative Commons license and your intended use is not permitted by statutory regulation or exceeds the permitted use, you will need to obtain permission directly from the copyright holder.

Multivariate Analysis: Causation, Control, and Conditionality

4.1 Causal Inference

4.1.1 Covariance and Causation

Theory building and data analyses based on three or more variables offer many possibilities for refinement and increased accuracy beyond what has been discussed in Chaps. 2 and 3. One of these involves "causal inference."

We know that a correlation between two variables, even a strong and statistically significant correlation—a correlation that justifies risking a Type I error—does not provide evidence that the relationship between the two variables involves causality. The distinction between a correlation and a causal connection is sometimes illustrated by silly, but humorous, examples. Here is one that we heard in the U.S. a few years ago.

Popular folktales pretend that newborn babies are brought to waiting parents by a stork. The image of a baby in a blanket hanging from the stork's beak is familiar, at least in the U.S. Of course, storks do not really deliver babies; but wait, it turns out that there is a strong and significant correlation across a sample of geographic localities between the presence of storks and a relatively high number of babies born each year.

Does this mean that we should not be so quick to dismiss the story in the folktale? Of course not. The correlation does not indicate a causal connection. It reflects the impact of a third variable, and that third variable is probably whether or not a locality is urban or rural. Birth rates are higher in localities that are more rural, and storks are more likely to be found in rural localities. Thus, whether or not there are both more babies and more storks, or fewer of each, depends on whether the locality is urban or rural. It is the impact of this third variable, rather than a causal relationship between the original two, that causes a measure of storks and a measure of babies to covary.

Well, maybe this folktale is not so humorous, after all! At least it is silly! There are many silly examples of things that covary but do not involve a causal relationship. Consider another example: wearing shorts and eating ice cream covary. Is it

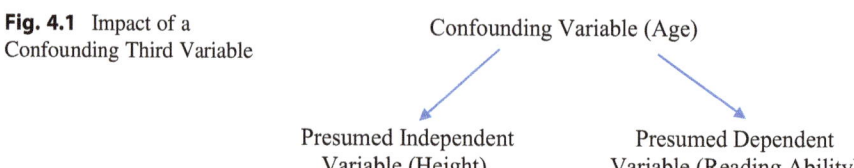

Fig. 4.1 Impact of a Confounding Third Variable

possible that there is something about wearing shorts that pushes a person dressed this way to eat ice cream, that wearing shorts causes a person to eat ice cream? The correlation, again, does not indicate a causal connection. It reflects, rather, the impact of a third variable, and that third variable might be the temperature outside a person's residence. When it is hot, people are more likely both to wear shorts and to eat ice cream; and so it is, again, the impact of this third variable, rather than a causal relationship between wearing shorts and eating ice cream, that causes the two variables to covary.

These examples, silly as they are, remind us that phenomena that vary together may do so for reasons having nothing to do with the variance on one variable determining, that is to say causing, the variance on a second variable. An online search of "correlation causation" yields many accounts and examples, some humorous and some less so, of strong bivariate relationships that do not involve causation. Among the examples given in a series of lectures entitled *Real Statistics: An Islamic Approach*[1] is the correlation between height and reading ability among school-aged children. An increase in height does not cause an increase in reading ability, as if books and other things to read were on the upper shelves of bookcases and could be reached only by taller individuals. Rather, as illustrated in Fig. 4.1, age is a confounding variable. As young people get older, their height increases, they go farther in school, and their reading skills improve.

Relationships that involve covariance, or association, but not causation are considered "spurious," meaning that the two variables may appear to be causally related but in fact are not. Spuriousness may result from co-variance that is coincidental,[2] or it may reflect the influence of a third variable that is connected to both of the two strongly correlated variables. The latter possibility explains the three previous examples, with the confounding third variable being, respectively, the urban-rural character of the locality, the outside temperature, and age. This phenomenon is also sometimes called "omitted variable bias."

---

[1] "Correlations & Common Cause: An Islamic Worldview," Lec. 9A of *Real Statistics: An Islamic Approach*, accessed at https://azprojects.wordpress.com/2020/12/25/correlations-common-cause/

[2] The following are two of the many examples posted online by a 17-year-old Egyptian science student: there is a relationship between US spending on science and suicide; there is a relationship between the consumption of cheese and the number of people who died by becoming tangled in their bedsheets; accessed at: https://www.arquestssern.org/post/correlation-causation-fallacy

4.1 Causal Inference

> **Exercise 4.1**
> Can you think of another three-variable relationship in which two of the variables might *appear* to be causally related but are not because the third variable is a confounding variable?
>
> - What are the two variables that appear to be causally related? Which is the presumed cause, and which is the presumed effect?
> - Why do they appear to be causally related? Why might it be reasonable to think they are causally related?
> - What is the confounding variable? How is the confounding variable related to the other two variables in a way that makes them covary without being causally related?

How can a researcher determine, and offer evidence, that a relationship involves causality and is not spurious? This is among the most salient and frequently asked questions that a social science investigator needs to answer, and it is among the most challenging. Social science research designs that incorporate experiments offer one strategy for determining whether a relationship between two variables is causal, and then for offering evidence of causality should that be found. Experiments—natural experiments, field experiments, and survey experiments, among others—are frequently conducted by social scientists, and the use of experiments in social science research will be very briefly discussed later in this chapter. With the possible exception of social psychology, however, other data collection and/or data analysis procedures are much more common, usually because the conduct of an experiment is not possible or not appropriate given the topic and hypotheses being investigated.

This brings the focus of our discussion to multivariate analysis when seeking to infer causality, when testing hypotheses that posit a causal relationship between a dependent variable and an independent variable. And take note, the use of the term "infer" is deliberate. Causality is usually inferred, not demonstrated or proved, meaning that the investigator seeks to determine whether or not an observed relationship is *probably,* or very likely to be, causal. Described as "causal inference," this involves elements both of theory and of research design. In quantitative studies, it will usually also involve multivariate statistical analysis. Analogous to the choice between Type I error and Type II error discussed in Chap. 3, the goal is to minimize the chance of error if causality is inferred, if an investigator concludes that a relationship is causal.

As discussed in the previous chapter, causal inference begins with the development of a causal story that is referenced by a testable hypothesis. Sources of the causal story, and therefore also the hypothesis, may include previous investigations by the researcher herself or other investigators, the researcher's knowledge and personal experience relating to the subject of the causal story and hypothesis, and new insights drawn from reflections and theorizing that call upon what is sometimes described as the "sociological imagination."

The important point here is that building a case for causal inference includes the delineation of a causal story that is at least very plausible and ideally very persuasive. While this might seem less rigorous than offering findings from a multivariate statistical test as evidence that a relationship is causal, a topic to which we turn next, it is actually no less important. In fact, the two must align; the causality attributed to a relationship whose statistical significance is confirmed must also make good sense. The fact that it does make good sense—that the causal story is coherent and persuasive, or at the very least plausible—is part of the case for causal inference that the researcher will need to build.

Against this background, we now turn to three interrelated considerations pertaining to causal inference. The first is the importance of a temporal sequence between the independent variable and the dependent variable. The second consideration is the use of multivariate statistical tests to derive probability values, which in turn give the researcher a basis for determining whether or not a hypothesized variable relationship that purports to be causal is very likely to be true—whether to risk a Type I error or a Type II error, in other words. The discussion focuses on multivariate regression, a widely used statistical technique that permits including and holding constant one or more control variables. Multivariate regression is the natural extension of bivariate regression, which was discussed in Chap. 3. The third consideration is a deeper look at control variables, including how they are defined and may be identified and why they are important. These three considerations are foundational elements of a convincing and robust causal story.

4.1.2 Temporal Sequence

Elements of research design that are relevant for causal inference include decisions related to the selection and measurement of key variables, beginning, of course, with the dependent variable and the independent variable. Further, there must be an appropriate temporal sequence between these two variables if causality is to be inferred. The cause of the independent variable, in other words, must precede the effect of the dependent variable.

Sometimes a temporal sequence occurs naturally given the structure of the study or the nature of the variables, and in these instances, the investigator need not do anything to ensure a sequential ordering. For example, an individual-level hypothesis that posits level of education as a determinant of current attitudes toward government held by adults posits a relationship between two variables that are by their nature sequentially arranged.

The requirement of a temporal sequence imposed by a concern for causal inference will very often determine the structure of an investigator's research design. Designs that incorporate some of the elements of an experiment, and that might, therefore, be described as quasi-experimental, constitute one possibility. For example, studies that seek to assess the impact and explanatory power of a particular action or event can measure the dependent variable at a time before the action or event and then measure it again at a time after the action or event. The difference between the two time-specific measures, hence the variance on the dependent variable, may be attributable to the impact of the intervening action or event, which in this instance is the independent variable, the presumed cause.

The variance on the dependent variable might also be attributable to other things that took place during the time between the two measures; and for this reason, other elements will need to be included in the analysis before a persuasive case for causal inference can be built. These elements, most notably the identification and inclusion of control variables, will be taken up later in this chapter. The point to be retained at present is that the existence of a temporal sequence, while not sufficient for advancing a claim of causality, is a necessary element of a research design concerned with a causal relationship.

It is not unusual to survey a country's population before and after a significant event, a national election for example, and then consider whether the attitudes or behavior of that population have changed in ways that might have been caused by the election. If the surveys are probability-based and nationally representative, the same population, although possibly not all of the same individuals, will have been surveyed at two points in time. Country is the unit of analysis in such studies, as illustrated by the meta-analysis described below.

An interesting variation on this country-level "Before and After" research design is provided by a meta-analysis that seeks to assess whether and how the Arab Spring uprisings in Tunisia, beginning at the end of 2010, contributed to changing, and improving, the status of women. The specific two-stage causal story to be assessed posits greater social media freedom both as a determinant of reduced violence against women and as a consequence of political changes brought by the country's Arab Spring experience. Several studies have suggested this causal story, or some variation of it.

A review of these studies prepared by Lilia Labidi, a prominent Tunisian social psychologist, looks at research projects undertaken both before and after Tunisia's Arab Spring uprisings. These uprisings, frequently described as the "jasmine revolution," brought the fall of the country's authoritarian government and, most relevant for the hypothesis, the removal of Internet censorship and restrictions on access to social media. Labidi reports that a number of private television and radio stations were started, and social media opportunities multiplied, with one individual able to maintain several Facebook accounts; and she then gives examples of the ways that advocates of women's rights and gender equality used the new media freedoms to advance their cause.[3]

One common criticism of a proposed causal story is the possibility that the direction of the causal relationship is actually reversed. With regard to the previous example, a critic might argue that increased support for women's rights and gender equality pushed toward media reform, thus reversing the direction of the causality.

---

[3] Lilia Labidi. 2020. "Violence against Women in Tunisia Before and After January 2011: The Role of Social Media." Wilson Center: Washington, DC; at https://www.wilsoncenter.org/blog-post/violence-against-women-tunisia-and-after-january-2011-role-social-media

But while worthy of consideration in the case of some hypothesized relationships, in this particular example Labidi calls attention to the temporal sequence, the before and after structure of the data. This helps to stave off criticism and strengthens her causal story.

Lagging independent variables, often referred to simply as lags, are a common way to ensure that a temporal sequence is built into the data and analysis used to test a hypothesized causal relationship. Lags provide the analytical structure, for example, in country-level studies in which both variables are time-specific, most often yearly, measures of aggregate national or societal performance or status. If, for example, a country-level study sought to test the hypothesis that Foreign Direct Investment (FDI) reduces a country's level of unemployment, and if the study's investigators had obtained or collected data on both variables for the 5 years between 2015 and 2020, the following are among the measures that might be used to test the hypothesis:

Dependent Variable

- The dependent variable might be the difference between the percent unemployed in a given year and an earlier year
- The specific year could be any in which the researcher has a particular interest or considers particularly important
- The magnitude of the time between the 2 years will be specified by the researcher based on her knowledge of the data and the mechanisms of her causal story
- The dependent variable might thus be the difference between unemployment in 2020 and 2019, or in 2020 and 2018, or even in 2020 and 2015, whichever best captures the variance for which the researcher seeks to account

Independent Variable

- The measure of the independent variable might be the difference in FDI as a percentage of Gross National Product (GNP) between the earliest of the years on which the dependent variable is based and an earlier year
- If the dependent variable is the difference between unemployment in 2020 and 2019, the independent variable might be the difference in FDI between 2019 and 2018
- As in the case of the dependent variable, the magnitude of the time between the two measures of the independent variable will be specified by the researcher based on her knowledge of the data and the mechanisms of her causal story

In this hypothetical example, as noted, the specifics of the hypothesis to be tested might be that an increase in FDI between 2018 and 2019 caused the level of unemployment to decrease between 2019 and 2020. Notice the careful choice of the years for the independent and dependent variables. If a researcher were to claim that the increase in FDI between 2019 and 2020 caused the level of unemployment to decrease between 2019 and 2020, a critic would immediately respond that not enough time could have passed for the increase in FDI to be the driver of the change in unemployment. By lagging the independent variable and looking at FDI between the years 2018 and 2019, the researcher creates a temporal sequence between the independent and dependent variables and thus a much more convincing causal story. This example is hypothetical, of course, and it is also simplified. But in fact, there have been serious tests of the proposition that an increase in FDI brings about a decrease in unemployment. A 2019 macroeconomic study of unemployment rates in general and youth unemployment in particular in eight Arab countries reports, "A positive impact of FDI on reducing national unemployment is proven in the group as a whole and individually in Jordan, Morocco, and Tunisia while it leads to an increase in unemployment in Egypt. The impact of FDI on reducing youth unemployment is not proven."[4]

This might be the place to introduce readers to the Cairo-based Economic Research Forum.[5] The ERF commissions and makes available numerous studies based on aggregate data with variables measured sequentially over time. A large proportion of these studies have an applied and policy-relevant focus. Among the ERF publications and working papers are, in fact, several studies that examine the relationship between FDI and unemployment in Arab countries. One of these compares and contrasts the impact of FDI in Arab countries and Asian countries.[6] The ERF website gives access to many other country-level studies that use aggregate data over time and lagged independent variables to test hypotheses about determinants of the variance associated with important economic and societal features, behavior, and performance.

4.1.3 Multivariate Regression

Multivariate regression is one of the inferential statistics most commonly used to test hypotheses in social science research. There are other statistical tests, of course, but attention to regression will be sufficient for present purposes, particularly because it has been used in many of this chapter's examples of causal stories that involve more than two variables. Among the kinds and purposes of the additional variables that a multivariate regression analysis might include, beyond the dependent variable and one independent variable, are the following:

---

[4] Ahmed Mohamed Ezzat. 2019. "The Impact of Foreign Direct Investment on Unemployment: Evidence from Arab Countries." *Scientific Journal of Economic & Commerce* (December); at https://journals.ekb.eg/article_94610_c9c12c652d5f8447d0b27e502309d122.pdf

[5] Economic Research Forum, Cairo, Egypt; at https://erf.org.eg

[6] See, for example, Brahim Elmorchid, Nouira Ridha and Khalid Sekkat. 2013. "A Comparative Analysis of the Determinants of Foreign Direct Investment in the Arab World and in Asia." Economic Research Forum Working Paper No. 811; see also Pierre-Guillaume Méon and Khalid Sekkat. 2014. "The Impact of Foreign Direct Investment in Arab Countries." Economic Research Forum. Working Paper No. 9.

- Multiple independent variables. Multivariate regression allows the researcher to test each of several hypotheses by considering one independent variable at a time with any others held constant
- Control variables, which are discussed later in this chapter
- Multiple indicators of the same, more abstract concept, or concepts, in order to consider the possibility that explanatory power resides in some dimensions of the concept but not in other dimensions
- Other "third" variables, to which we turn in the section of this chapter devoted to "Third Variable Possibilities."

These possibilities are not mutually exclusive. It would not be unusual for an investigator to include in her regression analysis variables selected for several of these objectives, or possibly even all of them.

Social science researchers, and certainly those that work with quantitative data, need to be broadly knowledgeable and competent with respect to inferential statistics, including, but not limited to, multivariate regression. Would-be researchers without this knowledge and competence should consult one of the many books on social statistics. With respect to the present discussion, only a cursory introduction to multivariate regression is offered, with an emphasis on how the statistic is used and how the results of its use should be understood. The goal of the present discussion is only to give readers enough familiarity with regression to understand and find instructive its use in the "third variable" designs to be introduced. The term "third variable" refers, generically, to the variable or variables that are added to the dependent variable and the independent variable in an analysis in order to enrich and/or increase confidence in a hypothesized bivariate relationship.

Ordinary least squares (OLS) regression is a statistical method of analysis used to estimate whether and to what extent a change in one or more independent variables brings a change in a dependent variable. This is sometimes described as estimating the strength of a relationship or predicting the effect that an independent variable has on a dependent variable. OLS is the most commonly used method for estimating the parameters of the linear regression model, and perhaps the most commonly used method overall in the social sciences. In addition to linear regression, which is used in the examples in this chapter, there are logistic and non-parametric forms of regression. These kinds of regression will be described very briefly following the discussion of OLS regression.

Linearity OLS regression is a linear statistic, meaning that its estimates pertain to variable relationships that are presumed to be linear, or in a straight line. As discussed in Chap. 3, a linear relationship may be direct, or positive, in which case an increase in the independent variable brings an increase in the dependent variable, or it may be inverse, or negative, in which case an increase in the independent variable brings a decrease in the dependent variable. Figure 4.2 illustrates several different degrees to which a relationship may be linear, either positive or negative. These figures are called scatter plots. Each individual plot in the two-dimensional space represents the values of the two variables defining, respectively, the vertical axis and horizontal axis.

4.1 Causal Inference

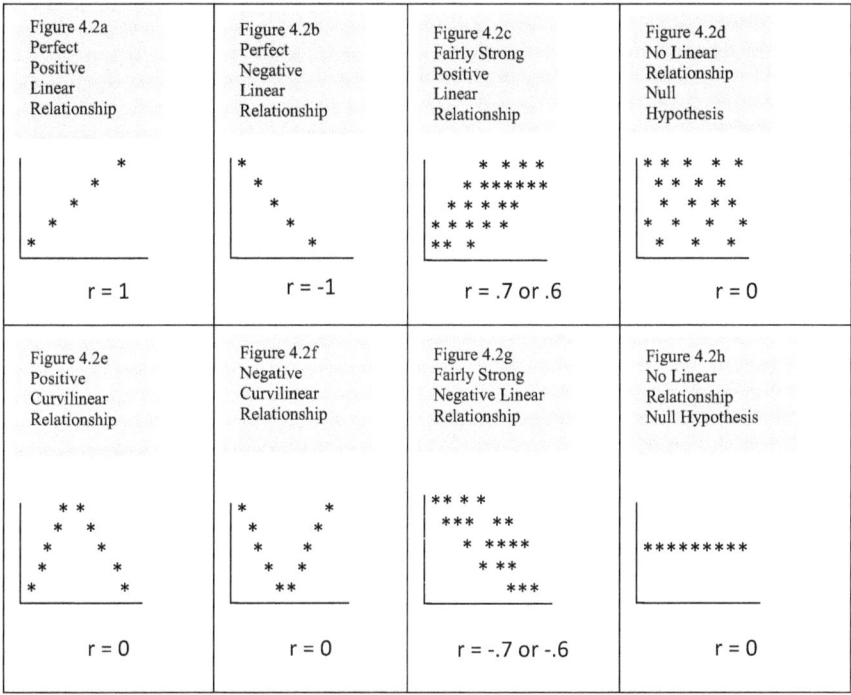

Fig. 4.2 Scatter plots showing degrees and direction of linearity

Generally, the vertical, or y, axis shows values of the dependent variable, while the horizontal, or x, axis shows values of the independent variable.

As an example, consider the hypothesis that in Arab countries there is a negative linear relationship between an individual's level of education and her satisfaction with the overall performance of the government. Accordingly, H1 posits that individuals who have had more education are more likely than individuals who have had less education to have an unfavorable judgment of the government's overall performance. Although a positive linear relationship between education and satisfaction with government performance might have been expected and might seem more plausible, Arab Barometer data from Wave 5 surveys will in fact confirm the existence of a negative relationship, and this is no less instructive for illustrating linearity.

Figure 4.3 shows the plots on education and satisfaction with government performance of two of the respondents in the Arab Barometer Wave 5 surveys. The dependent variable, satisfaction with overall government performance, is on the vertical axis and is an 11-point scale, with 0 = total dissatisfaction and 10 = total satisfaction. The independent variable, level of education, is measured by a 7-point scale, with 1 = no schooling and 7 = a postgraduate degree. In between are 2 = primary school, 3 = intermediate school, 4 = secondary school, 5 = some

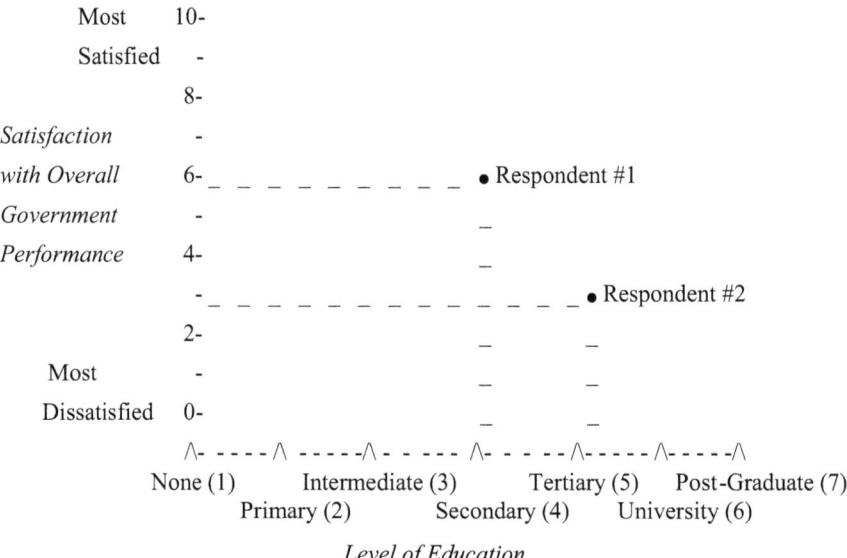

Fig. 4.3 Scatter plot with ratings of two respondents on level of education and satisfaction with overall government performance

post-secondary school education, and 6 = university bachelor's degree or a comparable degree.

One of the two respondents in Fig. 4.3 has completed high school and has a score of 6 on the 11-point scale of satisfaction. The other respondent has had tertiary education, meaning some post-secondary schooling, and has a score of 3 on the 11-point satisfaction scale. Once the ratings on both variables have been entered for all of the respondents in the Arab Barometer Wave 5 surveys, the scatter plot will be complete and ready for visual inspection. Tests of statistical significance will, of course, guide the researcher's decision about whether to conclude that the hypothesis has been confirmed, whether, in other words, to risk a Type I error. Visual inspection is often needed as well, however, in order to determine the structure of a relationship when the hypothesis of no relationship, the null hypothesis, has been rejected. The null hypothesis may have been rejected because the hypothesized linear relationship is true, or probably true. Or it may be rejected because the relationship between the independent and dependent variables appears to have a different structure than that proposed by the hypothesis.

Probability Values When researchers perform regression analyses, they are often most interested in the variable-specific coefficients and probability values, or p-values, that regression yields. A variable-specific coefficient, sometimes also called the slope, indicates the direction and magnitude of the relationship between an independent variable and a dependent variable. More specifically, as will be discussed more fully shortly, the coefficient provides an estimate of how much the dependent variable will change, either increasing or decreasing, in response to an increase of one unit in the independent variable.

The p-values associated with each coefficient indicate the likelihood that the researcher would have obtained the observed data, and thus the observed coefficients, from a population of units for which the null hypothesis, the hypothesis of no relationship, is true. Probability values are often of most immediate interest to an investigator because they provide her with a basis for deciding whether to reject the null hypothesis and accept her research hypothesis. Or, possibly, she may find a relationship between the variables in her hypothesis that differs significantly from the null hypothesis, hence a low p-value, but does not have the same structure as the one her hypothesis posits. In such a case, a scatter plot based on the independent variable and the dependent variable may help the researcher identify the structure of a variable relationship that differs from both the null hypothesis and the research hypothesis.

For example, suppose a researcher performs regression analysis using a sample from her population of interest and obtains a probability value of $p = .01$ for the independent variable in which she is interested. This indicates that were she to draw another 100 random samples from this population, most likely only one of these samples would be characterized by the null hypothesis. Conversely, 99 of the samples would be characterized by a relationship that differs from the null hypothesis and may lend support to the researcher's proposed hypothesis. Another way to think about this is that, with a p-value of .01, there is a 1 in 100 chance that the sample analyzed by the researcher differs significantly from the population of interest. Those are pretty good odds, and in the social sciences most researchers would confidently reject the null hypothesis upon obtaining a p-value of .01.

As discussed in Chap. 3, probability values that are usually considered low enough to reject the null hypothesis are $p < .05$, $p < .01$ and $p < .001$, each of which indicates the probability of a Type I error. In other words, if a researcher decides to set her confidence interval at $p < .01$, she is saying that she is willing to accept her research hypothesis, and reject the null hypothesis, if there is no more than a 1 percent chance that the null hypothesis is in fact true of the population from which her sample was drawn. The .05, .01, and .001 probability values are also sometimes described as levels of statistical significance, or alpha values. Lower alpha values (and p-values) give greater confidence in the researcher's findings.

Although widely used as standards for estimating statistical significance, the three alpha values are nonetheless arbitrary and subjective, as would be any other p-value. They are arbitrary since a p-value can be any number between 0 and 1. And they are subjective in the sense that the p-value does not tell an investigator how low is low enough to reject the null hypothesis and risk a Type I error. Other things being equal, the cost and consequences of making a Type I error will figure prominently in a researcher's decision about whether or not to reject the null hypothesis. The higher the cost and the more injurious the consequences of being wrong, the lower the probability value she will require before considering the research hypothesis to be confirmed and proceeding to act on this basis.

Table 4.1 Findings from regression analyses testing the hypothesis that individuals who are more educated are more likely than individuals who are less educated to judge overall government performance to be unsatisfactory

	Wave 5 11 countries	Wave 5 Iraq	Wave 5 Palestine	Wave 5 Lebanon
Higher level of education	−1.043***	−.318*	−.497**	−.018
	(.050)	(.140)	(.185)	(.077)
Constant	9.655***	5.414***	7.989***	3.270***
	(.213)	(.531)	(.805)	(.358)

Notes. Data are from Wave 5 surveys (2018–2019) of the Arab Barometer
Dependent variable: Judgments of overall government performance, 0–10 with 10 most satisfied
Standard errors in parentheses
*$p < .05$ ** $p < .01$ ***$p < .001$

Regression Results and Tables Table 4.1 shows the results of an OLS regression analysis that uses data from Arab Barometer Wave 5 surveys to test the hypothesis that individuals who have had more education are more likely than individuals who have had less education to have an unfavorable judgment of the government's overall performance. The hypothesis thus posits a strong negative, or inverse, relationship between the independent variable and the dependent variable. The table presents findings from a pooled analysis of data from 11 of the countries surveyed in Wave 5, the years of which are 2018 and 2019. The table also presents findings from single-country analyses of data from surveys in three of these 11 countries: Iraq, Lebanon, and Palestine. Importantly, the findings are not the same for the four sets of results presented in the table.

The numbers in the cells of Table 4.1 are regression coefficients and standard errors. The coefficients, as stated, express the magnitude and direction of a change in the dependent variable that is associated with an increase of one unit in the independent variable, with "caused by" replacing "associated with" if the relationship is very likely to be causal. As shown, a coefficient of −1.043 is obtained when judgments about government performance, the dependent variable, are regressed against education, the independent variable. This means that each increase in level of education decreases the value of the 11-point perception of government performance scale by 1.043.

The standard error, or standard error of the mean, is an estimate of the difference between the mean of an investigator's sample and the mean of the population that her sample purports to represent. Given this, the standard error is at the same time an estimate of how much difference there would be between the mean of a variable in her sample and the means of this same variable in other samples she might draw were she to repeat her study. As is implied by the term "error," lower values for standard errors indicate increased confidence in OLS results and hypothesized relationships.

The table also gives the value of the constant, also known as the intercept. This is the value of the dependent variable when the independent variable has a value of zero. As will be shown, a formula that includes both the constant and the regression coefficient can be used to estimate, or predict, hypothetical values of the dependent variable. Estimating or predicting values of the dependent variable might be, but very often is not, the objective of a social science research project that employs multivariate regression. Nevertheless, as in the case for the coefficient and the standard error, it is important to understand the kind of information that is provided by each value in a regression table.

The findings in Table 4.1 that are of most immediate interest are the probability values, which indicate the likelihood of being wrong if the research hypothesis is accepted and the null hypothesis is rejected. As discussed above, these p-values estimate the likelihood of finding the pattern an investigator actually observes if her sample has been selected from a population of units—of individuals, countries, or any other unit of analysis—that is characterized by the null hypothesis. The lower the likelihood that the population is characterized by the null hypothesis, the safer it is to conclude that the sample or subset of units drawn from that population depicts an existing, or true, relationship. And accordingly, then, the lower will be the likelihood of making a Type I error when concluding that the independent variable does in fact account for some of the variance on the dependent variable,.

As shown in Table 4.1, levels of statistical significance are often indicated by the presence and number of stars next to each variable in the table. A note at the bottom of the table indicates the p-values represented by one, two, and three stars. A variable next to which there are no stars is not strongly related to the dependent variable; the probability of finding a strong relationship involving this variable in a sample drawn from a population characterized by the null hypothesis is not low enough to reject the null hypothesis.

Several conclusions about the hypothesized relationship between level of education and satisfaction with overall performance of the government can be drawn from Table 4.1. First, focusing on the pooled analysis based on data from the Arab Barometer Wave 5 surveys in 11 countries, the hypothesized relationship between overall satisfaction with government performance and level of education is very strong and statistically significant at the .001 level of confidence. It is extremely unlikely that data exhibiting a relationship as strong as this were drawn from a population characterized by the null hypothesis. Accordingly, given these findings, the investigator would normally consider the research hypothesis to have been confirmed, reject the null hypothesis, and run the risk of a Type I error.

Second, findings about the hypothesized relationship found in the pooled analysis are not the same as the findings found in each of the countries. Sometimes the relationship between education and satisfaction with the government is also strong and statistically significant, as in Palestine. Sometimes it is statistically significant but at a lower level of confidence, as in Iraq. And sometimes, as in Lebanon, the relationship is not statistically significant and the researcher would probably choose to risk a Type II error, accepting the null hypothesis and rejecting the research hypothesis even though there is a chance that the latter might be true.

Third, given different findings across at least some of the countries included in the Wave 5 surveys of the Arab Barometer, the investigator might wish to reflect on, and perhaps offer hypotheses about, the determinants of this cross-country variance. Formulating, and perhaps also testing, such hypotheses would have country as the unit of analysis, have the bivariate relationship between education and satisfaction with the government as the dependent variable, and have country attributes or experiences as independent variables.

> **The Tradeoffs of Pooled Analyses**
>
> As Table 4.1 shows, findings from analyses that take together data from 11 of the countries surveyed in Wave V of the Arab Barometer, in what is called a "pooled" analysis, may not be the same as findings from analyses based on data from each individual country. This may or may not mean that findings from pooled analyses are misleading and that such analyses should not be undertaken.
>
> If the objective of a research project is to identify univariate, bivariate, or multivariate relationships that apply to all of the groups, countries in this case, on which an investigator has data, findings from a pooled analysis may be misleading. In this case, the researcher will need to consider each group, or country, separately in order to determine whether or not the same findings apply to each group. The researcher may still wish to carry out a pooled analysis, for convenience or other reasons, but she may not claim that findings produced by a pooled analysis apply to all of the groups that make up the pool unless she has analyzed each group separately and found this to be the case.
>
> If the objective of a research project is not to identify patterns that apply to all of the groups, countries in this case, on which an investigator has data, but rather to test hypotheses and offer insight and evidence about important causal stories, then pooled analysis will expand the data available and may be completely appropriate. Hypotheses being tested will, if confirmed, have been found to have substantial and broad explanatory power, even if they do not necessarily describe explanations of variance that obtain in any particular group.

The Slope-Intercept Equation There is a simple equation, frequently called the slope-intercept equation, that makes use of the information provided by the coefficient, or slope, and the constant, or intercept, to estimate the value of the dependent variable for a particular value of the independent variable: $y = mx + b$

Where:

- y is the value of the dependent variable, which is not known
- x is the value of the independent variable, which is known and specified
- m is the value of the change in y produced by a change of one unit in x; in regression, this is given by the coefficient, or slope, and frequently called the beta value or beta estimate
- b is the value of y when $x = 0$; in regression, b is given by the constant and is frequently called the intercept

4.1 Causal Inference

This equation omits a term that is ordinarily included in multivariate regression when the goal is to estimate the value of a dependent variable. This is called the "error term," and it is represented by "e" as shown in the following equation: y = mx + b + e. The error term is a value that represents the difference between the value of a population or universe, a value that can only be estimated and is therefore sometimes called the "theoretical value," and the actual observed value based on available data, usually a sample.

Note also that when referring to OLS, the slope-intercept equation, simplified here, is frequently rendered as: Y = Beta_0 + (Beta_x) (X).

Where:

- Beta_0 is the constant, or intercept
- (Beta_x) is the coefficient, or slope, for the variable(s) included in the regression
- (X) is an observed value of the independent variable

An application of the slope-intercept equation to predict a value of the dependent variable (y) based on the coefficient and constant in Table 4.1 is shown below. For this illustration, the value of the independent variable (X) is 4, meaning that the value of the dependent variable is being predicted for individuals with a secondary school education, those with a 4 on the 7-point education-level scale. The dependent variable, again, is an 11-point scale of satisfaction with overall government performance, with 0 = totally dissatisfied and 10 = totally satisfied. Application of the formula predicts that individuals with a secondary school education will have a score of 5.483 on this scale.

- y = mx + b
- y = 4 * coefficient + constant
- y = 4 * −1.043 + 9.655
- y = −4.172 + 9.655
- y = 5.483

The error term, as noted, is a value that represents the difference between the value of a population or universe, a value that can only be estimated, and the actual observed value based on an investigator's data. In the example above, 5.483 is the predicted value on the 11-point perception of government performance scale for individuals with a 4 on the 7-point level of education scale. However, not every individual with an education level of 4 surveyed by the Arab Barometer answered the government satisfaction item with a response of 5.483. In fact, obviously, a response of exactly 5.483 was not an option. The error term is the difference between an individual's actual response and the predicted response of 5.483. The error term for an individual who had a secondary school education and judged government performance to deserve a 7 on the 11-point scale would be 7 − 5.483, or 1.517. Further discussion of the error term is beyond the scope and purpose of the present account. Readers wishing additional information about the conceptualization and measurement of the error term, and about multivariate regression more generally, will find this readily available in books on multivariate statistics.

> **Exercise 4.2. Estimating Satisfaction with Overall Government Performance**
> Use the findings presented in Table 4.1 to estimate the satisfaction with overall government performance score of each set of respondents listed below. Satisfaction with overall government performance, the dependent variable, is measured by a 0–10 scale with 10 indicating the highest level of satisfaction. What is the score on this 11-point scale for each of the following:
>
> 1. All Wave V respondents with a rating of 6 on the 1–7 scale measuring level of education. A rating of 6 on the 7-point education scale indicates that an individual has had a university education.
> 2. Iraqi respondents with a rating of 4 on the 1–7 scale measuring level of education. A rating of 4 on the 7-point education scale indicates that an individual has had a secondary school education.
> 3. Palestinian respondents with a rating of 4 on the 1–7 scale measuring level of education. A rating of 4 on the 7-point education scale indicates that an individual has had a secondary school education.
> 4. In what way is satisfaction with overall government performance different for Iraqi respondents with a secondary school education and Palestinian respondents with a secondary school education?
> 5. Lebanese respondents with a rating of 2 on the 1–7 scale measuring level of education. A rating of 2 on the 7-point education scale indicates that an individual has had a primary school education.

Other Types of Regression Multivariate regression is a parametric statistic, meaning that assumptions are made about the distribution of variables in the population from which the data to be analyzed have been obtained. OLS regression is used when the dependent variable is continuous. It makes several strong assumptions, including, most importantly, that there is a linear relationship between the independent and dependent variables.

Although perhaps the most common, OLS regression is not the only regression model used to test hypothesized variable relationships. Another form of parametric regression is logistic regression, which is used when the dependent variable is a categorical variable. Binary logistic regression is used when the dependent variable has two categories, such as agree/disagree, present/absent, or high/low; multinomial logistic regression is used when the dependent variable has more than two categories; and ordinal logistic regression is used when the dependent variable has ordered categories, such as primary, secondary, and university levels of education.

There are also non-parametric types of regression, which require fewer assumptions about the shape or form of variable distributions in the population from which the data to be analyzed have been obtained. Non-parametric regression statistics are not as powerful with smaller samples.

Discussion of these other forms of multivariate regression is beyond the scope and purpose of the present account. They are mentioned only to alert readers to their existence. Readers wishing additional information, including about parametric requirements and assumptions, will find this readily available in books on social statistics.

4.1.4 Control Variables

Tests of hypotheses that posit variable relationships that purport to be causal usually require multivariate analysis. Along with the independent variable and the dependent variable, the analysis will require the inclusion of one or more additional variables. Control variables are of most immediate importance here, and it is here that the multivariate character of analyses devoted to causal inference comes into play.

Control variables are usually variables that are related to both the dependent variable and the independent variable and that, because of these parallel relationships, might cause the dependent variable and the independent variable to covary. Should this be the case, an investigator might be tempted to conclude, mistakenly, that the dependent variable and the independent variable covary because variance on the former is determined, or caused, by variance on the latter. However, should this be the case, such a conclusion would be wrong; as far as causality is concerned, the relationship would be spurious.

The reason that a relationship between two variables that covary might be spurious is illustrated by the stork-baby folktale and the shorts-ice cream story mentioned earlier. Despite the covariance of the stork measure and the baby measure, or of a wearing shorts measure and an ice cream measure, there is no causal connection between the measures in each pair. Rather, it is the impactful relationship of both variables in each pair to a third variable, rural-urban character of the localities in the first instance and temperature outside the home in the second, that produces the covariance.

This situation, or problem, where there is the possibility of attaching causality to a hypothesized variable relationship that is actually spurious with respect to causality, is often referenced by the term *omitted variable bias*, which is a form of *endogeneity*. A researcher has an endogeneity problem when there is a third variable, an endogenous variable, or a number of endogenous variables, that is related to her dependent variable and is also related to her independent variable but has not been identified and taken into consideration. It has not, more specifically, been included in a test of the hypothesized relationship between the investigator's independent variable and her dependent variable.

It is the designation "not taken into consideration" that makes endogeneity a problem. If a researcher knows that there is a third variable that affects both the dependent variable and the independent variable, she can include it in her analysis and treat it as a control variable. In this way, she can hold it constant and remove its impact. The challenge is to know, or identify, the third variable, or the fourth, fifth, sixth, and other variables, that fit this description and need to be included in the analysis and controlled.

In all probability, the researcher already knows some of the variables that need to be controlled. Research projects in which the individual is the unit of analysis very often include demographic attributes, like sex, age, education, and others as control variables. Studies in which country is the unit of analysis might include per capita gross national product, per capita national income, and position on a democracy-authoritarianism scale as control variables. Beyond these, however, and also in research projects that focus on other units of analysis, an investigator must be alert to less immediately obvious variables that may need to be controlled, perhaps interpersonal trust or civic engagement for individuals and ethnic diversity or percentage of women in the labor force for countries.

To identify other variables that may need to be controlled, an investigator will want to consult previous research on the subject of her study; and still others may suggest themselves as she continues to reflect and deepen her understanding of the causal stories that her hypotheses represent. In any event, to the extent that relevant variables are not identified and an endogeneity problem persists, findings about the researcher's hypotheses may be incomplete or even wrong.

After finding a strong and significant bivariate relationship between a dependent variable and an independent variable, identifying and adding one or more endogenous variables to the analysis as control variables—endogenous variables being, again, those that are related to the independent and dependent variables—will produce one of two possible results. Either the strong and significant relationship between the independent and dependent variables will remain strong and significant or it will cease to be strong and significant.

If the relationship between the independent variable and the dependent variable ceases to be strong and significant when a third variable, an endogenous variable, is included in the analysis and thereby controlled, it will become clear that the relationship found in a bivariate analysis was indeed spurious with respect to causality. To return for a moment to the humorous and silly examples previously used to illustrate the possibility of an endogeneity problem, the relationship between storks and babies will cease to be significant if the nature of the locality is considered as a control variable, as will the relationship between shorts and ice cream if temperature outside the home is considered. It will then be clear that the relationship between the independent variable and the dependent variable, however strong might be the bivariate correlation between them, is not a causal relationship.

Alternatively, if the relationship between the independent variable and the dependent variable remains strong and significant when one or more endogenous variables are included in the analysis and controlled, the case for causal inference will be strengthened. Whatever might be the impact of the control variable, or control variables, this is not the reason that the independent variable and dependent variable covary. More likely, the independent variable and dependent variable covary

4.1 Causal Inference

because the former is a determinant of the latter, because variance on the independent variable is a cause of variance on the dependent variable.

Causation cannot be proved, of course. It can only be inferred. And there may well be endogenous variables that have not been identified and controlled. Nevertheless, the case for causal inference will be stronger, and the probability of making a Type I error will be lower, if there is a strong and statistically significant relationship between the independent variable and the dependent variable, if there is a temporal sequence between these two variables, and if relevant and potentially endogenous variables have been identified and included in the analysis.

In multivariate statistical analysis, control variables are often included in the regression models that are run. Here *model* refers to a particular set of variables that are included in an analysis, along with the dependent and independent variables. It is not unusual for an investigator to run a number of models, one without any control variables in order to observe the strength and significance of the hypothesized relationship without any interference, and then one or more models with control variables, or different subsets of control variables, in order to see if the strength and significance of the hypothesized relationship change. As stated, whether a significant hypothesized relationship loses significance or remains significant in models that include control variables has clear implications for causal inference.

Procedures along these lines, with the goal being causal inference, are employed in numerous political and social science studies carried out in Arab countries and societies. One innovative and instructive study examines the behavior of members of parliament in Algeria and Morocco. It analyzes data from an original survey of 200 male and female parliamentarians.[7] Some of the study's hypotheses seek to account for variance in the kind or amount of constituent service work undertaken by different categories of deputies, variance associated with constituent service work being, therefore, the dependent variable. Below are two of these hypotheses. Each specifies a different independent variable, which it posits as one of the determinants, or causes, of the variance associated with the kind of constituent service work that deputies perform.

H1. Female deputies are more likely to serve female and less influential constituents than are male deputies.
H2. Quota-elected female deputies are more likely to serve female and less influential constituents than are non-quota-elected female deputies.

The table below is a reconstructed and simplified version of one of the tables in the article that describes this study and reports its findings. The table, based on an analysis of the 82 Moroccan deputies who were interviewed, presents the results of a multivariate statistical analysis, ordinary least squares regression, that tests the two

---

[7]Lindsay Benstead. 2016. "Why Quotas Are Needed to Improve Women's Access to Services in Clientelistic Regimes." *Governance: An International Journal of Policy, Administration and Institutions* 29:2, pp. 185–205.

Table 4.2 Some determinants of service work on behalf of female and less influential constituents by Moroccan deputies

	Model 1	Model 2
Independent variables: gender/quotas		
H1. Female (all)	2.77 (1.40)**	
H2. Female (no quota)		1.32 (1.73)
H2. Female (quota)		5.31 (2.29)**
Control variables		
Represents an electoral district with less than 100,000 urban residents	0.86 (0.79)	0.91 (0.79)
Represents electoral district with between 100,000 and 200,000 urban residents	1.08 (0.95)	1.20 (94)
Represents an electoral district with more than 200,000 urban residents	1.51 (0.72)**	1.64 (0.72)**
Deputy's age	0.14 (0.19)	0.17 (0.19)
Deputy had been elected in previous election(s)	.053 (0.53)	0.38 (0.52)
Member of an established center-left political party	−1.52 (1.06)	−1.75 (1.06)*

Note. The table presents the results of an ordinary least squares regression. Standard errors are in parentheses
Dependent variable: Degree of service work devoted to women and less influential constituents, 1–8 scale with 8 = more service work devoted to women and less influential constituents
Independent variables: Gender, 1–2 with 2 = female; elected on quota, 1–2 with 2 = on quota
*$p < 0.10$ **$p < 0.05$

hypotheses. Model 1 tests H1 and Model 2 tests H2. The dependent variable in both is the extent to which a deputy carried out service work on behalf of female and less influential constituents. The degree of service work devoted to these constituents is measured on an 8-point scale, with 8 = more service work on behalf of female and less influential constituents. Each model shows the relationship between the independent variable and the dependent variable. Each model also includes six control variables, a subset of those in the published article, and shows the statistical significance of each one's relationship to the dependent variable.

The findings presented in Table 4.2 show that the analysis supports both hypotheses. In both cases, the probability that the null hypothesis is true and that the researcher will make a Type I error if she rejects it and considers the research hypothesis to be confirmed, is less than .05. Note that in this table, the p-values have not been explicitly listed, so the reader must rely on the star system detailed in the note below the table and mentioned previously in this chapter in order to determine statistical significance.

With respect to H1, the probability that deputies who do more service work on behalf of female and less influential constituents are *not* more likely to be female is less than 5 percent ($p < 0.05$), and so the investigator concluded that the risk of making a Type I error is low and reported, accordingly, that H1 is confirmed. With respect to H2, the probability that deputies who do more service work on behalf of female and less influential constituents are *not* more likely to be female and to have entered the assembly through a quota of seats reserved for women is less than

5 percent (p < 0.05), and so the investigator again concluded that the risk of making a Type I error is low and reported, accordingly, that H2 is confirmed.

The six control variables in Table 4.2 are only some of the control variables in the table in the published article. As discussed, control variables are selected for inclusion in multivariate statistical analyses that test hypotheses because the investigator wishes to consider, and hopefully rule out, the possibility that a hypothesized variable relationship that purports to be causal is actually spurious. If the relationship between a dependent variable and a hypothesized independent variable is statistically significant when control variables are not included in the analysis but then ceases to be statistically significant when one or more control variables are included, the researcher will be forced to conclude that the relationship is not causal—or at least that it is not a direct causal relationship. The possibility of an indirect causal relationship will be discussed in the section of this chapter devoted to "Third Variable Possibilities."

> **Exercise 4.3 Connecting Hypotheses and Causal Stories**
> H1 and H2 in the study of constituent service work done by members of the Algerian and Moroccan national assemblies represent and call attention to a fuller causal story. Describe in two or three sentences what, in your best judgment, is a plausible causal story that tells *why* it is that Algerian and Moroccan members of parliament who do more service work on behalf of female and less influential constituents are more likely to be female and also more likely to have entered the assembly through a quota of seats reserved for women.

To select control variables, an investigator will reflect on and attempt to identify variables that may be related to both the dependent variable and the independent variable in ways that cause the two to covary or otherwise have an impact on the relationship between them. The impact of a potential control variable cannot always be known in advance, and it is unlikely that an investigator will be able to identify and include in a test of her hypotheses all of the control variables that might possibly be relevant. Nevertheless, confidence in a finding that her data support a hypothesized causal relationship will be much lower if plausible control variables have not been identified and included in her analyses.

Table 4.2 shows that the hypothesized causal relationships that H1 and H2 posit remain statistically significant at the .05 level of confidence when a number of control variables have been included in the analysis. Accordingly, this makes it more reasonable not only to risk a Type I error and accept the hypotheses but also to infer that the hypothesized relationships are very probably causal. When a hypothesized dependent variable-independent variable relationship is found to be statistically significant, in most cases with a p-value of .05 or lower, the inclusion of control variables increases confidence that this significant relationship is not due to the impact of one or more other variables and thus is probably not spurious.

In addition, however, confidence in causality when control variables are included in the analysis depends on the plausibility and relevance of the particular control variables that have been selected. On the one hand, variables that are known to be associated with both the dependent variable and the independent variable, or might reasonably and logically be thought to be associated, are those whose inclusion is most important. On the other hand, it is also important to have theoretical reasons for the control variables that are included, meaning that their connections to the dependent and independent variables should make sense in terms of the hypotheses and causal stories being investigated.

Researchers should be cautious about including additional control variables just in case they might have an unsuspected impact on the hypothesized relationship. Too many control variables can damage statistical estimates, particularly if the size of a researcher's dataset is small. By itself, the availability of data is not a good reason to include a control variable. Rather, if a researcher cannot explain why a particular variable should be included as a control, she probably should not include it in her analysis. In this way she avoids a common pitfall of multivariate analysis known as *overfitting*.

The control variables in Table 4.2, which are among those in the table in the published article, were selected with the previously mentioned criteria in mind. The author's rationale for including variables based on the urban population of the deputy's home district is given below. It suggests that these district-level attributes might influence the relationship between, on the one hand, a deputy's gender and/or whether or not she entered the assembly through a quota of parliamentary seats reserved for women and, on the other hand, the categories of constituents most likely to benefit from the deputy's service work. Without the inclusion of these variables as controls, the researcher's ability to conclude and then report that her hypotheses had been confirmed, including the causal connection that the hypotheses posit, would be very much weaker.

> [Measures of district population are among the variables related to perceived electoral incentives that have been included as controls.] Women elected in larger districts, including Algiers with 3 million residents and 32 seats, may be more responsive to females, due to greater ability to serve less influential constituencies, the presence of civil society organizations, and urban, employed female constituents. Women elected in small districts (e.g., Moroccan districts with 2 to 5 seats) may have stronger incentives to cultivate a personal vote among constituents of both genders and have lower responsiveness to women.

Exercise 4.4 Identifying and Selecting Control Variables
Table 4.2 includes six control variables, and the author's rationale for selecting some of them has been given. She states that they were selected because they are "*among* the variables related to perceived electoral incentives."

(continued)

Exercise 4.4 (continued)
One of the variables included as a control variable is whether or not the deputy is a member of an established center-left political party.

- Why do you think the researcher thought it necessary to control this variable? In what way might this variable be related to the dependent variable and the independent variable, possibly causing them to covary and, for this reason, making it necessary to include it in the analysis as a control variable?

The six control variables in Table 4.2 are only some of the variables the investigator deemed it necessary to control.

- Making your best guess, identify another variable that it would probably be necessary to control. Then give your reasons for selecting it; suggest how and why it might be related to the dependent and independent variables, thereby requiring that it be controlled.

4.2 Third Variable Possibilities

4.2.1 Other "Third" Variables

We turn now to ways that the refinement of a research design and the inclusion of additional variables, beyond those included for purposes of control, can enrich causal stories and/or make them more informative and more precise. These additional variables are frequently referred to as "third" variables, even though more than one of them may be added to the variables already included in the researcher's models. Table 4.3 identifies and describes the three components into which our discussion of third variables is divided. What the three third variable types and roles share is attentiveness to the possibility that a causal story may involve more than two variables that are significantly related and remain so when tested in analyses that include relevant control variables.

4.2.2 Direct and Indirect Relationships

A researcher might wonder not only whether the bivariate relationship she has observed is causal but also whether it is a direct or an indirect relationship, a distinction with very different implications about whether and how the independent variable impacts and accounts for variance on the dependent variable. Our discussion to this point has not made a distinction between direct and indirect relationships;

Table 4.3 Third variables in multivariate causal stories

Sub-section focus	Variable role	Contribution to causal story
Direct and indirect relationships	Mediator variable	We will consider the distinction between causal relationships that are direct and indirect. In indirect relationships, one or more mediator variables stands between, or mediates the relationship between, the independent variable and the dependent variable. Mediator variables shed light on causal mechanisms and pathways by which the independent variable influences the dependent variable.
Disaggregation/ conditional effects	Moderator variable (sometimes called interaction term)	We will consider the case where the significance, strength, and/or structure of a confirmed relationship between an independent variable and a dependent variable is not the same for all unit of analysis subsets on which an investigator has data. Moderator variables thus help to specify the locus of applicability of one or more causal stories. We will also consider the advantages and disadvantages of disaggregating multi-dimensional measures.
Scope conditions	Variable names substituted for proper names	We will consider the generalizability of one or more confirmed causal relationships and the role of scope conditions in specifying where and when, that is to say under what conditions, the relationship is and is not significant. To the extent that the specification of where and when involves proper names, such as Algeria in 2004, relevant attributes of this place and time may be expressed as variables and substituted for the proper names of Algeria and 2004. Scope conditions may enrich a causal story by specifying its applicability and thereby, in many cases, by adding a level of analysis.

we have for the most part proceeded as if our concern were only with direct relationships, relationships for which a change in the independent variable directly brings, and presumably causes, a change in the dependent variable. In this case, the causal story does not involve any other variables. The pathway from the independent variable to the dependent variable does not run through one or more other variables.

This is not the only possibility, however. The pathway at the center of a causal story may not lead directly to the dependent variable. Instead, it may initially lead to a third variable, making this third variable part of the causal story, and then lead from the third variable to the dependent variable. For example, the previously noted

4.2 Third Variable Possibilities

Fig. 4.4 Bivariate analysis finds a direct relationship

individual-level relationship between evaluation of the government's economic performance and the likelihood of voting might involve such a pathway. The hypothesis that posits evaluation of the government's economic performance as a determinant of the decision to vote or not to vote might actually involve an additional variable, such that the pathway leads from evaluation of government performance not to the decision about voting but rather to a third variable, perhaps trust in the government, and then from the third variable to voting.

This was, in fact, the finding of a study that used Arab Barometer data from five countries to test a hypothesis about the relationship between evaluation of government economic performance and voting and specifically to test the proposition that more favorable evaluations of government performance push toward greater likelihood of voting.[8] Bivariate analysis showed that the relationship between evaluation of government performance and voting had a very low probability of being spurious, and this remained the case in a multivariate analysis that included control variables. Accordingly, with the likelihood of making a Type I error very low, the researchers judged the hypothesized bivariate relationship to have been confirmed.

The figures below illustrate different possibilities with respect to direct and indirect relationships. An unbroken line between two variables indicates that the analysis has found a statistically significant relationship between these variables. X, Y, and M are the variables in this illustration; Y is the dependent variable; X is the independent variable; M is a third variable, trust in the government in this case.

- Figure 4.4 illustrates the results of a bivariate analysis that finds a statistically significant and direct relationship between X and Y. It is direct because there is not another variable in the pathway from X to Y. The researcher will recognize, of course, that the finding of an indirect relationship is not possible in bivariate analysis. The bivariate analysis can only determine whether or not the relationship between two variables is statistically significant, and also the structure and direction of the relationship. The structure and direction of variable relationships were discussed in Chap. 3.
- Figure 4.5 illustrates the results of a multivariate analysis that finds a statistically significant and direct relationship between X and Y. The analysis also finds a significant indirect relationship, wherein one of the pathways leads from X to M and then from M to Y. If all of the separate bivariate relationships are statistically significant, as they are in Fig. 4.5, the researcher can report that the causal story, in this case, includes both a direct way and an indirect way that the independent variable affects and accounts for variance on the dependent variable. The basis for

---

[8]Carolina de Miguel, Amaney A. Jamal, and Mark Tessler. 2015 "Elections in the Arab World: Why do citizens turn out?" *Comparative Political Studies* 48, no. 11, pp. 1355–1388.

Fig. 4.5 Multivariate analysis finds both a direct and an indirect relationship

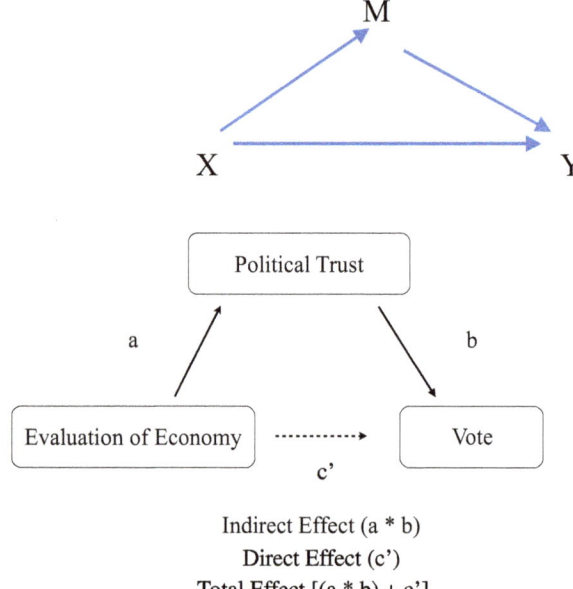

Fig. 4.6 Multivariate analysis finds only an indirect relationship

Indirect Effect (a * b)
Direct Effect (c')
Total Effect [(a * b) + c']

% Total Effect Mediated = Indirect Effect / Total Effect

attributing causality to these relationships will be much stronger if control variables are included in the analysis and the relationships shown in Fig. 4.5 remain statistically significant.
- Figure 4.6 is taken directly from the study, previously cited, that used Arab Barometer data to test the individual-level hypothesis that the more favorable an individual's evaluation of the government's economic performance, the more likely this individual will vote in national elections. In this case, in contrast to the relationships shown in Fig. 4.5, the multivariate analysis shows that there is only one statistically significant relationship involving the independent variable, and that this statistically significant relationship is not directly between the independent variable and the dependent variable.

Figure 4.6 shows that there is, nonetheless, a pathway leading from the independent variable to the dependent variable. It is indirect rather than direct, however, with the pathway running through a mediator variable, trust in the regime, in this case. The causal story to be reported by the investigators is, therefore: more positive evaluations of the government's economic performance increase trust in the government, and greater trust in government increases the likelihood that a citizen will vote. The dotted arrow leading from evaluation of the government's economic performance to likelihood of voting is intended to show that this relationship was significant in a bivariate analysis but ceased to be significant in a multivariate analysis that included trust in the governing regime, also sometimes called political trust.

4.2 Third Variable Possibilities

One way, and the most straightforward way, to test for the indirect effects shown in Figs. 4.5 and 4.6 begins with running three different bivariate regressions, one for each of the three relationships between X, Y, and M taken two at a time. There will be the possibility of a direct relationship if the X–Y connection is statistically significant, and there will be the possibility of an indirect relationship if the X–M connection and the M–Y connection are also both statistically significant.

The researcher will then proceed to multivariate analysis to see if these relationships remain significant in models that include all three variables—and also any relevant control variables. If all three two-variable relationships remain significant in the multivariate analysis, as shown in Fig. 4.5, the independent variable, X, will have been shown to have both a direct and an indirect effect on the dependent variable, Y.

Figure 4.6 depicts an alternative possibility: that there is an indirect relationship between the independent variable and the dependent variable but there is not a direct relationship between the two variables. This is the case if:

- the two relationships in Fig. 4.5 involving the mediating variable (M), trust in the governing regime, remain significant; and
- the relationship between evaluation of the government's economic performance and likelihood of voting, the X–Y relationship shown in Figs. 4.4 and 4.5, ceases to be significant when the multivariate analysis includes M.

As noted, this discussion of "Other Third Variables" seeks to introduce some of the ways that the addition of variables can produce instructive findings that might otherwise have been missed. Multivariate analysis makes it possible to test hypothesized bivariate relationships with control variables included in the analysis, and this can very significantly strengthen the case for causal inference. Beyond this, however, are many other ways in which a more sophisticated and nuanced, and hence more informative, causal story can be proposed and evaluated. Considering indirect as well as direct relationships is one such possibility. Moreover, indirect variable relationships can be proposed when hypotheses are formulated. In other words, unanticipated findings that result from data analysis are not the only way that attention might be called to such relationships. Indirect variable relationships may also, when relevant, deserve attention in the theorizing that precedes data analysis.

4.2.3 Disaggregation/Conditional Effects

Disaggregation refers to the process of separating something into its component parts. In social science research, an investigator may find it useful to consider disaggregation with respect to the population, or sample, of the units on which she has data. She may also find it useful to consider the disaggregation of the more abstract concepts, or the indicators of these concepts, that are important parts of the causal story she seeks to evaluate. Accordingly, the purposes for which an investigator may wish to disaggregate elements of a research project include more nuanced

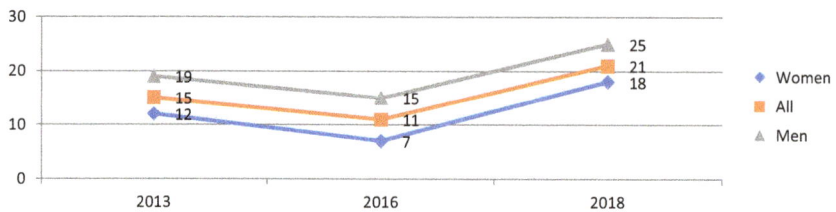

Fig. 4.7 Percent of Tunisians in 2013, 2016 and 2018 surveys agreeing that university education is more important for men

insights and greater precision in specifying the cases to which key findings apply. Disaggregation may also be undertaken to capture the dimensionality of key concepts and of associated variable relationships.

The line plot in Fig. 4.7 is based on Arab Barometer Waves 3, 4, and 5 surveys in Tunisia, which were carried out, respectively, in 2013, 2016, and 2018. The distribution based on all respondents (in orange) that is plotted over the three time periods shows the percentage of those who agreed or agreed strongly with a sentence stating that a university education is more important for men than for women. The line plot suggests questions that might be instructive to explore. Why, for example, was there a decrease in 2016 and an increase in 2018 of individuals who agreed with a proposition that is inconsistent with gender equality?

But while this and other questions raised by the line plot might deserve attention, the chart is presented here as a very simple example of disaggregation. The line plot shows that Tunisian men are significantly and consistently more likely than Tunisian women to agree with a proposition that favors men over women in university education. This is not the view of most men. Even at its highest level, in 2018, only 25 percent of Tunisian men expressed this view. Nevertheless, men in this instance are always less supportive of gender equality than are women, and this important finding would have been missed if men and women had not been analyzed separately, if there had not been disaggregation with respect to sex. The relationships that result from disaggregation are sometimes called conditional effects, with sex in this case being the conditioning variable.

This particular example is perhaps too simple; if support for gender equality were either the dependent variable or an independent variable, it is very likely that the analysis would at some point have compared the attitudes of men and women, perhaps by including sex as a control variable and thus making disaggregation superfluous. But the principle remains relevant and important: Distributions and relationships may appear one way for some subsets but not the same way for other subsets of the population or sample on which a researcher has data.

The following example also uses individual-level survey data, and the dependent variable is again views about gender equality. Based on a study published in 2017, the authors analyzed a dataset constructed from one or more surveys in 15 different

Table 4.4 Impact of personal religiosity and of economic circumstance on support for gender equality among respondents grouped by sex, age, and education

	Higher personal Religiosity	More favorable Economic circumstances
All Respondents	Significant, inverse $P < .001$	Significant, positive $p < .001$
Male, Age < 35 Education < secondary	Not Significant	Not Significant
Male, Age > 34 Education < secondary	Significant, inverse $p < .01$	Significant, positive $p < .01$
Female, Age < 35 Education < secondary	Not significant	Not significant
Female, Age > 34 Education < secondary	Significant, inverse $p < .001$	Significant, positive $p < .001$
Male, Age < 35 Education > intermediate	Not significant	Not significant
Male, Age > 34 Education > intermediate	Significant, inverse $p < .01$	Significant, positive $p < .001$
Female, Age < 35 Education > intermediate	Not significant	Not significant
Female, Age > 34 Education > intermediate	Not significant	Significant, positive $p < .01$

Arab countries,[9] and they tested hypotheses that posit religious, economic, and political factors as determinants of the variance associated with attitudes toward gender equality. The measures of some variables, including attitudes toward gender equality and personal religiosity, are indices based on a number of items in the survey instruments. Two of the hypotheses, one pertaining to religiosity and one pertaining to economic circumstance, are shown below. The table that follows shows the findings about each hypothesis, first for all respondents and then for subsets of respondents disaggregated on the basis of gender, age, and education taken together.

H1. Individuals who are more religious are less likely than individuals who are less religious to support gender equality.

H2. Individuals in more favorable economic circumstances are more likely than individuals in less favorable economic circumstances to support gender equality.

The table below, Table 4.4, shows that there is among all respondents and as hypothesized: (1) a significant and inverse relationship between personal religiosity and support for gender equality; and (2) a significant and positive relationship

---

[9] Mark Tessler and Hafsa Tout. 2017. "Religion, Trust, and Other Determinants of Muslim Attitudes Toward Gender Equality: Evidence and Insights from 54 Surveys in the Middle East and North Africa." *Taiwan Journal of Democracy*, Volume 12 No. 2, pp. 51–79. Weights controlling for sample size differences and for differences in the number of surveys conducted in any one country were carried out when the dataset was constructed.

between more favorable economic circumstance and support for gender equality. In addition, however, it also shows that there is more to be learned from disaggregation. The hypotheses are tested for subsets of respondents grouped according to sex, age, and level of education taken together, and the table shows that in only some of these demographic categories are the findings the same as those based on all respondents. For example, the hypothesized inverse relationship between religiosity and support for gender equality is confirmed when the analysis is based on all respondents, but in fact religiosity does not have explanatory power among younger men and younger women.

A fuller discussion of the nature and implications of these findings is beyond the scope of the present discussion. Nevertheless, it will be clear that the study would have reported findings that are at best incomplete had the authors not disaggregated their respondents. Rather than reporting that religiosity bears a statistically significant and inverse relationship to support for gender equality among citizens of the countries from which data have been collected, and also that economic circumstance bears a significant and positive relationship to support for gender equality among the same population, the investigators would be able, having disaggregated their respondents on potentially important demographic variables, to specify the characteristics of the respondents to whom these conclusions do and do not apply. This would permit the investigator to offer better insights and present a much richer and more fine-grained causal story about some of the determinants of support for gender equality.

As stated previously, a researcher may find it useful to consider disaggregation with respect to the population, or sample, of the units on which she has data. This does not mean that the units are always individuals, however, or that variables on which there is disaggregation are always demographic attributes. On the contrary, the potential utility of disaggregation is not limited to research in which the individual is the unit of analysis. There are numerous studies that analyze data on a different unit of analysis and report that their analyses and findings have been enriched by disaggregation. A few diverse and randomly selected examples are below:

- In a study of determinants of household poverty in Egypt, household was the unit of analysis. The attributes of the household considered included whether the head of the household was male or female, whether this person was in or not in the labor force, and if in the labor force, in what sector did the household head work. Most employed female heads were "blue collar workers," and to achieve a more fine-grained analysis, the investigator disaggregated this category by sector, including agriculture, fishing, service, and other.[10]

---

[10] Shireen AlAzzawi. 2015. "Endowments or Discrimination: Determinants of Household Poverty in Egypt." Economic Research Forum Working Paper No. 931; at https://www.researchgate.net/profile/Shireen-Alazzawi/publication/293486854_Endowments_or_Discrimination_Determinants_of_Household_Poverty_in_Egypt/links/56b8d2b208ae35670495b701/Endowments-or-Discrimination-Determinants-of-Household-Poverty-in-Egypt.pdf

4.2 Third Variable Possibilities

- In a study of the foreign policies of Arab countries, the unit of analysis is foreign policy output. The authors, two senior Egyptian political scientists, write that their study includes "disaggregation of foreign policy output into its relevant components: the actor's general objectives, orientation, or strategy and specific foreign policy behavior. The breaking down of foreign policy output into general objectives and concrete behavior draws attention to important questions for both the empirical analysis of foreign policy and theory-building."[11]
- A study of "Women's Empowerment and Political Voice" in Morocco considered many criteria, ranging from women in parliament to the Moroccan family code. Another important variable is public spending, which is the unit of analysis for this part of the research. The authors praised the recent introduction of "gender-responsive budgeting," with allocations and expenditures disaggregated by gender. They also complained that "inadequate disaggregated data on women's social and economic status limits the extent to which the state can be held to account."[12]

Finally, disaggregation is also potentially useful in measurement, especially the measurement of more abstract or multidimensional concepts. A good general example is the United Nation's Human Development Index (HDI). Created as an alternative to the economic indices that are frequently used to measure a country's level of development, the HDI seeks to measure the well-being of the ordinary citizens of a country. Toward this end, the index is composed of indicators pertaining to health, education, and standard of living, the latter measured by the GINI coefficient, which is a measure of income inequality. There is agreement that the HDI measures something important that is not captured by such economic indices as per capita gross domestic product or per capita national income. But while the HDI is frequently used, there are instances when it is useful to disaggregate the index and consider separately the explanatory power of one or two of its component indicators.

Personal religiosity, in Arab countries as elsewhere, is often measured by a composite index that includes behavior, such as prayer and reading religious books; belief in God and in the religion's central articles of faith; and other actions, such as preferring to consult religious officials to discuss personal problems. Construction of a scale based on all or at least some of these different indicators, perhaps by factor analysis or another scaling technique, provides a measure of personal

---

[11] Bahgat Korany and Ali E. Hillal Dessouki. 2008. "Foreign Policy Approaches and Arab Countries: A Critical Evaluation and an Alternative Framework." In Bahgat Korany and Ali E. Hillal Dessouki, eds., *The Foreign Policies of Arab States*. American University in Cairo, pp. 27–28; at https://books.google.com/books?hl=en&lr=&id=tpp8jYuH6vwC&oi=fnd&pg=PP9&dq=disaggregation+arab+country&ots=Ydot5td1z6&sig=YvbLg5ekWVdbc-yKvdzcRoBnf7w#v=onepage&q=disaggreg&f=false

[12] Claire Castillejo and Helen Tilley. 2015. "The Road to Reform: Women's Political Voice in Morocco." Development Progress, Overseas Development Institute; at https://cdn.odi.org/media/documents/9607.pdf

Table 4.5 Multiple regression showing the influence of attitudes toward political Islam on attitudes toward democracy

	Full sample	Full sample	Men only	Women only
Algeria				
Personal religiosity	−.06 (−1.55)	−.06 (−1.60)	.03 (.52)	−.15 (−2.82)***
Islamic guidance in public affairs	−.09 (−2.54)***			
• In politics and administration		.00 (.09)	−.00 (−.13)	.01 (.22)
• In economics and commerce		−.11 (−2.53)***	−.06 (.90)	−.15 (−2.56)***
Morocco				
Personal religiosity	−.01 (−.378)	.00 (.08)	.01 (.24)	−.00 (−.09)
Islamic guidance in public affairs	−.09 (−2.50)**			
• In politics and administration		−.06(−1.23)	−.11(1.67)	.01(−.15)
• In economics and commerce		−.12 (−2.43)**	−.08 (−1.20)	−.15 (−2.17)*

Survey items used to measure attitudes toward democracy and political Islam in Algeria and Morocco

Attitudes toward democracy:
• Openness to diverse political ideas is an important criterion for national leadership (ranks first or second on a list that also includes experience, a sense of justice, integrity, and human sensitivity)
• The development of democratic institutions is a high priority for government (ranks first or second on a list that also includes economic well-being, civil peace, and preservation of traditional values)

Attitudes toward "political Islam"
• Believes that religion should guide political and administrative affairs
• Believes that religion should guide economic and commercial affairs

Notes: Attitude toward democracy is the dependent variable. Table shows standardized coefficients (betas) and gives t-statistics in parentheses. Included in the analysis as control variables, but not shown, are age and education.
* $p < .05$, ** $p < .02$, *** $p < .01$

religiosity that is more complete and sometimes more useful. But in some instances, too, it may be more instructive to disaggregate the composite measure and consider relationships in which only religious action or only religious belief is a variable.

Table 4.5 presents findings from a research project that used survey data from Algeria and Morocco to explore the relationship between attitudes toward political Islam and attitudes toward democracy.[13] Support for political Islam is defined in this

---

[13] Mark Tessler. 2002. "Islam and Democracy in the Middle East: The Impact of Religious Orientations on Attitudes toward Democracy in Four Arab Countries." *Comparative Politics* 34 (April): 337–354.

4.2 Third Variable Possibilities

study as a belief that Islam and politics should not be separated and that the religion should play an important role in the governance of the respondent's country. Based on ordinary least squares regression analysis, the table presents standardized coefficients and gives t-statistics in parentheses. (t-statistics are an alternative measure of confidence in the coefficient estimates, similar and mathematically related to p-values.)

The table illustrates both measurement disaggregation and unit of analysis disaggregation in the analysis of both the Algerian data and the Moroccan data. More specifically, there is a composite measure of attitudes toward political Islam that has been disaggregated, with its political and economic dimensions considered separately; and the sex of respondents has also been disaggregated, with men and women considered separately.

The findings in Table 4.5 are the same for both Algeria and Morocco, and they are instructive findings that would have been missed had there been no disaggregation. There is a statistically significant inverse relationship between a favorable attitude toward democracy and a favorable attitude toward political Islam when the composite measure of attitudes toward political Islam is employed and the full sample of respondents is included in the analysis. The findings differ with disaggregation, however. It turns out that this significant inverse relationship only reflects the positive attitudes held by women toward the economic and commercial dimensions of governance that might be guided by Islam.[14] Had there been no disaggregation, the findings reported would have at best been incomplete and, in fact, actually somewhat misleading.

4.2.4 Scope Conditions

Scope conditions refer to the subset of cases, defined in terms of their most relevant attributes, to which a theory applies.

In positivist and empirical social science research, as discussed here, the goal of a research project is very often a causal story, that is to say a set of confirmed causal relationships and interrelationships. This is also frequently called a theory. Scope conditions are the characteristics, or parameters, that specify and describe in terms of concepts and variables the circumstances in which this theory is believed to apply. These concepts and variables are the conditionalities.

Scope conditions may be specified by an investigator prior to data collection and data analysis, in effect making them part of the causal story. In this case, the analysis will subsequently offer evidence about the degree to which the researcher's specification is correct. Alternatively, scope conditions may not receive serious attention until the research project's findings have become clear. In this case, the investigator will reflect on the attributes of the case or setting that has or has not lent support to

---

[14] Both attitudes toward democracy and personal religiosity have been measured by multi-item indices that have not been disaggregated. Perhaps findings would have been different had one or both of these composite measures been disaggregated.

her causal story and designate the case or setting attributes that she believes constitute appropriate scope conditions.

In many and probably most studies, an investigator will give attention to scope conditions both before the study has been conducted and after its findings are clear. Initially, her selection of the case or cases to be studied will almost certainly be based on her ideas about the conditions under which her hypotheses will have explanatory power. Subsequently, her findings will provide evidence about the accuracy of these ideas and a basis for thinking further about scope conditions. It is possible that some conditionalities will have been clarified and confirmed, that some will have been shown to be incorrect, and/or that some may be instructive but will need to be revised and refined.

Attention to scope conditions reflects the cumulative character of scientific research, including social scientific research. It recognizes that the work of an individual researcher or research project has increased value to the extent it contributes to the work of a community of investigators seeking to answer the same or very similar questions. This might not be the case if the objective of an investigation is to provide only thick description of a particular place and time. In fact, however, researchers usually aspire to identify generalizable insights, that is to say causal stories that have explanatory power in cases beyond those studied by any one investigator. To do this, except in the very unlikely event that the focus is on the rare causal stories that are believed to be universal and to apply in all times and places, the path toward cumulativeness lies with scope conditions. It is to say more than that the causal story sometimes applies and sometimes does not apply. It is to say, or to contribute to the research community's ability to say, that the causal story is disproportionately likely to apply in cases or settings that are characterized by specific attributes.

Cumulativeness also signifies that the identification of scope conditions is an ongoing process. Individual researchers or research teams undertake to reduce uncertainty and add to what is known about the conditionalities attached to a given explanation of variance—to a given causal story or theory. An investigator recognizes that she cannot offer definitive insights about these conditionalities. She also recognizes, however, that she can and should add to the insights about conditionalities that have been, are being, and will be added by other investigators. And so the contribution of her research, if successful, is not only a causal story that meaningfully accounts for variance, but also a delineation of the most relevant attributes of the case or setting for which she has found this causal story to have a high probability of being true.

A good example of attention to scope conditions comes from an individual-level study of the relationship between observing and participating in elections, the independent variable, and attitudes toward democracy, the dependent variable. Students of democratization argue that elections in non-democracies, particularly elections that are at least somewhat competitive, expose ordinary citizens to democratic principles and procedures and that the experience of electoral participation increases the likelihood that an individual will have a positive view of democracy.

4.2 Third Variable Possibilities

This is significant since public support for democracy appears to be necessary for a sustained and consolidated democratic transition.

A study in Algeria examined a modified version of this proposition, hypothesizing that the impact of electoral participation on attitudes toward democracy depends on whether the elections are, or are perceived to be, free and fair. Analyzing data from surveys both before and after a presidential election, the study found that the country's electoral experience decreased support for democracy among those Algerians who believed that the election was not free and fair. Accordingly, the take-away, at least in its basic formulation, is that if ordinary citizens observe and experience an important election that they judge to be fraudulent and unfair, their support for democracy as a desirable political system will then diminish significantly.[15]

Turning then to scope conditions, reflection is invited on the attributes of the cases or settings to which this analytical insight has been found to apply. In this instance, Algeria is the case to which a causal story about effect of elections on attitudes toward democracy has been found to apply. But "Algeria" is not a conditionality. It is rather the relevant attributes of the Algerian case that constitute conditionalities, and their specification is frequently described as replacing proper names with variable names.

So, what are the names of variables that might replace the name "Algeria" in order to specify the conditions under which what was found in Algeria might be found elsewhere? Among the likely scope conditions that specify the applicability of the Algeria study's findings are that they apply when the country is not democratic and is not actively engaged in a robust democratic transition, when the elections are at the national level and perhaps also are presidential, when the election is competitive to the extent that there are multiple candidates and/or political parties competing for votes, and when there are both candidates and parties aligned with the government and candidates and parties that are not aligned with the government.

Additional research, by others and perhaps also by the researchers themselves, will be necessary to determine whether these proposed scope conditions actually do specify when what was found in Algeria will be found elsewhere. Additional research on the relationship between elections and attitudes toward democracy will also be necessary to determine whether these are only some of the conditions under which the findings from Algeria apply, and whether all or only some of these particular scope conditions are necessary. That these determinations about scope conditions require additional research reflects the cumulative character of the production of knowledge in social science research.

Another opportunity to think about scope conditions is provided by a study in Tunisia, Algeria, and Morocco that tests hypotheses about the determinants of

---

[15] Michael Robbins and Mark Tessler. 2012. "The Effect of Elections on Public Opinion toward Democracy: Evidence from Longitudinal Survey Research in Algeria." *Comparative Political Studies* 45 (October): 1255–76. The study analyzed data from both the World Values Survey and the Arab Barometer.

variance in attitudes toward political Islam.[16] One of the several hypotheses that were tested is shown below, and the results of an OLS regression analysis are presented in Table 4.6. The hypothesis was tested at two points in time, 2013 and 2016.

H1. Individuals with lower levels of economic satisfaction are more likely than are individuals with higher levels of economic satisfaction to favor a political formula that gives Islam an important role.

The findings in Table 4.6 pertaining to H1 are straightforward. The hypothesis posited that higher levels of economic dissatisfaction push toward support for political Islam, and this was confirmed only in Morocco, and in Morocco for both 2013 and 2016. More research on the individual-level relationship between economic circumstance and attitudes toward political Islam will be needed before conclusions about scope conditions can be drawn with any degree of confidence. But the findings presented in Table 4.6 do contribute to this ongoing and cumulative enterprise. First, more often than not, economic circumstances do not have an impact on attitudes toward political Islam, and so it appears that H1 does not posit a relationship that is broadly applicable.

Second, in certain circumstances, that is to say under particular conditions, the relationship proposed in H1 does apply. And in the case being considered, the scope conditions are likely to be political and economic attributes of Morocco that are at least somewhat stable over time.

The place of Islamist parties and movements in Morocco points to what may be a conditionality. Extremist and anti-regime Islamist movements have been marginalized in Morocco. But the most important Islamist movement, the Party of Justice and Development, not only operates in the mainstream of Moroccan political life, it has in fact been victorious in elections and has led the government during the 2010s. Accordingly, a political situation that gives an Islamist party considerable influence may be an important conditionality.

Economic circumstances may also be a relevant conditionality. Given that Morocco is one of the poorest Arab countries, a likely scope condition is also that a significant proportion of a country's population is living in poverty. Both of these conditionalities, attributes that characterized Morocco but not Tunisia or Algeria at the time of the research, are discussed in the publication from which this example is taken. What distinguishes Morocco and may constitute scope conditions favorable to the existence of the hypothesized causal relationship probably lies in "the interaction between Morocco's overall relative and absolute poverty and its experience with the Justice and Development Party."

---

[16] Mark Tessler, 2019. "Do Political and Economic Grievances Foster Support for Political Islam in the Post-Arab Spring Maghreb?" In Stephen King and Abdeslam Maghraoui (eds.). *The Maghreb after the Arab Spring: The Lure of Authoritarian Stability*. Bloomington, Indiana: Indiana University Press.

4.2 Third Variable Possibilities

Table 4.6 OLS Regression coefficients showing the influence of personal economic circumstance on attitudes toward political Islam among all respondents and among respondents grouped by country and year

	All	Tunisia 2013	Tunisia 2016	Algeria 2013	Algeria 2016	Morocco 2013	Morocco 2016
More positive economic circumstance	.016 (.014)	−.004 (.034)	.030 (.033)	−.021 (.039)	−.007 (.029)	−.143*** (.041)	−.094** (.032)
Constant	.575*** (.068)	.326 (.186)	.619*** (.176)	.362* (.188)	.697*** (.134)	.280 (.159)	.673*** (.144)

Note: Dependent variable: higher value is more positive attitude toward political Islam
Higher values on the dependent variable indicate higher support for political Islam; the table presents unstandardized coefficients; standard errors are in parentheses
Not shown are four control variables: religiosity, age, gender, and education.
*Significant at .05 level, **Significant at .01 level, ***Significant at .001 level

Exercise 4.5. Thinking about scope conditions in the Maghreb

Table 4.2 presents the results of an innovative study in Morocco and Algeria that tested hypotheses about determinants of variance in the constituent service work of parliamentary deputies. It found that female deputies are more likely to serve female and less influential constituents than are male deputies, and that quota-elected female deputies are more likely to serve female and less influential constituents than are non-quota-elected female deputies. But it found these relationships only in Morocco. These or very similar patterns were not found in Algeria.

- What might be scope conditions in this case? Offer your thoughts about the conditionalities that determine when this finding is disproportionately likely to be found elsewhere.

The relationships shown in Table 4.5 offer another opportunity to think about scope conditions. The study is based on surveys in Algeria and Morocco, and attitude toward democracy is the dependent variable. Attitude toward political Islam is the independent variable. Interestingly and quite significantly, in both countries, attitudes toward one and only one of the two dimensions of political Islam were found to have explanatory power, and this was found to be the case only for women. This is a somewhat particular and unusual finding, reflecting both unit of analysis disaggregation and measurement disaggregation. To identify scope conditions, an investigator must consider whether there are attributes of both Algeria and Morocco, or of the situation of the two countries with respect to political Islam and to women, that may specify the conditions under which the same or very similar variable relationships will be found elsewhere.

- What might be scope conditions in this case? Offer your thoughts about the conditionalities that determine when this particular and somewhat unusual finding is disproportionately likely to be found elsewhere.

Table 4.5 also shows that personal religiosity has explanatory power among women but not men in Algeria and does not have explanatory power among either sex in Morocco. For women in Algeria, greater personal religiosity pushes toward unfavorable attitudes toward democracy.

- What might be scope conditions in this case? Offer your thoughts about the conditionalities that determine when this finding is disproportionately likely to be found elsewhere.

4.2.5 Experiments

Although controlling for potentially confounding variables helps to establish that a relationship is not spurious, there are often variables that a researcher cannot control due to measurement limitations or the absence of relevant data. In addition, there may be variables that could produce a spurious relationship that an investigator did not think to include in the causal story she proposes to test and, therefore, are not included as control variables in her hypothesis-testing analyses.

Experiments offer an alternative approach to controlling sources of extraneous variance and, thereby, reducing the chance of making a Type I error or a Type II error. Experiments also significantly strengthen the basis not only for concluding that an observed variable relationship very likely represents accurately the population of cases of which it is a subset, but also for establishing that the relationship is very likely to be causal. Accordingly, when appropriate given the hypothesis and causal story to be evaluated, experiments offer a powerful methodology for generating and analyzing data.

Experiments have traditionally been used more frequently in some social science disciplines than others. They have been conducted most frequently in psychology and educational psychology. Although not entirely absent, experimental research designs have been less common in political science and, to some extent, sociology. In recent years, however, the conduct of experiments has become much more common in the latter disciplines, and it has also become common to include an experiment as one element of a multi-method research design. Thus, although a thorough discussion of experiments in social science research is beyond the scope of this guide to social science research, political scientists and researchers in other social science disciplines should be familiar with at least the basic elements of experiments. A short overview of these elements, along with a few examples, is presented here for this purpose.

The basic structure of an experiment is simple and straightforward. To begin, an investigator randomly assigns the units of analysis on which she has data and that she plans to use in the experiment to two or more groups. One group will be designated the control group and it will not be subject to the treatment, or treatments, associated with the experiment. A second group will be exposed to the experimental treatment, and if the experiment involves more than one treatment, there will be more than one treatment group. After this group(s) has received the treatment, the researcher can easily compare the measures of the dependent variable in the control group and the treatment group(s) in order to measure the effect of the treatment.

Survey Experiments An example of a survey experiment is provided by a study pertaining to attitudes toward the Islamic State (Daesh) that was embedded in the 2016 Wave 4 Arab Barometer surveys. With attitudes about Daesh the dependent variables, the purpose of the experiment was to determine whether receiving different kinds of information about the goals and tactics of the Islamic State affected the attitudes toward the terrorist group held by ordinary citizens in the Arab world. In this experiment, as shown in Table 4.7, there were four treatments. One treatment

Table 4.7 Control group and treatment groups in an Arab Barometer Wave 4 experiment on the influence of information about the Islamic State (Daesh) on attitudes toward the terrorist group

Control group:
No added text
Treatment A:
As you may know, Daesh has emerged as a potent force in the region and the world. In 2014, it declared a caliphate based in Raqqa, Syria. Daesh's goal is to extend the caliphate across the Muslim world. It has killed many Muslims and non-Muslims in pursuit of this aim.
Treatment B:
As you may know, Daesh has emerged as a potent force in the region and the world. In 2014, it declared a caliphate based in Raqqa, Syria. Daesh's goal is to extend the caliphate across the Muslim world. It has killed many Muslims and non-Muslims in pursuit of this aim. Another of Daesh's stated objectives is to limit Shia influence across the Muslim world as well as opposing Iranian-led Shia forces in Syria, Iraq, Yemen, and elsewhere.
Treatment C:
As you may know, Daesh has emerged as a potent force in the region and the world. In 2014, it declared a caliphate based in Raqqa, Syria. Daesh's goal is to extend the caliphate across the Muslim world. It has killed many Muslims and non-Muslims in pursuit of this aim. Another of Daesh's stated objectives is to defend Islam from attacks by secular leaders and other elites whose goal is to limit the role of Islam in government and public life.
Treatment D:
As you may know, Daesh has emerged as a potent force in the region and the world. In 2014, it declared a caliphate based in Raqqa, Syria. Daesh's goal is to extend the caliphate across the Muslim world. It has killed many Muslims and non-Muslims in pursuit of this aim. Another of Daesh's stated objectives is to counter intervention in the region by the United States and other Western powers who have engaged in military attacks against it.

called attention to the group's claim to be establishing a caliphate and its use of violence against both non-Muslims and Muslims in pursuit of this objective. Each of the three remaining treatment groups received the same information about the pursuit of a caliphate and the use of violence, and then received additional information about one of the goals that was espoused by the Islamic State and emphasized in the group's social media messaging.

As noted, it is essential that group assignments be random. This assures that the groups, five in this example, are comparable with respect to anything other than the treatments that might affect the attitudes of the respondents. To measure their attitudes, respondents were asked to indicate their agreement or disagreement with a number of statements, three of which are listed below. These statements were presented to respondents after the experimental treatments had been introduced, and the influence of the information provided by each treatment was measured by comparing the responses of individuals in each treatment group to the responses of individuals in the control group. As long as assignments to the control group and the four treatment groups are random, the groups are almost certainly comparable with respect to other possible determinants of attitudes. And with other possible determinants thus held constant, control group-treatment group attitudinal

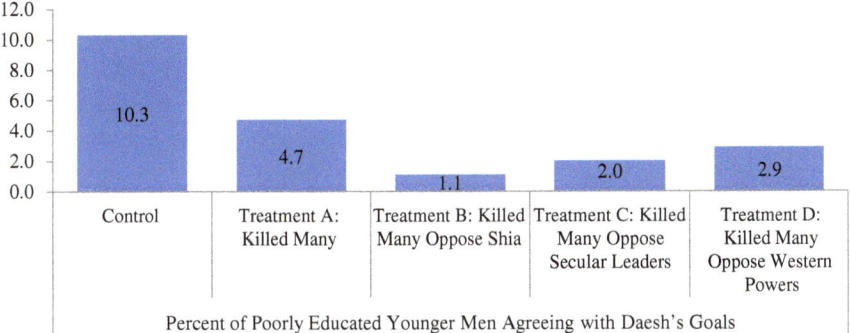

Fig. 4.8 Support for Daesh's goals by treatment among younger less educated men

differences can be attributed to the explanatory power of the treatment, rather than to any confounding variable, with a low likelihood of error.

- To what extent do you agree with the goals of the Islamic State? (3.1 percent of the individuals in the control group agree or somewhat agree)
- To what extent do you agree with the Islamic State's use of violence? (2.9 percent of the individuals in the control group agree or somewhat agree)
- To what extent do you agree that the Islamic State's tactics are compatible with the teachings of Islam? (5.3 percent of the individuals in the control group agree or somewhat agree)

A fuller account of this experiment is beyond the purview of the present discussion.[17] A few points may nonetheless be briefly noted. First, the proportion of respondents expressing even somewhat positive attitudes toward the Islamic State is very low. The percent agreeing to a large extent or to some extent is given in the parentheses after each statement. Second, the impact of the experimental treatments sometimes does but sometimes does not push the percentage of individuals with positive attitudes even lower, and the impact of some treatments varies from country to country.

Finally, some of the most instructive findings emerge when control group and treatment group comparisons are made for subsets of respondents, rather than for all respondents. This involves disaggregation, as discussed earlier in this chapter. Figure 4.8 offers an example and further illustrates the use and utility of experiments. It considers the attitudes of younger and less well educated men, a prime target of Islamic State recruitment efforts, and it shows that the proportion of individuals with positive attitudes toward the goals of the Islamic State is somewhat higher among

---

[17] Mark Tessler, Michael Robbins and Amaney Jamal. 2021. "Mapping and Explaining Arab Attitudes Toward the Islamic State: Findings from an Arab Barometer Survey and Embedded Experiment. In Melani Cammett and Pauline Jones (eds.). *The Oxford Handbook of Politics in Muslim Societies*. New York: Oxford University Press.

those in the control group but significantly lower among those in each of the treatment groups. It is also lower in some treatment groups than in others.

Another interesting example of an experiment embedded in a survey addressed determinants of attitudes toward gender equality. The survey was conducted in Egypt in 2013, and the dependent variable was the views of ordinary citizens toward women's roles in public and political life.[18] The specific question to be answered by the experiment was whether support for female political leadership would increase among individuals, Egyptians in this case, if they were exposed to arguments in favor of women's political equality that were grounded in the Qur'ān, Islam's holiest text. The authors write in this study that they draw on recent scholarship on religion and politics, including work by some who describe themselves as "Islamic feminists," to hypothesize that such exposure would increase support for women's political equality.

There were two treatment groups and a control group in the experiment. One of the treatment groups gave respondents a statement in support of gender equality based on Islamic sources. The other treatment group gave respondents a statement in support of gender equality based on scientific research. Both statements are shown below.

Treatment 1. Some say that there is no problem if a woman assumes a position of authority, such as the presidency of the republic or the prime ministership. And they rely on a verse from Sūrat al-Tawba (Chapter of Atonement) in the Holy Qur'ān that says, "Believing men and believing women are protectors of one another." And they interpret it to mean that God does not distinguish between men and women in their capabilities.

Treatment 2. Some say that there is no problem if a woman assumes a position of authority, such as the presidency of the republic or the prime ministership. And they rely on the results of numerous scientific studies. For example, in 2010, a group of leading scholars completed a study that showed that women and men have the same leadership capabilities.

Following the treatments, the survey continued and respondents were asked to respond to the item shown below. To test their hypothesis about the impact of religious discourse on attitudes toward political leadership by women, the authors compared the post-treatment attitudes of respondents who received Treatment 1 to the attitudes of respondents in the control group. The post-treatment attitudes of respondents who received Treatment 2 were similarly compared to the attitudes of respondents in the control group. The difference between each treatment group and the control group were then compared to see not only whether the religious treatment made a difference but also whether it made more of a difference than the non-religious treatment.

---

[18] Tarek Masoud, Amaney Jamal, Elizabeth Nugent. 2016. "Using the Qur'an to Empower Women: Theory and Experimental Evidence for Egypt." *Comparative Political Studies* 49 (12): 1555–1598.

4.2 Third Variable Possibilities

Between the following two opinions, which one is closer to your personal opinion?

(a) It is not good for a woman to assume a position of authority, such as the presidency of the republic or the prime ministership, or
(b) There is no problem if a woman assumes a position of authority, such as the presidency of the republic or the prime ministership.

The findings of the experiment supported the authors' hypothesis that religious discourse can be used to make inroads against conservative attitudes. Among respondents in the control group, 32.6 percent chose the statement that there is no problem if a woman assumes a position of authority. Among respondents in the treatment group receiving a statement in support of female political leadership based on scientific research, 34.3 percent agreed that there is no problem if a woman assumes a position of authority. This is only slightly higher than the percentage of respondents in the control group who took this position, a difference that is not statistically significant. By contrast, this position was taken by 40.5 percent of the respondents in the treatment group given a religious basis for gender equality. Both the difference between this treatment group and the control group and the difference between this group and the other treatment group were statistically significant, the former at the .01 level and the latter at the .05 level of confidence.

Conjoint Experiments The two experiments described above illustrate what are sometimes called "discrete" experiments or "unidimensional" experiments. This refers to the fact that questions measuring the dependent variable are asked and answered one at a time. Participants are not asked to consider the interaction between the subjects about which different questions ask.

In conjoint experiments, sometimes described as "multi-dimensional" experiments, participants are asked to respond to questions that propose a number of alternatives based on two or more variables taken in combination. This allows the investigator to assess the impact of experimental treatments on concepts that are complex and multidimensional.

An example of a conjoint experiment is provided by a study in Tunisia of the way that voters evaluate candidates running for office based on their gender and their religiosity taken together.[19] Respondents in a nationally representative survey conducted in 2012 were randomly assigned to one of two treatment groups. Both groups were shown two pictures of possible candidates for office and asked to indicate for each whether they definitely would, probably would, probably would not, or definitely would not vote for the person in the picture. In one treatment group, respondents were shown pictures of a secular man and a secular woman. In a second treatment group, respondents were shown pictures of a religious man and a religious

---

[19] Lindsay Benstead, Amaney Jamal, and Ellen Lust. 2015. "Is It Gender, Religiosity or Both? A Role Congruity Theory of Candidate Electability in Transitional Tunisia." *Perspectives of Politics* 13 (March): 74–94.

woman, with dress and appearance indicating religiosity. In both cases, the researchers were very careful to make the pictures clear and believable and otherwise comparable.

Examining support for men and women with religiosity taken into consideration, the authors found different patterns in the two treatment groups. In the second treatment group, those who gave a high score to the religious male candidate gave an even higher score to the religious female candidate. In the treatment group with secular candidates, those who gave a high score to the secular male candidate did not give a higher score, and sometimes gave a lower score, to the female secular candidate. The larger theoretical goal of the study was, first, to identify demographic and ideological factors that account for variance across the four candidate preference types; and second, to use the profile of supporters of each candidate type to assess the relevance and explanatory power of three theoretical frameworks: modernization theory, role contiguity theory, and social identity theory.

Natural Experiments and Matching Natural experiments are very similar in design to other experiments in that they rely on randomization to ensure that treatment and control groups are comparable. The main difference is that in natural experiments, the randomization of the treatment occurs "naturally" in the world, instead of being done by the researcher herself. Matching may be used in instances where assignment to the control and treatment groups is not based on randomization.

Suppose, for example, that the Ministry of Education in your country has been planning to develop a new set of high school textbooks that present a new interpretation of important events in your country's history. However, the ministry does not have enough copies of the new textbooks for all of the schools in the country, and so it decides for this reason to select a subset of high schools to receive and use the new textbooks. This creates the foundation for a natural experiment. Schools in which the old textbook continues to be used constitute, in effect, the control group of an experiment, and schools using the new textbook constitute, in effect, an experimental treatment group. An investigator could use this opportunity to conduct a natural experiment by surveying students in schools that did and in schools that did not receive the new textbooks, and she could then compare the students in the two groups to see whether and how using the new textbooks affected the knowledge, attitudes, and/or behavior of the students.

In this example, the way that the ministry selected the schools that received the new textbooks would have important implications for the experiment. In order to draw conclusions about whether and how the new textbooks affect student knowledge, attitudes, and behavior, the control group and the treatment group must be comparable. In other words, factors other than the textbook used must be held constant and thus be deprived of any possible explanatory power. If use of the new textbooks is the only difference between the control and treatment schools, any difference in the knowledge, attitudes, or behavior, which are the dependent variables, cannot be attributed to any confounding variable.

Randomization in assigning schools to either the old textbook control group or the new textbook treatment group is the best way to create groups that are comparable apart from the treatment. As in other types of experiments, randomization in

4.2 Third Variable Possibilities

group assignment should be used whenever possible. But randomization is not always possible, especially in natural experiments since group assignments are made in a way and for reasons having nothing to do with an experiment. In this case, it may be possible to use matching to establish comparability between the control group and the treatment group or groups.

Matching uses observational data where the treatment and control groups are not randomly assigned. Based on observable pre-treatment covariates, meaning variables that need to be held constant, each unit of analysis in the treatment group is paired (matched) with a very similar unit of analysis in the control group. These matched pairs are then used to assess the explanatory power of the experimental treatment. Units of analysis that cannot be matched are not included in the analysis. Matching does not provide the same degree of comparability as randomization. Nevertheless, the degree to which matching makes the treatment and control groups very similar, and similar especially with respect to variables that may be sources of extraneous variance, will increase the researcher's confidence in her findings about the impact of the treatment.

An interesting and potentially important finding comes from a natural experiment in the Israeli-occupied West Bank.[20] Matching was used to establish the treatment group and the control group in this experiment. The groups were two West Bank Palestinian villages that had many similar characteristics and thus matched one another and were broadly comparable.

Among the elements of the occupation that are particularly problematic and oppressive for West Bank Palestinians are the checkpoints through which they must pass when traveling in many areas. Although it is not always the case, Palestinians may be interrogated, searched, or otherwise detained at checkpoints, sometimes for a long time. It is not surprising that checkpoints contribute to anti-Israel attitudes among Palestinians.

In 2009, Israel decided to remove a checkpoint that monitored traffic on an important highway and through which travelers into and out of a large Palestinian village were obliged to pass. To make this the basis for a natural experiment, with removal of the checkpoint as the treatment, the research team identified another village with very similar characteristics that could serve as a control group. The second village was affected by a checkpoint that was not being removed, which qualified its residents as a control group. The research team then interviewed a representative sample of Palestinian residents in each village several months before the checkpoint was removed and then again several months after it had been removed. The survey questions asked about various aspects of the Israeli-Palestinian conflict in general and about the degree of militancy of respondent attitudes in particular.

---

[20] Matthew Longo, Dafna Canetti, and Nancy Hite-Rubin. 2014. "A Checkpoint Effect? Experiment on Travel Restrictions in the West Bank." *American Journal of Political Science* 58 (October): 1006–1023.

The data were analyzed using a "difference in differences" model, often called simply dif-in-dif or DID. The dif-in-dif analysis involved measuring the difference in treatment village attitudes before and after removal of the checkpoint, measuring also the difference in control village attitudes before and after removal of the checkpoint in the other village, and then comparing these two measures of difference. To the extent that the two villages are broadly comparable, and to the extent that attitudes changed significantly more among residents of the treatment village than among residents of the control village, the researchers were able to conclude that the presence or absence of a checkpoint is a significant determinant of variance in the attitudes of West Bank Palestinians toward the conflict with Israel.

More specifically, the attitudes about the Israeli-Palestinian conflict of the treatment village residents were less militant and hostile in the post-treatment survey than they had been in the pre-treatment survey. Among control village residents, by contrast, attitudes toward the conflict were actually more militant and hostile in the post-treatment survey than they had been in the pre-treatment survey. Among the study's conclusions: Checkpoints have a significant effect on West Bank Palestinian attitudes toward their conflict with Israel, and the nature of this effect involves making Palestinians more militant and hostile in their views about the conflict.

* * *

This chapter has discussed many different types and goals of multivariate analysis, and it has provided a diverse array of examples for purposes of illustration. The discussion in the section on "Causal Inference" is primarily concerned with the requirements for establishing that a bivariate relationship very probably involves causality. Identifying relationships that are causal, that have explanatory power, in other words, is a central preoccupation in social science research. This is not the goal of all social science research. Some studies simply seek to better understand variance and are primarily descriptive; they seek to provide information and insight about *what* the variance looks like or how it is distributed, not *why* a variable behaves as it does or with what consequences. And variance itself is not the preoccupation of all social science research.

Nevertheless, formulating and testing theories and hypotheses that purport to account for variance, that seek to discover determinants, that seek to explain, remain one of the most widespread and important dimensions of positivist social science. Multivariate analysis is required to determine whether a variable relationship is indeed causal, or very likely to be, and to inspire confidence in an investigator's claim that her findings demonstrate causality. The concepts and procedures discussed in the section of this chapter on "Causal Inference" are the elements of a research design to which an investigator must be attentive in order to build a case for causal inference.

The section on "Third Variable Possibilities" discusses some of the important ways that multivariate analysis, meaning the addition of one or more "third" variables, can enrich the sophistication and shed light on the applicability of a causal story. A distinction between direct and indirect relationships, the concept of disaggregation, and attention to scope conditions all contribute to these important goals.

4.2 Third Variable Possibilities

This does not exhaust the list of ways that the inclusion of one or more additional or "third" variables can contribute to the refinement of a causal story or to increased understanding of the conditions that specify when the causal story probably does and probably does not have explanatory power. Again, however, the topics covered in the section on "Third Variable Possibilities" are widely used in social science research and constitute powerful methodologies with the potential to significantly enhance the value of any research project.

Numerous real-world examples of social science research projects carried out in the Arab world have been provided to illustrate these points about causal inference and the addition of "third" variables. Interested readers, or perhaps students reading this guide in a classroom setting, might find it useful to consult and discuss some of the original publications that have been cited in this chapter. Or, such readers might find it profitable to seek out and review additional examples of relevant research reports, especially those designed and conducted by Arab social scientists. More examples of research projects designed and carried out by Arab social scientists will contribute to a fuller understanding of the application in Arab environments of the concepts and procedures discussed in this and other chapters.

Open Access This chapter is licensed under the terms of the Creative Commons Attribution 4.0 International License (http://creativecommons.org/licenses/by/4.0/), which permits use, sharing, adaptation, distribution and reproduction in any medium or format, as long as you give appropriate credit to the original author(s) and the source, provide a link to the Creative Commons license and indicate if changes were made.

The images or other third party material in this chapter are included in the chapter's Creative Commons license, unless indicated otherwise in a credit line to the material. If material is not included in the chapter's Creative Commons license and your intended use is not permitted by statutory regulation or exceeds the permitted use, you will need to obtain permission directly from the copyright holder.

5. Reprise and Conclusion: Overview, Audience, and Uses of the Guide

It will be useful in concluding this guide to social science research to return to some of the points made in the Introduction, reminding readers about the origins of this guide to social science research in the Arab world and about the choices that have been made with respect to coverage and emphasis. The way that the information and insights presented in Chaps. 2, 3, and 4 come together and cumulate should also be noted. Finally, and importantly, we offer very briefly some thoughts about the audience for whom the guide is intended, about the ways in which the guide might be productively used, particularly in education, and about the ways in which and the degree to which the guide possesses an Arab sensibility.

The Carnegie Grant and Project The writing of this guide was made possible by a generous grant from the Carnegie Corporation of New York in 2017. The principal investigators were members of the Arab Barometer's U.S.-based leadership team: Amaney Jamal, Michael Robbins, and myself.

Preparation of the guide is not the only activity that the grant supported. Ambitiously entitled "Understanding Marginalized Communities in the Arab World through Social Science Research: Gaining Insight, Enhancing Capacity, and Building Collaborations to Impact the Region," the project brought together young Arab scholars and professionals for two years of workshops and a final international conference. The last workshop and the conference were held virtually in 2020 because of the coronavirus pandemic.

Workshop participants worked with one another and with the organizers of the project to design and then carry out original data-based research projects on marginalized communities, broadly defined. For example, one of the participants, a Tunisian economist, chose to focus on intimate partner violence and used survey data from Tunisia to test the hypothesis that education decreases the likelihood that a woman will experience this kind of violence. Another, a political scientist from Morocco, conducted an original survey of Sub-Saharan migrants in Morocco in order to map and then account for variance in their perceptions of Moroccan society and culture. A third, a sociologist from Jordan, focused on Syrian refugee women in

Jordan and built a database from the transcripts of audio-recorded interviews with a sample of these women. All three of these young scholars, like some of the other participants, are university professors in a social science department.

Working with these young women and men on the theory and method of research design and development over 2 years contributed to our understanding of the kind of guide to research that would be helpful to these and other young Arab social scientists, a community of scholars whose members vary considerably in their knowledge and experience with hypothesis-driven, quantitative inquiry. As elsewhere, some are quite advanced, others less so. We often thought about the interests and needs of the Carnegie project participants when making decisions about what to include, and in what detail, in the present volume.

The Arab Barometer Many of the explanations, examples, and exercises in this guide to social science research focus on public opinion research with the individual as the unit of analysis. This is partly, but not solely, because a ready resource is provided by the Arab Barometer survey project.

As many readers already know, the Arab Barometer has been carrying out nationally representative face-to-face public opinion surveys since 2006. Dozens of surveys have been conducted in Arab countries and tens of thousands of ordinary citizens have been interviewed about their social and political attitudes and values. Data from these surveys can be downloaded without charge from the Arab Barometer website (arabbarometer.org), and an online analysis tool on the website makes it possible to carry out univariate and some bivariate analyses without downloading the data.

Choices The enterprise of social science research is vast and there is no way to avoid choosing some approaches and topics for coverage and setting aside others. For reasons discussed in the Introduction, the present guide to social science research in the Arab world has focused on positivist, quantitative research and has sought the middle ground in depth and breadth.

- *The Middle Ground.* Our experience with the Carnegie project, as well as our previous research in Arab societies, led us to focus on what in the Introduction we called the "middle ground" with respect to both depth and breadth. This, in our understanding, is the space between a comprehensive textbook, on the one hand, for which these chapters are by no means a substitute, and, on the other, study guides that are little more than checklists of key concepts and terms or glossaries with two- or three-paragraph definitions.

  The goal has been to find the sweet spot between too little information and too much information. Readers should, therefore, approach this guide with the sense of a continuum ranging from a detailed and very thorough approach, on the one hand, to a limited and introductory approach, on the other. The present volume seeks to make its contribution at an intermediate point on this continuum, a point that is distant to an appropriately equal degree from each of the two poles. This

does mean that some readers may find the text to be a little too advanced and that others may judge the text to be a little too elementary.
- *Positivist Research.* Choosing to situate Chaps. 2, 3, and 4 in the middle ground with respect to depth and breadth is not the only decision that shapes the content that this guide seeks to deliver. It has also, and self-consciously, decided to focus on positivist research, even while acknowledging that other approaches to social science investigation are also useful and legitimate.

  We associate a positivist approach with empirical, evidence-based, or data-based, inquiry that seeks to describe and/or explain variance. The concept of variance occupies a place of pride in positivist research, and for this reason it provides the structure for Chaps. 2, 3, and 4, which deal, respectively, with univariate analysis, bivariate analysis, and multivariate analysis. Again, however, the volume's emphasis on positivism does not reflect a belief that other research methodologies are necessarily less useful or that other research objectives are necessarily less worthwhile.
- *Quantitative and Qualitative Research.* The present guide also emphasizes quantitative research. Again, however, this should not be understood as arguing that qualitative research is less valid than quantitative research. Both have their place and have contributions to make, and qualitative research can also be positivist and have describing and/or explaining variance as its goal. To illustrate this point, Chap. 2 includes a short digression that includes an account of several qualitative studies in Arab countries that were based on empirical evidence and sought to offer explanatory insights about variance.
- *Unit of Analysis.* The unit of analysis is often the individual in many of the examples and exercises included in this volume. This is, in part, because Arab Barometer survey data have been used to illustrate many points. This has worked well so far as providing information and advancing understanding of concepts and procedures are concerned. Of course, other units of analysis are frequently the focus of social science inquiry as well, and other units of analysis are also the focus of some of the research included in this volume as examples of concepts or procedures.

  Notwithstanding a disproportionate number of examples in which the individual is the unit of analysis, many other units of analysis are frequently the focus of social science research. The take-away, as emphasized in the Introduction and in Chap. 2, is that studies concerned with describing or explaining variance must be clear and specific about the unit of analysis, the unit that is doing the varying along the range of possible values defined by each variable the investigator includes in her study.

The Chapters Chapters 2, 3, and 4 deal, respectively, with univariate analysis, bivariate analysis, and multivariate analysis. Each chapter introduces concepts and procedures that can stand alone as a basis for meaningful analysis. More specifically, the central themes of Chap. 2 are measuring and describing variance; the central themes of Chap. 3 are hypothesized variable relationships and probability; and the central themes of Chap. 4 are causation, control, and conditionality.

Beyond the stand-alone analyses associated with the concepts and procedures introduced in each chapter, Chap. 2 also lays a foundation for Chap. 3, and Chap. 3 in turn lays a foundation for Chap. 4. Accordingly, the chapters cumulate. In order to understand and apply the information and insights provided in Chap. 3, in order to formulate hypothesized bivariate relationships and assess their statistical significance, in other words, knowledge and mastery of the elements of defining and measuring variance discussed in Chap. 2 are essential. Similarly, Chap. 4's attention to causation, control, and conditionality is, in each case, about adding to, refining, or making more precise what can be learned about a hypothesized bivariate relationship.

An Arab Sensibility A legitimate question about this guide to social science research is whether and in what sense does the guide display an Arab sensibility, or an Arab feel. One part of the answer concerns the circumstances that led to its creation and the author's experiences both before and during its drafting. As stated, the drafting of this guide was coterminous with working with a group of young Arab social scientists and reflecting on what they would find most useful as they designed and carried out original projects dealing with marginalized communities in one or more Arab countries.

A more specific way in which this guide endeavors to embed an Arab sensibility has to do with the text itself. On the one hand, mention is made of the Arab Barometer when discussing a number of concepts or procedures, and a number of exercises are based on survey data from the Barometer. Some exercises ask the reader to log onto the Barometer's website and use the online analysis tool. On the other hand, almost all of the examples used to illustrate other concepts and procedures draw upon published reports of research carried out in one or more Arab countries.

Some of the published research reports cited for purposes of illustration in Chaps. 2, 3, and 4 report on projects designed and carried out by Arab scholars. But many are not by Arab scholars; many are by Western social scientists, and they are published in Western and in many cases disciplinary journals. These examples are valuable and should be effective in promoting a better understanding of relevant concepts and procedures. At the same time, it would be useful to have more examples of research carried out by Arab social scientists. Should this guide at some point be used for instructional purposes, perhaps in university classes in social science research design and methodology, an assignment might be for students to seek out and evaluate published reports of research conducted in Arab environments by Arab social scientists.

Audience The guide is intended, of course, for those interested in social science research in the Arab world. This applies in particular to those interested in an approach to research that is positivist, data-based, and quantitative.

- *Practitioners of Qualitative Research.* Although much of the volume's content deals with describing, presenting, and analyzing quantitative data, very substantial attention is also devoted to broader conceptual considerations relating to hypothesis formation, causal inference, probability, measurement, and conditionality. These latter considerations make the volume relevant for social scientists who collect and work with qualitative data.

- *Consumers of Research.* Consumers of social science research are much more numerous than practitioners of this research, and these individuals must be able to understand and evaluate the research reports they read. Consumers cannot be well versed in the specific methodology of every study they read. But they should at a minimum be familiar with foundational conceptual and methodological considerations. The present volume devotes significant attention to these foundational concerns.
- *Instructors and Students.* Another audience for which this guide is intended, and perhaps the most important, is composed of students and instructors, particularly at the university level, who are learning or teaching about social science research and its application in the Arab world. Providing a resource for classroom use is among the motivations for creating this guide.

One possibility is that instructors will find it useful to borrow heavily from the guide as they decide what to cover, and what specific information to provide, in their lectures about data-based and quantitative social science research.

But the volume's chapters lend themselves to classroom use as well, and they might be included in the readings an instructor assigns. That the volume is available without charge removes what might otherwise be a serious impediment to such an assignment. Beyond simply reading and discussing the chapters, or sections of the chapters, there are exercises that students can profitably do and discuss with classmates and the instructor. Students can also read the published research reports that the chapters cite for purposes of illustration and make these the basis for additional class discussion. And students can also be asked to search out and then report on additional publications based on quantitative social science research carried out in the Arab world, perhaps giving special attention to projects and publications by Arab scholars.

Open Access This chapter is licensed under the terms of the Creative Commons Attribution 4.0 International License (http://creativecommons.org/licenses/by/4.0/), which permits use, sharing, adaptation, distribution and reproduction in any medium or format, as long as you give appropriate credit to the original author(s) and the source, provide a link to the Creative Commons license and indicate if changes were made.

The images or other third party material in this chapter are included in the chapter's Creative Commons license, unless indicated otherwise in a credit line to the material. If material is not included in the chapter's Creative Commons license and your intended use is not permitted by statutory regulation or exceeds the permitted use, you will need to obtain permission directly from the copyright holder.

Appendices

Appendix 1: Fieldwork and Ethics

Abdul-Wahab Kayyali

For a considerable number of social science researchers studying the Middle East and North Africa (MENA), doctoral and post-doctoral research entails an element of fieldwork, broadly construed. This fieldwork typically entails either within-country or cross-country data collection and involves work in environments that are likely to present obstacles and challenges to even the most seasoned researchers. Social science being what it is, these obstacles and challenges typically involve human subject research with ethical constraints and considerations.

This appendix addresses these issues; it considers best practices and offers helpful hints for social science fieldwork. It is based on the field research experience of four early career social scientists during their doctoral fieldwork research. Notably, it does not focus on Western researchers traveling to an Arab country but draws upon the fieldwork of four Arab social scientists, one of whom is the author. It addresses the following issues:

- Pre-arrival and preparation
- First steps in the field
- Best practices of data collection and preservation
- Managing subjectivity and ensuring the safety of collaborators
- After the field

Pre-Arrival and Preparation

Many social scientists spend significant resources preparing for field research, regardless of the level of familiarity with "the field." Even if researchers don't have to worry about language training and acquisition or navigating transportation and logistics, there is still much to be planned for to make the most of time in the field. Those studying their own country or locale should be particularly mindful of their own assumptions. "The fact that you're from somewhere can lead you to sometimes overestimate how much you know it," says Thoraya El Rayyes, who studies state-society relations in Jordan and Egypt with a political economy bent. "You actually need to break out of [your positionality]," she adds.[1]

A researcher still has to invest in learning the social norms, behaviors and red lines that help them manage their profile. "It is important to do the stakeholder mapping, to figure out the different types of groups you want to interview/study," says El Rayyes, "especially if you don't have much time to spend in the field." "If possible, carry out preliminary research in the field to see what is feasible and what isn't," says Omar Sirri, who studies the security infrastructure in Iraq, "even if you're from the site or have spent a lot of time there."[2] "Prepare your questions before you go and try talking to some people on the ground before you get there," he adds. You also want to access people who are "at the crux of academic, policy making and politics, who can tell you what you can and can't do," says El Rayyes.

In terms of logistical planning, if you are leaving your home country or country of study you would benefit greatly from seeking local affiliation with a university or research center. The purpose of this is to be as transparent and visible as can be, to alleviate people's concerns about you and your research. Sirri has another practical tip regarding transparency: "The thing that hurt me the most is not having business cards, because no one is just going to believe you!" Business cards communicate a level of transparency but also formality and seriousness that you need in the field. You want to be reassuring and develop a reputation as "the newcomer/foreigner who is studying X." People will be suspicious, especially in the MENA, and your anonymity might be a hindrance.

Funding is also a consideration, as research requires some basic financial resources, and the researcher must utilize their network to explore pots of money—regardless of their size. It is worthwhile to lay out the financial obligations that the research might entail and to plan according to different budget sizes and contingencies.

First Steps in the Field

Once in the field, the learning curve is going to be very steep. Nonetheless, you want to look for and talk to people who are going to facilitate your research and help you access different sources of information. Even if you're studying your own country, El Rayyes says, "you want to take advantage of two-step ties to access key informants and interlocutors who can help you build trust in your field community." Many researchers first talk to academics, to discuss their projects and solicit feedback. Interlocutors are often not chosen but are products of "an organic process"

---

[1] Thoraya El-Rayyes. 2021. Unpopular Protest: Mass Mobilization and Attitudes toward Democracy in Post-Mubarak Egypt." *Journal of Politics* 83 (1): 291–305.

[2] Omar Sirri. 2019. "Siting the State: Intersections of Space, Religion and Political Economy in Baghdad." In *Religion, Violence, and the State in Iraq*. Project on Middle East Political Science (POMEPS) Studies, 35:33–37.

where you find people willing to share their social network and are interested in the research and have insights. At the same time, you don't want to rely on interlocutors too much or to rely on only one interlocutor, says El Rayyes.

Your initial instinct might be to seek out leaders of official institutions related to your topic of study. Even if that's not helpful in getting information, says Sirri, you have to exhaust the possibility and you "might get lucky with access." You are also collecting data from these interactions, he adds—and that is where your data collection starts. "Listen and observe," he encourages. Create contacts of people you trust, and ideally have a home institution (not necessarily a university). Institutional affiliation, whether with a think tank, NGO, university, or media outlet can help open doors and connect you with primary interlocutors.

It is typical that "reality does not map your planning," according to Annelle Sheline, who studies official religious discourses in the MENA.[3] It is advisable to leave room for contingencies, where things go off plan but are still informative. Civil society groups and journalists can be just as valuable as academics to reach out to initially, so, like Sirri, she also advises not to constrict yourself to academic circles.

If you are a foreigner in a country different than your country of citizenship and plan on spending a significant amount of time, consider obtaining a residency permit. When doing my dissertation research in Morocco, this was one of the first things I set out to do in order to get access to the country for 1 year without constantly having to renew the visa, as well as to announce my arrival and my intentions to the security establishment. That way, I thought, no one can question the legality of my presence or my research in the field.

Best Practices of Data Collection and Preservation

At some point, you will have to decide what data to include in your study and what to leave out. Nevertheless, there is widespread agreement among MENA researchers today that data collection starts even before arrival in the field. "When you're doing qualitative fieldwork, the data starts on your way to the field, before you even get there," says Sirri. As for what counts as data, El Rayyes says "Everything is data, and you can't just take what people say at face value," especially when the methods involve ethnographic fieldwork and interpretation.

It is important to be as transparent as possible with your subjects and set a formal tone for your work. Everyone in your field site must know who you are and what you're doing, and this is where business cards and ethical consent forms come in handy. They establish the nature of your relationship with the field site.

Collection and preservation should be standardized, says El Rayyes, in terms of recording certain interviews and not recording others. How anonymous or public the

---

[3] Annelle Sheline. *ND. Traditions of Tolerance: Constructing Moderate Islam in the Arab Monarchies*, book manuscript in preparation that devotes a section to fieldwork; http://www.annelle-sheline.com/about

data are should depend on the topic and the risks entailed to interview subjects. El Rayyes takes contemporaneous handwritten notes, types them up, shreds the originals, and saves everything to the cloud—with a password and two-factor authentication. Recorded interviews are transcribed in full—to avoid confirmation bias and "cherry picking data." Sirri takes notes and transcribes Arabic interviews in English, translating in real time.

Recording interviews and transcribing them subsequently is a choice that a researcher needs to make depending on the topic, the risks entailed to interview subjects, and the amount of time the researcher has to sift through the data. Regardless of the choice, the researcher must systemically go through the data in its entirety. "Be diligent about your note taking so that you can decipher your notes later," says Sheline, and if need be "sacrifice that next interview to make sure you go over your notes or transcribe the recording," she adds.

Resources and hardware/software factor into the collection and preservation of data. It is important to have the necessary hardware and software, whether it be a voice recorder, a computer, or a statistical software package, and to allocate ample resources towards this hardware/software. At every junction, the researcher has to manage the tension between collecting as much data as possible and ensuring the quality of the collected data. In that sense, more is not necessarily better, and data saturation can (and often does) occur. "When you start understanding the agenda of your interlocutors is when you are probably reaching data saturation," says El Rayyes.

Managing Subjectivity and Ensuring the Safety of Collaborators

Subjectivity and positionality are bound to influence the data collection process. Apart from visible identifiers which could include class, gender, religiosity, ethnicity, and race, there are also non-visible identifiers that can and often do impact the process of data collection and channel or limit a researcher's access to certain spaces, influencing the collection process. Researchers must recognize their subjectivity and be cognizant of how that shapes the data collection effort. "The data will be skewed by your identity, but it will be so systematically," says Sheline.

Even in societies that the researcher is familiar with, there is a degree to which differences with subjects in the field are non-reconcilable. Researchers must balance between trying to relate to some interview subjects versus accepting their "foreignness" and just attempting to show empathy and understanding rather than relatability. Some of this can be managed with socially desirable dress and behavior, but some of it cannot. What Sirri recommends is the expression of a long-term commitment, especially in a place like Iraq which is "a fly by night place for foreign researchers." In such a place, you always have to answer for your presence at a place where you choose to be, rather than are born into. You either have to manage your anonymity or identity, depending on how well the community knows you, or comfort your subjects and mitigate their concerns. "At the same time you can't predict what's going to happen and assume you're going to be treated one way or another based on who you are," says Sheline.

In societies with securitized approaches to information such as most MENA countries, profile management is key to managing your subjectivity and ensuring your safety and that of your collaborators. It doesn't matter how benign you seem and how benign you act: it is important to manage the changing risk landscape, which—as we've learned from the tragic case of Giulio Regeni—cannot be assumed to remain constant. Researchers must always balance between lowering their profile and being transparent, which is the result of dynamic rather than static processes, according to El Rayyes.

As for guaranteeing your security and that of your subjects, if your university has an institutional review board office or ethical review process for human subjects research, you will be obliged to map out the risks and obtain the necessary approval. One good way to start is by obtaining all the legal permissions necessary for your research in the field site itself. That was my rationale behind obtaining a local university affiliation and obtaining a residency permit. Sirri followed a similar path: "Permission from authorities is a form of protection for everyone involved in the research," he says.

If your research involves interviews, you want the location of the interviews to be secure. Meeting at an office would make sense, but also any private place that subjects are comfortable with. Depending on the topic and the risks involved, you may want to anonymize your interviews using different levels. Your notes also must be anonymized for the sensitive interviews. Give your subjects control over topics to be covered, as they are more likely to know what is sensitive and what is not, says El Rayyes. "Time, honesty, empathy and solidarity ... are part of guaranteeing the safety of your interlocutors," says Sirri.

After the Field

After you're done with collecting the data, it is perfectly normal for your topic to change. That is why Sirri recommends taking time away from the data (if possible), to reflect on what you actually have. He has another practical piece of advice: "Read, read, read," before and after you go to the field. "It is critical to help you figure out how you want to frame your arguments and how you want to write them up," he says. "Consider using the writing as a way to think with the data, thinking with the texts, and thinking with your interlocutors," he adds. Don't wait to start writing, certainly not until you're done reading. You have to choose the audience of your writing, both within academia and more broadly, and the earlier you start the earlier you can iterate your writing to multiple audiences.

Lastly, you want to maintain and manage your relationship with the field site. This does not mean absolving yourself from any commitments to the site, but rather figuring out a healthy relationship by which you can maintain your independence and critical distance as a researcher while also continuing to have access to your subjects without jeopardizing yourself or jeopardizing them.

Appendix 2: Research Ethics

Rebecca Savelsberg

How does our research affect others? What responsibility do we have toward our research subjects, the communities we study, and those who help us conduct our research? No matter whether we are conducting research with a pre-existing dataset, constructing a new dataset, perhaps based on a public opinion survey, or conducting in-depth interviews for purposes of thick description and/or attention to underlying mechanisms, we must consider these questions. Accordingly, this brief overview of research ethics discusses the following topics:

- Informed Consent
- Protecting Confidentiality
- Trauma and Sensitive Topics
- Fieldwork as an Unequal Exchange
- Internal Review Boards
- Ethics and the Bigger Picture

No matter if our research is based on fieldwork or other methods, one of the most important ethical guidelines is to do no harm. This means that it is our ethical duty to protect research subjects and anyone else who assists us in our research from psychological, social, physical, and legal harm. Furthermore, since our work as social scientists often affects more than individuals, we must consider the impact that our research (both conducting and publishing it) has on the communities, countries, and societies we study. This is especially important for those doing research in a country very different from their own.[4]

Informed Consent

Informed consent is the idea that research subjects must be fully informed about the possible costs and possible benefits of participating in a research study and must give their voluntary consent to participate in a study before commencing the research. Depending on the modality of the research, informed consent can be obtained orally, by explaining the terms of participation to the participant and having them agree out loud to continue, or it can be obtained in writing, by having the participant sign an informed consent statement. If a research project involves human beings, it is essential to obtain informed consent prior to starting the study with a participant.

Informed consent becomes trickier when working with vulnerable populations. Vulnerable populations are generally groups that cannot speak for themselves or lack certain legal protections. These might include institutionalized persons, prisoners, or

---

[4] Anna Getmansky. 2019. ""Englishman in New York": Conducting Research in the Middle East as a Foreign Scholar." *PS: Political Science and Politics.*

children. Some fall into more of a grey area, e.g. those in refugee camps. If you are using connections through the government or NGOs to find your research subjects, you must also make sure that your research subjects do not feel obligated to participate due to a feeling of duty toward those making the connections (either in general, or because they feel like they won't get certain services in the future).

When dealing with vulnerable populations, researchers must make a serious effort to identify the conditions under which a vulnerable individual can engage fully and freely in the informed consent process. A researcher may have to come up with creative solutions when involving these types of participants and ought to document which solutions worked well and which did not for the benefit of future researchers. As part of this process, it can also be helpful for researchers to engage with individuals and organizations on the ground that already work with the vulnerable population of interest, as they will be aware of common pitfalls that ought to be avoided.

Protecting Confidentiality

Another key ethical consideration when conducting research is protecting the confidentiality of your research subjects. This is especially important if you are asking participants about sensitive topics or if they are in danger of any kind of retaliation as a result of their participation in your study. Think carefully about the location in which you will conduct your research; a participant's home may feel safer and more private than a crowded café, for example.

Conducting research about sensitive topics can also restrict which research methods you consider using. For example, while focus groups can be a great research tool, they may be unwise to conduct when addressing sensitive topics such as political opinions in an authoritarian context, or subjects with social stigma attached, such as sexual violence. Research subjects will no longer be anonymous, at least to the other members of the focus group, which could expose them to retaliation later on (in addition to also compromising the type of information they will be willing to share).

Once you have collected your data, whether through interviews, archival research, or other methods, there are multiple things you can do to protect confidentiality. The best practice is to save any data you collect (e.g. notes, audio recordings) in a cloud-based service (e.g. Dropbox) that is only accessible with a password and two-factor authentication. Depending on how sensitive the data is that you are working with, you may want to type up and/or take pictures of handwritten notes and then destroy your notes, or delete audio files on devices you cannot protect (e.g. your phone or a tape recorder). You can also further ensure the confidentiality of your research subjects by assigning them code names or numbers. If it is necessary to save the real names of your research subjects and which code names they correspond with, save the names in a separate cloud-based and password protected service. That way, if one of your accounts is hacked, it will be more difficult to connect sensitive information to your research subjects.

Trauma and Sensitive Topics

Some research addresses sensitive topics, such as physical or sexual violence, that could bring up traumatic memories for respondents. This poses ethical quandaries with respect to which methods to use, which questions to ask, how to act while conducting interviews, and should there be support for those involved in your research. Practical advice is offered by Jesse Driscoll, a political scientist at the University of California, San Diego:

> Revisiting difficult memories with an authority figure can yield unpredictable emotions. There can be tears, followed quickly by shame at the tears and intense anger at the researcher for causing the shame. Maintaining professional distance in these delicate moments is important. Do not interrupt. Do not touch your subject until the moment has passed and you are concluding the interview. Do not be afraid to stop or end the interview. Remember: You are not a counselor and you did not initiate this conversation in order to provide healing. When questions involve emotionally intense subject matter, including personal tragedy and trauma, researchers have a primary responsibility to try to hold interviewees on the interview track, *not* to allow them to explore depths of trauma with you.[5]

Depending on context, researchers must give careful thought to what may be considered a sensitive topic and must recognize that an uncontroversial topic in their home country may well be controversial in a different country or context. Sensitive topics can include seemingly mundane issues, such as voting or general questions about everyday behavior. In politically repressive contexts, participants may be unwilling to answer certain questions out of fear of retaliation by state security services.

Fieldwork as an Unequal Exchange

As a way to attract and retain research participants, researchers often offer financial incentives to participants. Research projects with large budgets may in theory be able to offer large rewards to less privileged participants. In reality, however, researchers are encouraged to strike a balance between financial incentives and intrinsic incentives for participants. If researchers offer large amounts of money, participants may join the study for the wrong reasons or may provide false answers simply in order to receive the reward at the end. Participants may also feel that they need to answer the research questions in a particular way in order to please the researcher. Ideally, researchers want the financial incentive to convince potential participants who are "on the fence" about joining the study to participate, but they do not want the financial incentive to attract large amounts of people who weren't really close to the "fence" in the first place.

---

[5] Jesse Driscoll. 2021. Doing Global Fieldwork: A Social Scientist's Guide to Mixed-Methods Research Far from Home. Columbia University Press.

While the issues discussed above are ethical obligations involved in conducting fieldwork, researchers should also consider how they interact with the community and the individuals involved in their research once their fieldwork is over. Fieldwork is almost always an unequal exchange, as researchers benefit academically and professionally (and thus indirectly usually financially) from the information their research subjects share with them. Researchers should thus create or take advantage of opportunities to make the exchange more equal.

One broad way to do so is to make the research accessible to the public, such as through op-eds, blog posts, and public lectures or discussions. This should be written in language non-academics will understand, and also offered in the language(s) of the research population. Researchers can also offer assistance to research assistants and other people or organizations that helped with their fieldwork. This may be in the form of aiding in writing grant proposals, or providing professional help such as feedback on written work or network connections. Some believe that the ethical opportunities of researchers should go further and exit the realm of neutral observation by participating in activism related to the issue they are researching. Others warn that this sort of behavior should be avoided as it can seem patronizing or produce backlash against local activists.

Internal Review Boards

In Western research institutions, researchers who conduct research with human beings often find themselves in contact with the institution's Internal Review Board (IRB) committee. This committee is responsible for reviewing and approving research projects in advance in order to ensure that they comply with common ethical guidelines. When the IRB approves a researcher's project, she may feel that she has fulfilled her ethical obligations and has nothing more to worry about. Many reject this carefree approach and argue instead that researchers must continually reassess the ethics of their projects as new information emerges.

Additionally, when it comes to research in the Middle East and North Africa (MENA), IRBs at Western institutions are often ill equipped to assess the ethics of a project, as the members of these committees tend to be general social scientists who do not necessarily understand the cultural and political context of the MENA. Researchers who work outside of their home country may need to have projects approved both by their home institution's IRB and an IRB within the country where they want to conduct the project. In MENA, some universities have created IRBs and others have not. In cases where an institution has no IRB, it is even more essential for the researcher to think carefully about the ethics of her project and perhaps consult seasoned researchers in the field for additional advice.

Ethics and the Bigger Picture

While most research ethics review committees focus on preventing harm to individuals, the ethical considerations of conducting social science research do not stop there. Researchers should also consider their obligation as researchers to "get the story right." This means being transparent about their evidence and discuss honestly the limitations of their data and methodology.

Appendix 3: Survey Research

Michael Robbins

This appendix details the Arab Barometer survey project and provides some guidance for those who wish to contemplate conducting an original survey as part of their research. It briefly discusses the following topics:

- The Arab Barometer
- Sampling Methods
- Survey Mode
- Survey Questions

The Arab Barometer

Established in 2006, Arab Barometer is a comparative research project that seeks to understand the views of ordinary citizens across the MENA region. To date, it has conducted 68 nationally representative public opinion surveys in 16 countries and interviewed more than 100,000 respondents. The survey is comparative in nature, asking similar questions across the countries where the survey is fielded to allow researchers to better understand differences across countries. The project is also longitudinal, meaning it seeks to understand how views of publics change over time.

Arab Barometer also seeks to place MENA within a global perspective. It is a member of the Global Barometer Survey, which brings together six comparative survey research projects covering approximately 100 countries and covering all major world regions with the exception of Europe and Oceania. Comparing the results of Arab Barometer with those from other regions allows researchers to understand how MENA publics are similar to or different from those around the world.

Sampling Methods

Perhaps the most essential element to consider when conducting a survey is the sample. Defining and executing the sample is essential to being able to make claims about the external validity of the causal claims of the research project. Key considerations are both the feasibility of carrying out the sample and the degree to which the researcher hopes to make claims about the generalizability of the findings from the survey.

Representative Sampling A representative sample is one that possesses the same attributes and orientations as the larger "population" from which it has been drawn. This usually involves the use of random, or probability-based, procedures to select the members of the population who will be included in the sample. To the extent that a sample is representative, the univariate distributions and variable relationships that characterize the sample can be assumed to be those of the population from which the sample was drawn.

Historically, many social science surveys relied on probability-based samples, meaning each respondent has a known and calculable probability of selection. Because of these factors, it is possible to calculate the degree to which the findings of the survey represent the views of the target population. For example, if well executed, it is possible to calculate a margin of error, which by convention provides a range for which the results of the survey would fall 19 out of 20 times if the survey were repeated.

For this reason, high quality surveys take great care in designing and executing the samples. Arab Barometer typically relies on face-to-face surveys in the respondent's place of residence. The samples are multi-stage area probability samples with stratification and clustering, meaning areas of the country are selected at random at multiple levels until a small cluster of about 250 houses is selected. Within each cluster, eight or ten households are selected.

This design ensures that the sample is spread out across the country but also is not prohibitively expensive as a result of the clustering. It ensures that each member of the target population, typically citizens of the country ages 18 and above, has an approximately equal probability of selection. As a result, it is possible to generalize the findings to citizens ages 18 and above at the national level within the reported margin of error.

Other approaches can be used, however, to yield a representative sample. For example, due to health measures associated with COVID-19, it was not possible to conduct in-person surveys during 2020–2021. To yield representative surveys, Arab Barometer shifted to phone surveys using a random-digit dial technique. This approach means that phone numbers are randomly selected from the known universe of possible numbers with calls placed to these numbers. This approach means that all of those with a phone number in the country have a chance of being selected, and so the results from the sample can be generalized to the population.

Non-representative Surveys Representative samples, especially at the national level, tend to be significantly more costly than non-representative surveys, which makes alternative approaches of particular interest to many researchers. A number of approaches fall under this rubric, including convenience sampling, purposive sampling, referral sampling, volunteer sampling, and some forms of quota sampling. What these forms have in common is that the selection process is not random, meaning that each respondent does not have a known or calculable probability for inclusion in the survey. In turn, although it is *possible* for the results to be representative of a larger population, it is not possible to calculate a traditional margin of error or determine whether the sample is significantly biased in some manner. As a result, researchers are limited in their abilities to make broader generalizations about the findings to a larger population.

However, this caution is not to say that there are not clear uses or even times when a non-representative sampling approach may be preferable to one that is representative. One example is if the focus of research is a survey experiment, meaning that part of the sample receives a treatment of some kind while the rest serves as a control. Such examples include but are not limited to question wording experiments, list experiments, or other randomized experiments to determine how responses differ between two groups.

Recruiting a convenience sample for an experiment has many benefits, including the ability to conduct the research on an established panel of respondents or to recruit respondents to a research lab where the experiment is administered. If the respondents are randomly assigned to two (or more) groups for the experiment, it is possible to determine if there is a causal effect from the treatment using proper approaches. Although the results are not necessarily generalizable to the population as a whole, this approach is a more cost-effective way to determine if there is a causal effect from the treatment. If there is, additional research can determine whether or not this result is generalizable more broadly.

Additional reasons to use a non-randomized sample might be to study a rare population. If the survey is only relevant to one percent of a general population, it can be very challenging and costly to reach this group using standard probability-based approaches. Instead, a researcher might pay for an already existing convenience sample from this group or recruit respondents through referrals from other members of this group who have already been interviewed. These approaches can yield a sufficient number of respondents to provide insight into the research question, although there will remain questions about the generalizability of the results.

Survey Mode

An additional consideration for researchers is the survey mode, which has important implications for researchers working on MENA. Historically, the dominant mode of survey collection for researchers focusing on this region has been in-person or face-to-face in the respondent's place of residence. If done properly, this mode has a number of benefits. Namely, it ensures that all respondents (who are home) can be reached instead of depending on them to have access to a phone or internet connection, for example. This method is more likely to reach populations that have a lower socio-economic status, especially in rural areas where limits to existing infrastructure may make access by phone or internet less likely.

This approach also has a number of other advantages. When being interviewed in-person, respondents are typically willing to be interviewed for a longer period of time than by other modes. This tendency allows for significantly longer survey instruments than surveys conducted by phone or internet, for example. Face-to-face surveys also tend to have significantly higher response rates than other modes and completion rates given that respondents are less likely to turn down someone at the door or end the interview with the enumerator present than they are to hang up the phone or close a browser window. Given these advantages and the fact that costs per interview in MENA have been affordable for many researchers, this mode remains common in MENA today, though it is less popular in the U.S. and Europe.

However, there are also some important challenges. For one, oversight tends to be more complicated than other modes. Enumerators are typically dispersed across large areas to cover the target population, making it difficult for the researcher or firm to oversee them directly. Interviews in respondents' place of residence are especially difficult to monitor, meaning even honest supervisors cannot observe them all. The challenges of quality control have been significantly improved with the rise of computer-assisted personal interviews (CAPI), meaning interviews conducted by computer tablets. Tablets can automatically collect vast amounts of paradata, including exact times, locations, and possibly even recordings of parts of the interview to help validate that interviews were done according to the sampling plan and interview schedule. Nevertheless, software exists that can be used to compromise these devices, meaning that oversight still remains more challenging for this mode than for others.

Another consideration is the interview setting. In most face-to-face interviews, enumerators ask questions to respondents directly. In this setting, interviewer effects tend to be greater as respondents tend to adjust their answers to what they think would be more acceptable to the interviewer. For example, a respondent may be less likely to say they oppose women's rights if the enumerator is a woman rather than a man. Additionally, in face-to-face surveys, other people such as the respondent's family may be present in the place of residence. Even if not in the same room, fears about a potential lack of privacy from other members of the household could affect answers. If a conservative member of the family might hear some of the questions and answers, it might lead the respondent to provide more conservative answers to certain questions to avoid upsetting their relative. The presence of more liberal family members could have the same effect.

Increasingly, phone and internet are becoming more common modes in MENA for a number of reasons. Before 2020, the relative cost and ability to circumvent government restrictions were major reasons for considering alternative modes. For the former, surveys conducted by phone and internet tend to be cheaper (in absolute costs) than face-to-face surveys, meaning they are often preferable for short survey instruments. Additionally, since it is possible to conduct the survey from a call center based in another country or on the internet, there is not a requirement for formal governmental approval. Given that many governments across MENA place restrictions on the questions that can be included on the survey if done in-person or by a research organization based in their country, conducting surveys by phone or internet provides a way to include certain questions that would otherwise not be possible to ask.

There are a number of potential limitations, however. For one, phone surveys are typically relatively short with a maximum recommended time of about 15 minutes. Internet surveys are even shorter (without incentives) with respondents typically not remaining engaged for more than about ten questions.

A related challenge relates to recruitment. For phone surveys, using the relatively standard random-digit dial approach for a phone survey typically yields relatively low response rates. Many targeted respondents, especially on mobile devices, are unlikely to pick up an unknown number or hang up when the interviewer introduces the survey.

For internet surveys, it is extremely challenging, especially in MENA contexts, to find a way to randomly select respondents using e-mails or other online tools. Instead, it is more common to use a pre-existing panel of respondents provided by a survey firm. Although firms often claim to provide a sample that resembles the target population, thereby implying the findings are generalizable, in reality panels were recruited using incentives and are opt-in, meaning members have chosen to take part. In virtually all cases, there is no known, or even estimated, probability of selection, making internet surveys effectively convenience samples. Although now commonly used in the U.S. and some other contexts where survey research is well-developed as a means of generalizing about a broader population, at the time of writing existing online panels in MENA are not sufficiently established to viably do the same.

Other approaches to recruit online may be through social media websites whereby users are informed about the survey. These ads can be targeted to specific groups, but the methodology of such approaches is questionable. For example, a Facebook ad targeting members of certain groups could be seen by other groups on the same platform who might then take the survey and skew the results. This outcome would mean that responses do not necessarily reflect the actual views of potential targets, compromising or at least strongly calling into question the survey results.

An additional consideration for phone or internet surveys relates to privacy considerations. It can be more difficult to gain the trust of the respondent in both modes. By phone, it may be unclear who is making the call and whether the enumerator might be misrepresenting the purposes of the survey. Or, respondents may fear that the regime might tap the phone call, increasing the likelihood of preference falsification on certain questions about the government.

These concerns also exist for internet surveys to varying extents, and internet panels pose an additional challenge. Members of the panel are typically compensated for taking multiple surveys. They can, in effect, become "professional" survey takers. They may also fear that they must provide the "correct" or desired response in order to remain in the panel, thus affecting their responses. Internet surveys also provide opportunities for government surveillance.

However, there is an additional benefit to phone and internet surveys, which is that they are more likely to provide the respondent with privacy from others in the household. On the phone, others in the household are unlikely to hear the question being posed, meaning the respondent can simply provide their answer with the knowledge that others in the vicinity will not be able to hear the response. This could provide more truthful measures for questions of particular sensitivity within the household setting. The same is also true of internet surveys where, presumably, respondents can fill them out without others watching.

Other survey modes are also possible, including self-administered surveys. These are less common in MENA to date, excepting for internet surveys. Self-administered surveys have some additional challenges, including, for example, literacy limitations for surveys that are written.

Survey Questions

Another critical element of a survey is developing the instrument, which is the schedule of questions asked of the respondent. There are many different approaches, but in surveys with a large number of respondents, sometimes called large-n surveys, the survey instrument, or questionnaire, is usually mostly composed of close-ended questions. This makes the aggregation of responses much easier, and it also reduces the possibility of bias in the interpretation of responses. As a result, it is possible to place respondents into a set number of pre-determined response patterns that can then be analyzed by the researcher.

Most questions in surveys are either ordinal, nominal, or numerical. Ordinal means there is a natural order to the questions, such as a scale ranging from strongly agree to strongly disagree or one's level of concern about a certain problem. A nominal question lacks a natural order, such as what is the greatest challenge facing one's country or a preferred political party. The responses do not come in any order. A numerical question is one that can be counted, such as the number of hours per day spent engaging in an activity or the number of elections in which an individual has voted.

Ordinal questions are frequent on surveys but present a set of challenges. Perhaps the most important is how to determine the range of the scale. Five- and seven-point Likert scales are particularly common as a means to scale responses. A five-point scale, for example, might offer respondents a choice between strongly agree, agree, neither agree nor disagree, disagree, and strongly disagree. Seven-point scales might add somewhat agree and somewhat disagree to this list.

Although common, Likert scales present certain challenges, including measuring the difference between two responses, especially if the survey is conducted in multiple languages. The difference between "strongly agree" and "agree" may not be the same as the difference between "agree" and "somewhat agree," meaning the scale is not equidistant between response options.

Translating adjectives across languages to ensure equivalency can also yield discrepancies in comparative survey research. Another common dilemma is whether or not to include a neutral category, as many respondents may choose it because they are not paying sufficient attention, satisficing, or preference falsifying. Not including a neutral category may increase the percentage who say "don't know," but can also incentivize those who lean one way or the other, even slightly, to select a positive or negative response option.

One potential solution to some of these challenges is to introduce a numeric scale where only the extreme values are defined. For example, it would be possible to create an eleven-point scale where zero is strongly disagree and ten is strongly agree with no other values being defined. Of course, this also has challenges with some respondents not being familiar with such scales. Additionally, there tends to be selection of certain values, as respondents may understand zero, five, and ten clearly, but are less certain of the difference between two and three.

For nominal questions, there are also multiple approaches. One is to ask respondents to choose the category or response they think best expresses their views or situation. But it can be challenging to make the response options exhaustive, especially without creating a list of items that is too long to be read out or for the respondent to remember. Often, researchers will try to identify the most common expected responses and then have an option for "other—specify."

Yet, this approach can also create biased responses. Experiments have shown that respondents are more likely to choose an item from the list than specify their own other, in part thinking that they should choose from this list since the researcher has highlighted these topics. Additionally, including "other—specify" can create a number of challenges in coding. For example, if asked about the greatest challenge facing their country, two options might be the economy and corruption. The respondent might then give "the economy of corruption" as her response, leaving a difficult choice for the researcher to determine how to handle this response.

Other approaches include ranking nominal questions. For example, respondents could be asked to rank candidates for political office from most to least favored. However, this assumes that respondents have an opinion about each candidate. It may be that there is one particularly loved and one particularly hated candidate, with the respondent being completely ambivalent between the remaining ones. Yet, each candidate must receive a ranking so that the respondent can show that one candidate is the most and one the least preferred.

Beyond close-ended responses, open-ended questions may also be included. These present a potential challenge for surveys in general and large-n surveys in particular. Respondents may be reluctant to answer open-ended questions if the wording gives too little guidance about what is being sought. Further, if respondents do provide an answer, it may be long and winding and only vaguely responsive to the question. The response may also be ambiguous, making coding difficult and subject to bias when comparing the responses of different individuals.

Fortunately, computer-derived text analysis is becoming more common, which provides additional leverage for analyzing and coding open-ended responses. Computer algorithms can assist researchers in looking for common words, phrases, or other parts of the response and help them categorize open-ended responses efficiently.

Researchers also need to be alert to the possibility of question order effects, meaning that responses to a question may be influenced by where it is placed in the survey instrument or its position in a group of questions. Careful pretesting will often enable the researcher to identify question order effects and if necessary make adjustments in the placing of questions.

Finally, in surveys where the individual is the unit of analysis, questions about the attributes of the respondents will be included. The researcher will need to decide how detailed she needs this demographic information to be, whether and how to ask more personal questions, and where to place demographic questions in the instrument. Potentially sensitive questions, perhaps about income, for example, are often put at the end of the survey instrument.

Conclusion

Conducting high quality surveys is challenging and requires significant attention to many details throughout the process, some of which are described here. This appendix is not intended to be a complete guide, but rather a general overview of some important considerations for researchers seeking to conduct their own surveys.

Given the complications of conducting surveys, it is strongly recommended that researchers work with an organization that has experience operating such projects. They can serve as a valuable resource to a researcher and help the researcher through country- or population-specific challenges they might encounter.

Additionally, survey research is a growing field in the MENA region. There are now a number of high quality and reliable surveys that are regularly conducted in many countries across the region. Arab Barometer is one of these. Beyond documenting the views and attitudes of MENA publics, the project is designed to build capacity across the region to conduct survey analysis. Researchers associated with the project routinely share best practices and guidance with other researchers and can provide resources for the field.

Appendix 4: Software for Statistics and Data Analysis

Irene Morse

As the social sciences have become more advanced with respect to data collection and data availability, researchers have increasingly turned to software packages to assist them in analyzing data. In the past, a researcher might have to calculate a statistical test by hand and then look up significance values in a table at the back of a statistics textbook. Nowadays, by contrast, all this and much more can be done with a few keystrokes. Below, we identify, briefly describe, and outline the advantages and limitations of four of the statistical software packages that are most widely used by social scientists.

Stata

Stata is a proprietary software first released by StataCorp in 1985 and updated approximately every 2 years. The pricing for this software varies by country but generally costs about $100 per year for a student. Costs for others are substantially higher, but universities often purchase this software and place it on university computers so that researchers do not have to individually buy it. Stata is easy to use because it uses a clickable interface, meaning that the user does not need to understand much, if any, computer code. It also produces high-quality charts and graphs that the user can save for publication in a research paper. It is capable of conducting all major statistical calculations and running all major statistical models, including regression. It also allows the user to view the data set while performing computations.

The primary advantage of Stata is definitely its user interface. Stata has much less of a learning curve than some other statistical software; almost anyone can get started with data analysis and modeling immediately. The primary disadvantage is its cost, which could be prohibitive for many students, and especially for those who are not students. Stata is a popular choice for data analysis among economists and political scientists.

Learn more or purchase at stata.com.

R

R is an open-source programming language that was created by statisticians Ross Ihaka and Robert Gentleman and launched in 1995. It is free to download via the Comprehensive R Archive Network (CRAN), which is easily found online. Many R users also choose to download and use a free software called RStudio, which provides a user-friendly interface for writing, saving, and running code in R. Writing code in R has a slight learning curve, especially for those with no prior exposure to computer programming. However, the basics can be learned quickly and easily through free or paid online tutorials, such as Code Academy and Data Camp. R code can produce high-quality charts and graphs that the user can save for publication in a research paper. R is capable of conducting all major statistical calculations and running all major statistical models, including regression. Users can also download additional R "packages" that permit the conduct of more complex or unique analyses; this makes R a highly versatile option.

The primary advantage of R is that is free and readily available to anyone. There are also many free resources for learning R online. The primary disadvantage is the learning curve. Writing code in R can be a frustrating experience, and new users will regularly encounter confusing error messages that must be addressed. As one learns to use R, one must also learn how to troubleshoot errors by searching online. Although it has a learning curve, R is a popular choice for data analysis among almost all types of social scientists because it is free and capable of a wide range of statistical operations.

Learn more or download at r-project.org and at rstudio.com.

SPSS

Statistical Product and Service Solutions (SPSS) is a proprietary software developed by Norman H. Nie, Dale H. Bent, and C. Hadlai Hull and first released in 1968. It was purchased by IBM in 2009, and a new version is released approximately every year. The pricing for this software varies depending on the version purchased but generally costs between $50 and $100 per year for a student. Universities often purchase this software and place it on university computers so that researchers do not have to individually buy it. SPSS uses a spreadsheet-style interface, which may be more familiar to users than the interfaces of the previous options. However, it is more powerful than the typical spreadsheet software and can carry out all major statistical calculations and run all major statistical models, including regression. SPSS users must learn some very simple programming commands in addition to using the dropdown menus and buttons provided by the software. SPSS can also produce high-quality charts and graphs that the user can save for publication in a research paper. Like Stata, SPSS allows the user to view the data set while performing computations.

The primary advantage of SPSS is its user interface; viewing data in a spreadsheet will be familiar for many users, and the learning curve will be less steep. The primary disadvantage is its cost, which could be prohibitive for many students. Luckily many universities purchase SPSS for the university computers, which can make the software more accessible. SPSS is a popular choice for data analysis among psychologists and business researchers.

Learn more or purchase at ibm.com.

Excel and Google Sheets

Excel is a software for the creation and editing of spreadsheets launched by Microsoft for Macintosh computers in 1985 and for Windows computers in 1987. It is a proprietary software and is part of the Microsoft Office Suite, which is often pre-installed on new computers. In addition, Google Sheets offers a free alternative to Excel that provides most of the same functionality. Performing computations in Excel requires knowledge of very simple programming commands that can be learned through free online tutorials. Excel can produce very high-quality charts and graphs that the user can save for publication in a research paper. Unfortunately, however, because it is a spreadsheet software rather than a statistical software, it lacks many functions that the previous options have, and it does not support regression.

The primary advantage of Excel is that it is readily accessible on many computers. Many researchers may also have had exposure to Excel in the past and therefore may find it easier than some other options. The primary disadvantage is that it is not nearly as powerful a software as the previous options mentioned. It cannot handle large datasets, and its computational ability is limited. Therefore, most social scientists have moved away from using Excel except for conducting small computations or occasionally making an attractive chart or graph.

Learn more or purchase Excel at microsoft.com or use Google Sheets at docs.google.com.

GPSR Compliance

The European Union's (EU) General Product Safety Regulation (GPSR) is a set of rules that requires consumer products to be safe and our obligations to ensure this.

If you have any concerns about our products, you can contact us on

ProductSafety@springernature.com

In case Publisher is established outside the EU, the EU authorized representative is:

Springer Nature Customer Service Center GmbH
Europaplatz 3
69115 Heidelberg, Germany

www.ingramcontent.com/pod-product-compliance
Ingram Content Group UK Ltd.
Pitfield, Milton Keynes, MK11 3LW, UK
UKHW021952040925
462611UK00004B/408